D0934991

POETRY'S PLEA FOR ANIMALS

*An anthology of justice and mercy
for our kindred in fur and feathers*

Collected and edited by
(Elizabeth)
FRANCES E. CLARKE

With an introduction by
EDWIN MARKHAM
Author of "The Man With the Hoe"

ILLUSTRATED BY W. F. STECHER

**GRANGER BOOKS
MIAMI, FLORIDA**

FIRST PUBLISHED 1927
REPRINTED 1976

POETRY'S PLEA FOR ANIMALS

*An anthology of justice and mercy
for our kindred in fur and feathers*

From Painting by Giotto.

ST. FRANCIS AND THE BIRDS.

Dedicated
To the memory and achievement of
HENRY BERGH
(1813 – 1888)
First pioneer in humane work in the United States
and
Founder and first President of
The American Society
for the
Prevention of Cruelty to Animals

FOREWORD

THE quest for poems for this anthology has provided convincing proof that the poetry of the early English-speaking centuries is lacking in the spirit humane. Down to the middle of the eighteenth century no poet voices protest against cruelty to the lower creatures as did Montaigne in French literature, two hundred years before. Out of the ranks of the poets who sought inspiration in nature, birds, and the more beautiful of the wild animals, as the deer, no champion of humaneness arises till the age of romanticism. Occasionally a gentle note is heard, but it is quickly lost in the mighty orchestration of classical content and form. James Thomson in *The Seasons* makes ready the way. In his criticism of this work, Samuel Johnson remarks: " The reader of *The Seasons* wonders that he never saw before what Thomson shows him, and that he never felt what Thomson impresses."

Cowper and Burns are the first to denounce man's inhumanity to birds and other animals, and even to the lowest forms of life.

> " I would not enter on my list of friends,
>   (Though graced with polish'd manners and
>   fine sense,
>   Yet wanting sensibility) the man
>   Who needlessly sets foot upon a worm,"

declares Cowper. And Burns, with a sob in his voice, cries in *The Wounded Hare:*

> " Inhuman man! curse on thy barbarous art,
>   And blasted be thy murder-aiming eye."

In gentler strain Burns quickens sympathy for helpless creatures with here a line and there a line, and now and then an entire poem; while Cowper consecrates much of his verse to a cause that received no legal recognition in his country till twenty-five years after his death.

The poetry of the gentle William Blake is suffused with loving pity for the little inhabitants of earth and air. Byron in casual flashes, but especially in his vituperative fling at mankind in the epitaph to his dog Boatswain, testifies to his affectionate sympathy for animals. Coleridge's masterpiece has for its theme:

> " He prayeth well who loveth well
> Both man and bird and beast."

But the humane trend in the poetry of the first half of the nineteenth century finds fullest expression in Wordsworth's nature poems.

The Brownings, Tennyson, Swinburne, Christina Rossetti, William Morris, and Leigh Hunt, and lesser Victorian poets, have occasional verse pointedly humane.

In America, Longfellow, Holmes, Emerson, and several humbler poets were awakening sentiment chiefly through legend. *The Birds of Killingworth, The Emperor's Bird's Nest, The Bell of Atri, Walter von der Vogelweid* are a few of Longfellow's tales of justice. He states with characteristic sincerity:

> " Among the noblest of the land,
> Though he may count himself the least,
> That man I honor and revere,
> Who, without favor, without fear,
> In the great city dares to stand
> The Friend of every friendless Beast."

Holmes pitied the caged lion. Emerson found a lesson in the brave gymnastics of the cheery little chickadee, and wrote *The Titmouse;* and in *Forbearance*, he asks his reading public:

" Hast thou named all the birds without a gun? "

But not till the twentieth century is the humane cause consummated in both British and American poetry. In England, Arthur Symons proclaims:

> "——— When I hear
> Crying of oxen, that, in deadly fear,
> Rough men, with cruel dogs about them, drive
> Into the torture-house of death alive,
> How can I sit under a tree and read
> A happy idle book, and take no heed? "

Ralph Hodgson defines his attitude toward the world's unthinking cruelty in his lovely lyric, *Stupidity Street:*

> " I saw with open eyes
> Singing birds sweet
> Sold in the shops
> For the people to eat,
> Sold in the shops of
> Stupidity Street.
>
> I saw in vision
> The worm in the wheat,
> And in the shops nothing
> For people to eat;
> Nothing for sale in
> Stupidity Street."

And again in *The Bells of Heaven:*

> " 'Twould ring the bells of Heaven
> The wildest peal for years,
> If Parson lost his senses
> And people came to theirs,
> And he and they together
> Knelt down with angry prayers
> For tamed and shabby tigers
> And dancing dogs and bears,
> And wretched, blind pit ponies,
> And little hunted hares."

In the same slender volume, *Poems*, is *The Bull*. " The poet," says William Lyon Phelps in commenting on this poem in *The Advance of English Poetry in the Twentieth Century*, " draws us for the moment from all other tragedies in God's universe."

James Stephens, the Irish poet, sings his devotion with plaintive tenderness in poem after poem, *The Cage*, *The Lark*, *Little Things*, and *The Snare*, to list only a few.

> " And I cannot find the place
>   Where his paw is in the snare:
> Little one!   Oh, little one!
> I am searching everywhere."

William H. Davies expresses his humane creed nowhere else so succinctly as in the following lines:

> " When I give poor dumb things my
>   cares,
>   Let all men know I've said my
>   prayers."

Walter de là Mare in many a poem reveals a gentle understanding of " little things," as in *The Mother Bird*, *The Titmouse*, *Summer Evening*, *Earth Folk*, *Five Eyes*, and *All But Blind*. One poem of whimsical charm is *Nicholas Nye*, in which a child, perhaps child Walter de la Mare, holds silent and secret communion with a donkey, " Lame of a leg and old." In a concluding stanza their mutual regard attains perfect consummation:

> " Seem to be smiling at me, he would,
>   From his bush in the corner, of may,—
> Bony and ownerless, widowed and worn,
>   Knobble-kneed, lonely and grey;

And over the grass would seem to pass
'Neath the deep dark blue of the sky,
Something much better than words between me
And Nicholas Nye."

Occasionally Mr. de la Mare is frankly outspoken; to
wit,—the opening lines of *I Can't Abear*:

" I can't abear a Butcher,
I can't abide his meat,
The ugliest shop of all is his,
The ugliest in the street."

Again his sentiment makes playful threat, as when
Nemesis, in *Tit for Tat*, stalks after Tom Noddy, who
" trod like a murderer through the green woods."

Thomas Hardy has dedicated many lines to the lowly
wee inhabitants of his famous shire, declaring that
posterity should know that " he strove that such innocent creatures should come to no harm." For the celebration in 1924, in London, of the centenary of The
Royal Society for the Prevention of Cruelty to Animals, the world's oldest animal welfare organization, he
wrote an ode, *Compassion*. The following are the opening and concluding stanzas:

" Backward among the dusky years
A lonesome lamp is seen arise,
Lit by a few fain pioneers
Before incredulous eyes.
We read the legend that it lights:
' Why should throughout this land of historied rights
Mild creatures, despot-doomed, bewildered, plead
Their often hunger, thirst, pangs, prisonment,
In deep dumb gaze more eloquent
Than tongues of widest heed? '

. . . .

Cries still are heard in secret nooks
Till hushed with gag or slit or thud;
And hideous dens whereon none looks
Are blotched with needless blood.

But here, in battlings, patient, slow,
Much has been won—more, maybe, than we know—
And on we labour stressful. ' Ailinon! '
A mighty voice calls: ' But may the good prevail! '
And ' Blessed are the merciful! '
Calls yet a mightier one."

Rudyard Kipling through living individualities portrayed in prose and verse in *The Jungle Book* has, without doubt, influenced reading interest in animal intelligence. *Toomai of the Elephants, The White Seal, Tiger-Tiger, Letting in the Jungle, The Miracle of Purun Bhagat, Outsong in the Jungle,* and " *Lukannon* " are unrivalled among masterpieces of their kind. " *Lukannon* " pleads more powerfully for conservation in the seal industry than tons of propaganda.

*"Wheel down, wheel down to southward!   Oh, Gooverooska go!
And tell the Deep-Sea Viceroys the story of our woe;
Ere, empty as the shark's egg the tempest flings ashore,
The Beaches of Lukannon shall know their sons no more! "*

is the final warning. *The Parade-Song of the Camp-Animals* in its kineographic review of animal service in the British army receives the reader's repeated applause as each division swings into line, from the cavalry horses, cantering to the tune of *Bonnie Dundee,* to the screw-gun mules, grateful if they arrive on a mountain height " with a leg or two to spare! " " *The Power of the Dog* " evokes poignant reminiscence for every one who has loved and lost a dog.

John Galsworthy arraigns the human race in *Pitiful.* Each stanza is an indictment, to which incriminating testimony compels " This man of God's " to plead guilty.

Norman Gale is one of the most generous contributors in poetry to the cause of animal welfare.   There is a

singing quality in the verses in *A Merry-Go-Round of
Song* and *A Flight of Fancies* that makes one wonder
why musical settings have not been written for them.
His *Collected Poems* adds to his humanitarian contribu-
tion such lyrics as *A Bird in the Hand*. A few lines
are:

> " Nay, polished beak, you are pecking a friend!
>   Bird of the grassland, you bleed at the wing!
> Stay with me, love; in captivity mend
>   Wrong that was wrought by the boy and his sling.
> Oh for a Priest of the Birds to arise,
>   Wonderful words on his lips that persuade
> Reasoning creatures to leave to the skies
>   Song at its purest a-throb in the glade! "

The Quails, published in the *London Mercury* in 1921,
and later in John Collings Squire's *Second Anthology
of Modern Verse*, proclaims a poet in passionate revolt
against cruelty as the offspring of deplorable ignorance.
The author is Francis Brett Young, British novelist and
poet. In a prefatory note to *The Quails*, Mr. Young
states: " In the South of Italy the peasants put out the
eyes of a captured quail so that its cries may attract
the flocks of spring migrants into their nets."

> "All through the night
> I have heard the stuttering call of a blind quail,
> A caged decoy, under a cairn of stones,
> Crying for light as the quails cry for love."

These are the opening lines. They are followed by
forty more as tender in their pathos, and then the concluding lines:

> " Why should I be ashamed? Why should I rail
> Against the cruelty of men? Why should I pity,
> Seeing that there is no cruelty which men can image
> To match the subtle dooms that are wrought against them
> By blind spores of pestilence: seeing that each of us,

> Lured by dim hopes, flutters in the toils of death
> On a cold star that is spinning blindly through space
> Into the nets of time?
>
> So cried I, bitterly thrusting pity aside,
> Closing my lids to sleep. But sleep came not,
> And pity, with sad eyes,
> Crept to my side, and told me
> That the life of all creatures is brave and pitiful
> Whether they be men, with dark thoughts to vex them,
> Or birds, wheeling in the swift joys of flight,
> Or brittle ephemerids, spinning to death in the haze
> Of gold that quivers on dim evening waters;
> Nor would she be denied.
> The harshness died
> Within me, and my heart
> Was caught and fluttered like the palpitant heart
> Of a brown quail, flying
> To the call of her blind sister,
> And death, in the spring night."

Another noteworthy poem by this young author is *Bête
Humaine* in *Five Degrees South*.

Alfred Noyes, G. K. Chesterton, Christopher Benson, Wilfred R. Childe, John Collings Squire, D. H. Lawrence, Harold Monro, Winifred M. Letts, and Dorothea
MacKellar are among British poets who, in occasional
poems, are arrayed on the side of pity and justice for
animals.

In America there seems to be a steadily increasing
interest in the humane theme. Perhaps no poet chal-
lenges attention more courageously than Henry Herbert Knibbs, author of *Riders of the Stars, Songs of the
Outlands, Songs of the Trail*, and *Saddle Songs*, volumes
of western verse. He stands four square in his denun-
ciation of " Braves of the Hunt " who go out with

> ". . . . . . guides and gold and the polished
>   tube of steel,
> Playing safe with the hunting-pack, the trap and the
>   prism-glass; "
>
>   .   .   .   .

" Not with the strength of your brawn and thew matching
   the fury-fire
   Of the beast that fights for the life it loves; nay! but
   with sneaking skill."

The following line affirms the need for conservation of
wild animal life:

"   .   .   .   . So do our monarchs pass."

The American antelope, buffalo, and grizzly are passing, as are several species of bird life. The carrier
pigeon has become extinct. " Hunt with the camera "
is a timely slogan. American citizenship should have
regard for the preservation of its country's natural
beauty and wild life, if not for its own enjoyment, then
for the pride of posterity.

" O beautiful for spacious skies,
   For amber waves of grain,
   For purple mountain majesties
   Above the fruited plain!
   America! America!
   God shed His grace on thee
   And crown thy good with brotherhood
   From sea to shining sea! "

sings Katharine Lee Bates, another poet whose verses
express a noble regard for the native beauty of her
country. She, too, is quick to denounce needless destruction. *The Horses* and *Only Mules,* deploring the
sufferings of mute victims of warfare, had considerable
popularity during the World War. The former was
written in reply to the news item: " Thus far 80,000
horses have been shipped from the United States to the
European belligerents." The latter took exception to
the " rights " in the authorized statement: " The submarine was quite within its rights in sinking the cargo
of the Armenian,—1,422 mules valued at $191,400."
To Sigurd and *Laddie* are two elegies that hold solace

for readers bereft of dog companions. They are comforting sequels to Kipling's *The Power of the Dog.*

The author of *The Man with the Hoe* might be expected to enlist in service that looks toward higher civilization. Not a few of his poems bear testimony to such activity. *The Fate of the Fur Folk* was written in ardent protest to the use of the steel trap, " one of the most diabolical instruments of prolonged torture ever invented by the human mind." Well may Mr. Markham ask:

> " Ladies, are the furs you wear
> Worth the hell of this despair? "

This poem was read at the world convention of societies for the prevention of cruelty to children and animals, held in New York City in 1923. It was later published by *The Ladies' Home Journal*, and is printed entire in Mr. Markham's introduction to this book.

The steel trap calls to mind another poet and another poem. The poet is Lew Sarett, whose volume, *Slow Smoke*, received in 1924 the annual award of *The Poetry Society of America*. The poem is *Four Little Foxes*, which appeared first in *The Atlantic Monthly*.

> " Speak gently, Spring, and make no sudden sound;
> For in my windy valley, yesterday I found
> New-born foxes squirming on the ground—
> Speak gently.
>
> Walk softly, March, forbear the bitter blow;
> Her feet within a trap, her blood upon the snow,
> The four little foxes saw their mother go—
> Walk softly.
>
> Go lightly, Spring, oh, give them no alarm;
> When I covered them with boughs to shelter them
> from harm,
> The thin blue foxes suckled at my arm—
> Go lightly.

> Step softly, March, with your rampant hurricane;
>   Nuzzling one another, and whimpering with pain,
>   The new little foxes are shivering in the rain—
>   Step softly."

From his forest retreat in northern Wisconsin, Mr. Sarett writes: " And, peculiarly, many of the poems I plan to do lie in the field of your interest—poems on and for animals,—dogs, horses, deer,—creatures hunted and hurt." In his rare volume, lyric compassion sings on page after page in such poems as,—*Breakers of Broncos, When the Round Buds Brim, Blacktail Deer, Ghost, Readers of Loam, Dynamite, Colloquy with a Coyote,* and *To a Wild Goose Over Decoys.*

Mahlon Leonard Fisher, editor of the brochure entitled *The Sonnet,* and author of *Sonnets: A First Series,* is another American poet endowed with humanitarian perception. Verification of this statement is provided by his companion sonnets, *Oxen* and *The Old Plough-Horse,* and by such lyrics as *In Cool, Green Haunts:*

> " A sweet, deep sense of mystery filled the wood.
>   A star, like that which woke o'er Bethlehem,
>   Shone on the still pool's brow for diadem—
>   The first to fall of summer's multitude!
> In cool, green haunts, where, haply, Robin Hood
>   Ranged royally, of old, with all his train,
>   A hushed expectance, such as augurs rain,
>   Enthralled me and possessed me where I stood.
>
> Then came the wind, with low word as he went;
>   The quick wren, swift repeating what he said;
>   A chattering chipmunk lured me on and led
> Where scented brakes 'neath some wee burden bent:—
>   One look—'t was this those wild things yearned to say:
>   ' A little brown-eyed fawn was born to-day! ' "

Several poets have written poems of humanitarian import, but probably not with humanitarian intent. One is Vachel Lindsay, who, in *The Broncho That Would Not Be Broken*, has given the world not only an immortal poem but a heart-breaking picture of broncho training. There is something to ponder in the bitter contrast of broncho and breaker:

> " You were born with the pride of the lords great and
>   olden
> Who danced, through the ages, in corridors golden.
> In all the wide farm place the person most human."
>
> .   .   .   .
>
> " But arch were your thoughts, all malice displacing,
> Though the horse-killers came, with snake-whips
>   advancing.
> You bantered and cantered away your last chance.
> And they scourged you; with Hell in their speech
>   and their faces,
> O broncho that would not be broken of dancing."

Richard Burton, Robert Carr, James Beebe Carrington, Arthur Chapman, Francis Holman Day, Glenn Ward Dresbach, Louise Driscoll, Hamlin Garland, Strickland Gillilan, Charlotte Perkins Gilman, William Griffith, Edgar Guest, Arthur Guiterman, John Russell Hayes, DuBose Heyward, Charles Keeler, Jeannette Marks, Gertrude Huntington McGiffert, Angela Morgan, Christopher Morley, Cale Young Rice, Clinton Scollard, George Sterling, Charles Hanson Towne, and Florence Wilkinson are in the increasing number of American poets who are helping to create a new era for what is popularly known as the lower creation.

Frances E. Clarke

INTRODUCTION

BY EDWIN MARKHAM

Author of " The Man With the Hoe,"
and other poems

GLIMPSES of animal life are woven into the race memory. Looking back over the vista of history, we find that the earliest traditions and records of the race reveal men at work with the animals about them as friends and servants.

An ancient tablet in Egypt, for instance, shows a man and an ox in the threshing field, the workman cheering on his patient work-mate with the words:

> " Step along, step along faster . . .
> The husks for yourself:
> The corn for the master."

Indeed, Egypt went to the length of deifying certain animals for their strength or sagacity, and punished all who violated this sacredness.

Animals were lifted into a high place in all the ancient sacrifices intended to appease the anger of the gods. The Greeks offered to their hungry deities the savor of fat bulls,—offered the animals most prized and precious. In our own Scriptures, we find intimations of an old and tender bond between man and the animals. To appease and to please Jehovah, the ancient Hebrews brought to the sacrificial altar their most innocent and lovely possessions, the dove and the lamb.

So in the long march of the ancient religions, as well

as in the misty whirl of myth and fairy tale, animals have been man's comfort, man's help, man's hostages to the gods.

The dog was one of man's earliest companions. When Azarias and Tobias went forth, as told in the Apocrypha, "The young man's dog went with them." When in the Odyssey, Ulysses returned after his long absence in the Trojan war, his old dog welcomed him back.

And the horse has been loved and honored even from the ages of heroic myth. You remember the horses of Apollo. The shining Hours led them forth from the lofty stalls, led them forth harnessed and fed full of ambrosia; whereat the beamy God, seizing the reins, sprang to his place in the car and leaned forward as he urged across the perilous heavens the chariot of the sun.

At a later epoch in Egypt, we are told that Joseph gave corn in return for horses; and all through the Bible sounds the pleasant or terrible tramp and snort of these faithful multipliers of the strength and the speed of man.

The ancient teachers seem never to have forgotten utterly to impress upon men the duty of considering the rights of animals. We all remember that in the Ten Commandments it was ordained that cattle as well as menservants and maidservants should have their rest on the Sabbath day. We are told that in the destruction of Nineveh "much cattle" were spared; and we are told—with a touch of sweet humanity—that Jacob led the cattle softly on "as they were able to endure." We are also assured that the ox and the ass were not to plow together because of the unequal strain.

Turn now to India, and you will find that love and care for animals are urged upon men by the great Buddha Sakyamuni, that immortal prophet of the Orient. You remember how beautifully his early ministry began in that earnest protest, defending the swan injured by the flying arrow of the hunter. He finds the dying bird beside the way, and lifts it gently. You have read the story in *The Light of Asia:*

> " Then our Lord
> Laid the swan's neck beside his own smooth cheek
> And gravely spake: ' Say no! the bird is mine,
> The first of myriad things which shall be mine
> By right of mercy and love's lordliness.
> For now I know by what within me stirs,
> That I shall teach compassion unto men
> And be a speechless interpreter,
> Abating this accursed flood of woe,
> Not man's alone.' "

It has been said that Buddha, more than Christ, has expressed a sympathy for our kindred of fur and feather. This is not the case, for Christ's love and tenderness for these lesser kindred are expressed in His habitual word and attitude toward them.

So true is this that we feel that it was most appropriate that the birth of Jesus should have been in a manger in close neighborhood with the watching ox and ass. It appears at a later time that He approved of the recovery of the ox and ass when fallen into the pit, even upon the Sabbath day. He noted the sparrow on the wing, and He bears tender witness to the fact that a sparrow never falls without the Father's notice. In His effective speech, He expresses His desire to inbrother the people of His disturbed chaotic Jerusalem. So He cries out: " How often would I have gathered thy chil-

dren together even as a hen gathereth her chickens under her wings!" He could not have conceived of this
touching and powerful image unless He had often
watched with tender interest the mother-hen gathering
her chicks under her sheltering wings at the fall of the
night.

Yes, His eye of compassion was ever alert to behold
our humbler kindred. He saw the dove on the house-
top. He saw the shepherds passing with their flocks
in search of new pastures; and He noted with compassion a sheep which wandered lost and unshepherded
on the perilous hillsides. He not only beheld the strayed
sheep, but He also commemorates the shepherd who
leaves his safely folded flock to go out to seek and recover the wandered one.

Besides all this, we find His ever-devoted follower, St.
Francis of Assisi, turning with tenderness toward all
animals, seeing in them our lesser brethren of the common way.

If the followers of Jesus have not always been kind to
animals, we cannot charge their inhumanity to the compassionate One, the heart-warm nature-lover of Galilee.

Whatever else Jesus was, He was a poet; and the
poets have always been on the side of the angels, on the
side of humanity. Yet only in recent times have they
spoken so frequently and so forcibly in defense of the
oppressed.

However, as long ago as that old time when Greece
was in her glory, we hear Æschylus in *Prometheus Bound*
telling us that one of the three laws " of most revered
righteousness " demands that we hurt no living thing.
In little flashes of phrase, Shakespeare also lets out his

sympathy with animal life. He knows the nesting-place of the martlet or swallow on the castle eaves, and he pictures it for the heart as well as for the head:

> " This guest of summer,
> The temple-haunting martlet, does approve,
> By his loved masonry, that the heaven's breath
> Smells wooingly here: no jutty, frieze,
> Buttress, nor coign of vantage, but this bird
> Hath made his pendent bed and procreant cradle:
> Where they most breed and haunt, I have observed,
> The air is delicate."

And Shakespeare puts these compassionate words into the lips of Lear:

> " Mine enemy's dog,
> Though he had bit me, should have stood that night
> Against my fire."

Two hundred years later, we hear cries of protest out of the wild heart of William Blake:

> " A robin redbreast in a cage
> Puts all Heaven in a rage.
>
> A dog starved at his master's gate
> Predicts the ruin of the State.
>
> A skylark wounded on the wing
> Doth make a cherub cease to sing."

Long ago, all enlightened men realized that God is not pleased with blood sacrifice in His honor. But they have not yet fully learned that no harmless creature should be hurt or slain for any caprice of pleasure. Nor have certain women altogether learned that no little creature should be tortured or slaughtered to secure the feathers or the furs that contribute to the vanity of adornment.

In defense of these defenseless creatures, many of our

modern poets have spoken in impassioned terms. I myself in *The Fate of the Fur Folk* and in other verses have tried to cry protest against the immense cruelty of the steel-trap and other engines of animal suffering.

THE FATE OF THE FUR FOLK

Early, while the east is pale,
The trapper is out on the frozen trail;
Cruel traps are on his back,
Snares to line the woodland track;
Day by day he links the chain
Of these grim machines of pain,
In whose merciless iron jaws
Little fur folk die, because
Men must high on Fortune ride,
Women have an hour of pride.

Squirrel, ermine, sable, mole,
Out for food from cliff and hole;
Muskrat, silver fox and mink,
At the stream for evening drink—
All are tempted to this hell
That some bank account may swell.

Ladies, do you think of this—
Up where tempests howl and hiss,
Where the folk of hill and cave
Scream with no one there to save?
Do you see them crunched and lone,
Steel teeth biting into bone?

Ladies, did you ever see
An otter gnawing to get free?
Gnawing what? His fettered leg,
For he has no friend to beg.
Do you see that tortured shape
Gnaw his leg off to escape?

Have you seen these creatures die
While the bleeding hours go by—
These poor mothers in the wood
Robbed of joy and motherhood?
Do you, when at night you kneel,
See them in their traps of steel—
Not alone by pain accurst,
But by hunger and by thirst?
Do you hear their dying cries
When the crows pick out their eyes?

Yes, sometimes in dreams you hear
Yells of agony and fear
From the snare of iron teeth,
With that panting thing beneath.
For all night, where storms are whirled,
Groans are curdling the white world—
Groans of mothers dying so,
Groans of little ones that go
Homeless, hungry in the snow.

Ladies, are the furs you wear
Worth the hell of this despair?

NOTE—The above poem will lead off the group of humane
verses in Edwin Markham's *Collected Poems* to be printed
in the Autumn of 1927. Free copies of this poem for dis-
tribution can be secured by writing—with self-addressed
envelope—to Edwin Markham, West New Brighton, N. Y.

Frances E. Clarke has been touched by the pathos of all this Iliad of suffering. Helped by many comrades in this great compassion for the defenseless, she is working for the humane cause. And she has now compiled and edited this anthology of poems, selected from distinguished poets, living and dead.

This is the only anthology of its kind in America. The time is opportune for its appearance, for a great wave of humane sentiment is sweeping over the continent. We see this in the recent formation of a national society to abolish the use of the steel trap; we see it in the soaring membership of the Jack London Society, organized to protest against the training and exhibition of performing animals.

It is needless to say that all persons in sympathy with the animal kingdom will wish to do all in their power to make this volume a triumphant force in materializing and perpetuating the gospel of loving kindness.

CONTENTS

PRELUDE

CONTENTS

SONGS IN MANY KEYS

CONTENTS xxix

THE HORSE

"MY DOG AND I"

THE CAT

CONTENTS

BURDEN-BEARERS

SMALL CREATURES

"UPON A THOUSAND HILLS"

OXEN

"THE LAST AND LEAST OF THINGS"

Poetry

PRELUDE

Yet, taught by time, my heart has learned to glow
For other's good, and melt at other's woe.

Odyssey, BOOK XVIII.

Translation by Alexander Pope.

PRELUDE

TEWKESBURY ROAD

By John Masefield

It is good to be out on the road, and going one knows
    not where,
  Going through meadow and village, one knows not
    whither nor why;
Through the grey light drift of the dust, in the keen
    cool rush of the air,
  Under the flying white clouds, and the broad blue lift
    of the sky.

And to halt at the chattering brook, in the tall green
    fern at the brink
  Where the harebell grows, and the gorse, and the fox-
    gloves purple and white;
Where the shy-eyed delicate deer come down in a troop
    to drink
  When the stars are mellow and large at the coming on
    of the night.

O, to feel the beat of the rain, and the homely smell
    of the earth,
  Is a tune for the blood to jig to, a joy past power
    of words;
And the blessed green comely meadows are all a-ripple
    with mirth
  At the noise of the lambs at play and the dear wild
    cry of the birds.

A SONG OF SOLOMON

By Josephine Preston Peabody

King Solomon was the wisest man
    Of all that have been kings.
He built an House unto the Lord;
    And he sang of creeping things,

Of creeping things, of things that fly,
    Or swim within the seas;
Of the little weed along the wall,
    And of the cedar-trees.

And happier he, without mistake,
    Than all men since alive.
God's House he built; and he did make
    A thousand songs and five.

THE BROTHER OF A WEED

By Arthur Symons

I

I have shut up my soul with vehemence
Against the world, and opened every sense
That I may take, but not for love or price,
The world's best gold and frankincense and spice.
I have delighted in all visible things
And built the world of my imaginings
Out of the splendour of the day and night,
And I have never wondered that my sight

Should serve me for my pleasure, or that aught
Beyond the lonely mirror of my thought
Lived, and desired me. I have walked as one
Who dreams himself the master of the sun,
And that the seasons are as seraphim
And in the months and stars bow down to him.

II

And I have been of all men loneliest,
And my chill soul has withered in my breast
With pride and no content and loneliness.
And I have said: To make our sorrow less
Is there not pity in the heart of flowers,
· Or joy in wings of birds that might be ours?
Is there a beast that lives, and will not move
Toward our poor love with a more lovely love?
And might not our proud hopeless sorrow pass
If we became as humble as the grass?
I will get down from my sick throne where I
Dreamed that the seasons of the earth and sky,
The leash of months and stars, were mine to lead,
And pray to be the brother of a weed.

III

I am beginning to find out that there
Are beings to be pitied everywhere.
Thus when I hear, at night an orphaned sheep
Crying as a child cries, how can I sleep?
Yet the night-birds are happy, or I seem
To hear them in the hollow of a dream,
Whispering to each other in the trees,
And through the window comes a leaping breeze

That has the sea-salt in it. When I hear
Crying of oxen, that, in deadly fear,
Rough men, with cruel dogs about them, drive
Into the torture-house of death alive,
How can I sit under a tree and read
A happy idle book, and take no heed?

IV

Why is not sorrow kinder to all these
That have short lives and yet so little ease?
Life is but anxious fear to lambs and hens,
And even the birds are enemies of men's
Because they rob a cherry-tree; the mole
Cannot be left in quiet in his hole
Though he is softer than a velvet gown;
The caterpillar is soon trodden down
Under a boot's ignorant heel, though he
Is woven finer than old tapestry.
The worm is close and busy and discreet,
The foe of no man living: no man's feet
Spare him, if he but crawl into the sun.
Who can be happy, while these things are done?

V

Why are the roses filled with such a heat,
And are so gaudy and riotously sweet,
When any wind may snap them from the stem
Or any little green worm canker them?
Why is the dawn-delivered butterfly
So arrogant, knowing he has to die
Before another dawn has waked his brother?
Why do the dragon-flies outshoot each other

With such an ardour, knowing that the **noon**
Will put away his shining arrows soon?
Why is the seed that, having got to corn,
Must come to bread, so eager to be born?
Why is it that the joy of living gives
Forgetfulness to everything that lives?

A TULIP GARDEN

By Amy Lowell

Guarded within the old red wall's embrace,
  Marshalled like soldiers in gay company,
  The tulips stand arrayed.   Here infantry
Wheels out into the sunlight.   What bold grace
Sets off their tunics, white with crimson lace!
  Here are platoons of gold-frocked cavalry,
  With scarlet sabres tossing in the eye
Of purple batteries, every gun in place.
  Forward they come, with flaunting colours spread,
With torches burning, stepping out in time
  To some quick, unheard march.   Our ears are dead,
We cannot catch the tune.   In pantomime
  Parades that army.   With our utmost powers
  We hear the wind stream through a bed of flowers.

THE MARSH

By Glenn Ward Dresbach

Farmlands about the marsh are dreary
  With sameness and unending toil
But in the marsh are groups of willows
  And calamus grows in the treacherous soil.

A meadow brook through the cool lush grasses
  Makes pools where water lilies bloom,
And bob-o-links shake dewy music
  On marsh airs dreamy with perfume.

One farmer said, " The place is worthless—
  The bogs and rains must have their way."
Another said, " Our children plague us
  For sneaking to the marsh to play."

Some dreaming farm lad yet may wander
  Into the marsh and find the words
To make them love it and hear its whispers
  Above the lowing of the herds.

He may—I doubt it since so many
  Who left their chores and ran with me
Down to the marsh to play are dreary
  For beauty they no longer see.

Unheard the bob-o-links are singing,
  Unloved the willows sway in light—
All that the grown folks near the marsh know
  Is distant sound of frogs at night.

PITIFUL

By John Galsworthy

When God made man to live his hour
  And hitch his wagon to a star,
He made a being without power
  To see His creatures as they are.

He made a masterpiece of will,
  Superb above its mortal lot,
Invincible by any ill—
  Imagination He forgot!

This man of God's, with every wish
  To earn the joys of Kingdom Come,
Will prison up the golden fish
  In bowl no bigger than a drum.
And though he withers from remorse
  When he refuses Duty's call
He'll cut the tail of any horse,
  And carve each helpless animal.

No spur to humour doth he want,
  In wit the Earth he overlords,
Yet drives the hapless elephant
  To clown and tumble on " the boards."
This man, of every learning chief,
  So wise that he can read the skies,
Can fail to read the wordless grief
  That haunts a prisoned monkey's eyes.

He'll prate of " mercy to the weak "
  And strive to lengthen human breath,
But starve the little gaping beak
  And hunt the timid hare to death.
Though with a spirit wild as wind,
  The world at liberty he'd see,
He cannot any reason find
  To set the tameless tiger free.

Such healing victories he wins,
  And drugs away the mother's pangs,
But sets his God-forsaken gins
  To mangle rabbits with their fangs.
Devout, he travels all the roads
  To track and vanquish all the pains,
And yet—the wagon overloads,
  The watch-dog to his barrel chains.

He'd soar the heavens in his flight
  To measure Nature's majesty,
Yet take his children to delight
  In captive eagles' tragedy.
This man, in knowledge absolute,
  Who right, and love, and honour woos,
Yet keeps the pitiful poor brute
  To mope and languish in his Zoos.

You creatures wild, of field and air,
  Keep far from men, where'er they go!
God set no speculation there—
  Alack!—We know not what we do!

ON THE COMPANIONSHIP WITH NATURE

By Archibald Lampman

Let us be much with Nature; not as they
That labour without seeing, that employ
Her unloved forces, blindly without joy;
Nor those whose hands and crude delights obey
The old brute passion to hunt down and slay;
But rather as children of one common birth,
Discerning in each natural fruit of earth

Kinship and bond with this diviner clay.
Let us be with her wholly at all hours,
With the fond lover's zest, who is content
If his ear hears, and if his eye but sees;
So shall we grow like her in mould and bent,
Our bodies stately as her blessèd trees,
Our thoughts as sweet and sumptuous as her
    flowers.

THE SEEING EYE

By John Kendrick Bangs

Small things and humble greatest lessons hold,
Which to the seeing eye they soon unfold—
As on some thorny road my way I pass
I get new courage from a blade of grass,
Which 'mid the turmoil and the weeds that kill
Holds fearlessly its course appointed still.

BROTHER BEASTS

By Cale Young Rice

Winter is here
And there are no leaves
On the naked trees,
Save stars twinkling
As the wind blows.
Soft to the branches
The little screech-owl
Silently comes,
Silently goes,
With weird tremolos.

I would go out
And gather the stars
The wind shakes down,
Were they not scattered
So far in the West.
I would go ask
The little screech-owl
If he finds ease
There in his nest
After his quest.

I would go learn
If the small gray mouse
Who sets up house
In the frozen meadow
Dreams of the stars.
Or what he thinks
There in the dark,
When flake on flake
Of white snow bars
Him in with its spars.

I would go out
And learn these things
That I may know
What dream or desire
Troubles my brothers
In nest or hole.
For even as I
The owl and the mouse,
Or blinded mole
With unborn soul,
May have some goal.

THE BELLS OF HEAVEN

By Ralph Hodgson

'Twould ring the bells of Heaven
The wildest peal for years,
If Parson lost his senses
And people came to theirs,
And he and they together
Knelt down with angry prayers
For tamed and shabby tigers
And dancing dogs and bears,
And wretched, blind pit ponies,
And little hunted hares.

AN ANSWER

By S. St. G. Lawrence

You call them " beasts that perish," and you say
　That we, God's higher children, have the right
To trample our dumb brothers in the clay,
　And use against them all our greater might;

To force the horses on their weary way,
　Urged by the stinging whip and tight-drawn rein;
To take the slow, dull cattle for our prey,
　And slay the furry creatures for our gain.

They may not reach the heaven we hope to win,
　And so ten thousand of their lives are naught
Against one human life, though dark with sin—
　Their soulless sufferings are not worth a thought.

Not so, my friend; if this poor life be all
  Our Father has vouchsafed them, surely they
To whom no glad to-morrow may befall
  Have all the better claim to their to-day.

QUESTIONS

By Oliver Wendell Holmes

Is there not something in the pleading eye
Of the poor brute that suffers, which arraigns
The law that bids it suffer? Has it not
A claim for some remembrance in the book
That fills its pages with the idle words
Spoken of man? Or is it only clay,
Bleeding and aching in the potter's hand,
Yet all his own to treat it as he will,
And when he will to cast it at his feet,
Shattered, dishonored, lost for evermore?
My dog loves me, but could he look beyond
His earthly master, would his love extend
To Him who—hush! I will not doubt that He
Is better than our fears, and will not wrong
The least, the meanest of created things.

ONCE ON A TIME

By Margaret Benson

Once on a time I used to dream
  Strange spirits moved about my way,
And I might catch a vagrant gleam,
  A glint of pixy or of fay;

Their lives were mingled with my own,
   So far they roamed, so near they drew;
And when I from a child had grown,
   I woke—and found my dream was true.

For one is clad in coat of fur,
   And one is decked with feathers gay;
Another, wiser, will prefer
   A sober suit of Quaker gray:
This one's your servant from his birth,
   And that a Princess you must please,
And this one loves to wake your mirth,
   And that one likes to share your ease.

O gracious creatures, tiny souls!
   You seem so near, so far away,
Yet while the cloudland round us rolls,
   We love you better every day.

AN ANIMAL SONG

(For *Lone Hunter's Stories of the Fur Folk*)

By Kathleen Conyngham Greene

These are your brothers; listening you have heard
Their thin faint voice that speaks without a word,
That speaks from beast to beast since life began,
And oh! so rarely speaks from beast to man.

For you, I think, with open eyes have trod
The long, long road that leads at last to God:
And over all the centuries between
Look and remember where our lives have been.

And, seeing that we rose, can trust that they
Not unrecorded suffer day by day;
Can trace the purpose through their endless pain,
And hold their loves and labours not in vain.

These are your beasts. Too low, we say, for sin,
Unsharing in the fight the world must win:
We spurn them, scorn them, slaughter them for
    play—
Are we more fit for Heaven than such as they?

APRIL IN THE CITY

By Elisabeth Scollard

Her lyric laughter ripples down the street;
The echoing tread of feet
Goes surging by the door
As in the countless April tides of yore;
A tender touch of green
Amid the parks is seen,
And down the bay
The blue-gold flag of day
Has been unfurled across a height of sky;
A breeze drifts by . . .
Bringing a hint of dancing daffodils
And some quaint garden where the sunlight spills
Its mellow loveliness; the tired streets sing
Beneath the magic of another spring;
And yet how much, how more than much they miss
Who know no other April day than this
Deep in the heart of town!
Theirs is no wonder of green sprung from brown,

Music of melting snows
Or song of wind that blows
Across far hills where blue-eyed violets wake;
They see no pine grove bordering a lake;
The tragedy is theirs who never trod
Paths made by God;
An artifice of spring is all they know
Here in the city's endless ebb and flow.

A BROOK IN THE CITY

By Robert Frost

A farmhouse lingers, though averse to square
With the new city street it has to wear
A number in.   But what about the brook
That held the house as in an elbow-crook?
I ask as one who knew the brook, its strength
And impulse, having dipped a finger length
And made it leap my knuckle, having tossed
A flower to try its currents where they crossed.
The meadow grass could be cemented down
From growing under pavements of a town;
The apple trees be sent to hearth-stone flame.
Is water wood to serve a brook the same?
How else dispose of an immortal force
No longer needed?   Staunch it at its source
With cinder loads dumped down? The brook was
      thrown
Deep in a sewer dungeon under stone
In fetid darkness still to live and run—
And all for nothing it had ever done

Except forget to go in fear perhaps.
No one would know except for ancient maps
That such a brook ran water. But I wonder
If from its being kept forever under,
These thoughts may not have risen that so keep
This new-built city from both work and sleep.

THE SPIRIT OF NATURE

By Richard Realf

O Earth! thou hast not any wind that blows
  Which is not music; every weed of thine,
  Pressed rightly, flows in aromatic wine;
And every humble hedge-row flower that grows,
And every little brownbird that doth sing,
  Hath something greater than itself, and bears
A living word to every living thing,
  Albeit it holds the message unawares.
All shapes and sounds have something which is not
  Of them; a spirit broods amid the grass,
Vague outlines of the everlasting thought
  Lie in the melting shadows as they pass,
And touch of an eternal presence thrills
The fringes of the sunsets and the hills.

HIS EPITAPH

By Clarence E. Flynn

He wasn't rich; he wasn't great,
  His place was lowly and obscure.
His clothing was not up-to-date,
  His house was tumble-down and poor.

No special honor did he claim.
  He never walked with lords and kings.
No glory has illumed his name,
  But he was kind to helpless things.

He won no victories to boast.
  He made no conquests, waged no strife.
He never led a conquering host;
  He lived an unpretentious life.
But, when is writ the judgment scroll,
  And Time its final verdict brings,
This will be said of him: his soul
  Was rich in love for helpless things.

ON THE DEDICATION OF A DRINKING FOUNTAIN

ALAMEDA, CALIFORNIA

By Charles Keeler

The skies yielded up their bounty unto the earth;
In the Sierra heights the thunder-cloud gave of its
    plenty,
And the leaden curtain of the mist of the winter moons
From seaward and the south swept in to drench the
    valleys;
Yea, the teeming mothers of the heavens gave birth to
    the rain children,
And the earth was gladdened and sent up pæans of joy.
The grass-blades were the prayers of the grateful land,
And the happy flowers were the hymns of the exultant
    earth.

Then all the little rillets began to sing songs of praise;
Jubilant canticles of swelling brooks arose from every
    mountain side,
And the voices of streams all joined in a grand halle-
    lujah chorus,
And the rivers chanted in deep-voiced harmony thanks-
    giving to the Sender of Rain.

O ye babbling brooks and mellifluous rills,
O ye laughing waterfalls and crystal cascades,
O ye joyous life-giving waters, careering deliriously
    downward,
Sing Te Deums triumphal on the awakening of spirit
    from earth!

In the mountains loom the titan watchmen pine-trees,
And the vast Sequoias near their sentinel towers anear
    the streams;
In the valley-lands the oaks, benignant guardians,
Spread their gnarled boughs beside the rivers.
There the wild birds come to drink,
And the thirsty bear leads forth her cubs to lap the tide,
And the native woman, grinding acorns in potholes by
    the river,
Scoops up the water in the hollow of her hand to quench
    her thirst.

Then, lo, another day, another race, another world!
The white man, he who loves power more than beauty,
The ravager of nature, the destroyer of the forest,
The slayer of all wild things, of trees and flowers and
    birds,

Cometh unto the land, and, glorying in his might,
Lays waste all things most fair.
He buildeth cities and the joyous streams he leadeth
into murky sewers,
Yea, the sweet springs he polluteth and hideth beneath
the ground.
Where once were flower-starred banks and sighing trees
He buildeth drear walls and sad unlovely temples.
But the still small voice of the brooklet aye whispers
unto him,
And the mute appeals of thirsty brutes still clamor for
the life-giving water.
Though the deer and the mountain lion no longer roam
abroad,
The helpless beasts by man subdued look up into his face
And silent beg for drink.

Then somewhere in the great cold heart of man
Awakens the spirit of tenderness and compassion,
And the selfish monster arouses out of his lethargy,
And the God-spark kindles love in him,
And he knows that the beast is his brother;
Aye, he knows that there is but one family and one
Father,
And he loves the helpless ones and stretches out a hand
to them.
Come, come, O children, little brothers and great,
Let us drink together, for this is the holy sacrament,
This is the communion service in which we all may join,
This, the life-giving water, O my brothers, little birds
and faithful dogs and patient horses,
The same sweet water that quenches your thirst and
mine,

Drink of this holy fountain reared in the midst of the
    sordid city,
Drink that you may be appeased and satisfied,
Drink, for such is the will of God, my brothers,
And he who thinks of the least of the children of the
    all-merciful Father,
Aye he shall be rewarded with the gift of love from on
    high,
And the bond of fellowship shall gather him in with its
    benediction.

COMPASSION

AN ODE

*In Celebration of the Centenary of the Royal Society
for the Prevention of Cruelty to Animals*

By Thomas Hardy

I

Backward among the dusky years
A lonesome lamp is seen arise,
Lit by a few fain pioneers
    Before incredulous eyes.
We read the legend that it lights:
" Why should throughout this land of historied rights
Mild creatures, despot-doomed, bewildered, plead
Their often hunger, thirst, pangs, prisonment,
    In deep dumb gaze more eloquent
      Than tongues of widest heed? "

II

What was faint-written, read in a breath
In that year—ten-times-ten away—
A larger clearer conscience saith
    More sturdily to-day.
  But still those innocents are thralls
To throbless hearts, near, far, that hear no calls
Of honour towards their too-dependent frail;
And from Columbia Cape to Ind we see
    How helplessness breeds tyranny
      In power above assail.

III

  Cries still are heard in secret nooks,
  Till hushed with gag or slit or thud;
  And hideous dens whereon none looks
    Are blotched with needless blood.
  But here, in battlings, patient, slow,
Much has been won—more, maybe, than we know —
And on we labour stressful. " Ailinon! "
A mighty voice calls: " But may the good prevail! "
    And " Blessed are the merciful! "
      Calls yet a mightier one.
January 22, 1924.

The ADORATION of the TREES

There is nevertheless, a certain respect and a general duty of humanity that ties us, not only to beasts that have life and sense, but even to trees and plants.

Of Cruelty.   MICHAEL DE MONTAIGNE.

THE ADORATION OF THE TREES

GOOD COMPANY

By Karle Wilson Baker

To-day I have grown taller from walking with the trees,
The seven sister-poplars who go softly in a line;
And I think my heart is whiter for its parley with a star
That trembled out at nightfall and hung above the pine.

The call-note of a redbird from the cedars in the dusk
Woke his happy mate within me to an answer free and
    fine;
And a sudden angel beckoned from a column of blue
    smoke—
*Lord, who am I that they should stoop—these holy folk
    of thine?*

SERMONS IN TREES

By Florence Wilkinson

The purple of early November
    Lies like a dream on the hill;
In this basking hollow of woodland
    The berry-vines glitter and thrill,
And a maple is hushed to remember
Trancèd days of quiet September,
    And the gold that she used to spill.

My feet through the wood-path bearing
  Are an alien noise in the dale,
Stirring to wings of terror
  A partridge or two from the trail;
So with my uncourteous daring
I have hindered their leisurely faring,
  The pretty brown birds of the dale.

I am humbled and full of repentance
  For my race's enmity,
That these gentle-eyed wood-creatures
  Should whir from their hostelry;
And I fain would make their acquaintance
That they should reverse the sentence
  And not be afraid of me.

A tawny squirrel comes whisking
  Around the bole of a tree,
With his bright shy look untroubled
  And his tail a-quiver with glee;
I am glad of his billowy risking,
The trustful heart of his frisking;
And I thank my brother the squirrel,
  For his friendliness to me.

TREES

By Joyce Kilmer

I think that I shall never see
A poem lovely as a tree.

A tree whose hungry mouth is pressed
Against the earth's sweet flowing breast;

A tree that looks at God all day
And lifts her leafy arms to pray;

A tree that may in summer wear
A nest of robins in her hair;

Upon whose bosom snow has lain;
Who intimately lives with rain.

Poems are made by fools like me,
But only God can make a tree.

A WASTED MORNING

By Abbie Farwell Brown

I wasted a morning!
                    Where?   And Why?
I let swift hours go silently by,
As I lay at the foot of an ancient tree,
And let God's universe talk to me.

Wind and shadow, cloud and bird,
Spoke each to my heart a musical word.
The little brown cone that fell on my cheek,
The squirrel who mocked with an impudent squeak,
The golden mushroom brimmed with death,
The twin-flower blessing the air with its breath;
Old spider spinning above my head
A magical dream with her rainbow thread;
The liliput vases of moss below;
The sudden caw of a picket crow;

The rhythmical green of a supple snake
Quivering into a lair of brake;
The grumbling bee, the whispering pine—
What need had they for a word of mine?
They lived the poem; they wove the spell
No tongue could utter, no phrases tell;
And a human voice could but disgrace
The eloquent stillness of the place.

So I lay at the foot of the ancient tree,
And let God's free verse sing to me.

A B C'S IN GREEN

By Leonora Speyer

The trees are God's great alphabet:
With them He writes in shining green
Across the world His thoughts serene.

He scribbles poems against the sky
With a gay, leafy lettering,
For us and for our bettering.

The wind pulls softly at His page,
And every star and bird
Repeats in dutiful delight His word,
And every blade of grass
Flutters to class.

Like a slow child that does not heed,
I stand at summer's knees,
And from the primer of the wood
I spell that life and love are good,
I learn to read.

TREE FEELINGS

By Charlotte Perkins Gilman

I wonder if they like it—being trees?
I suppose they do. . . .
It must feel good to have the ground so flat,
And feel yourself stand right straight up like that—
So stiff in the middle—and then branch at ease,
Big boughs that arch, small ones that bend and blow,
And all those fringy leaves that flutter so.
You'd think they'd break off at the lower end
When the wind fills them, and their great heads bend.
But then you think of all the roots they drop,
As much at bottom as there is on top,—
A double tree, widespread in earth and air
Like a reflection in the water there.

I guess they like to stand still in the sun
And just breathe out and in, and feel the cool sap run;
And like to feel the rain run through their hair
And slide down to the roots and settle there.
But I think they like wind best. From the light touch
That lets the leaves whisper and kiss so much,
To the great swinging, tossing, flying wide,
And all the time so stiff and strong inside!
And the big winds, that pull, and make them feel
How long their roots are, and the earth how leal!

And O the blossoms! And the wild seeds lost!
And jewelled martyrdom of fiery frost!
And fruit-trees. I'd forgotten. No cold gem,
But to be apples—And bow down with them!

THE HEALING OF THE WOOD

By Clinton Scollard

To heal mine aching moods,
Give me God's virgin woods,
His cloistral solitudes,
　　Where none intrudes!

A dim sequestered place,
With leaves that link and lace,
Where peace and primal grace
　　Meet face to face.

There would I gain heart's-ease
From the sweet calm of trees,
And the low melodies
　　Of birds and bees.

There would the balm distill
A soothing for all ill;
With cheerfulness the rill
　　My heart would fill.

I would go softly thence
With a far kindlier sense;
With more benevolence,
　　And less pretence.

Fairer the sky would ope;
Less would I, faltering, grope;
But tread life's onward slope
　　With surer hope!

MY LEGACY

By Ethelwyn Wetherald

The little tree I planted out
  And often muse upon,
May be alive to grow and thrive
And out into the sunlight strive,
  When I am dead and gone.

So it shall be my legacy
  To toilers in the sun,
So sweet its shade, each man and maid
May be induced to take a spade
  And plant another one.

THE TREE'S WAY

By George Cronyn

The high trees are honest folk;
They do not stand so much aloof
Up under heaven's roof,
Altho' they are earth's fairest cloak.
Their lives are very calm and slow;
They wait for coming things to come,
They wait, they rest, they ponder some
Purpose forgotten long ago
Like quiet folk;
And sometimes I am moved to stroke
Hand-greeting as I pass them near,
And often I am sure I hear
An answer from these stately folk!

TREES

By Angela Morgan

Trees are astronomers, benign and hoary,
Tellers of tall antiquity, who stand
Bastioned upon the bosom of the land
Yet freed eternally from earth's red story.
No lowly secrets of the dark soil
Command their toil;
Their learnèd eyes
Fastened in solemn rapture on the skies
Witness the bright procession of the stars move on
From early dark till dawn.
Seeing Orion with his blazing shield
Marshal his hosts upon the battlefield.
Beholding Perseus, whose winged leap
Turns the devouring demon into stone,
Melting the while a virgin heart from sleep
That fair Andromeda shall be his own.

Trees are historians who tell upon their pages
The pageantry of ages.
No earthly dwellers they
Who watch all day
The scenic splendor of the sky
Drifting by.
Battles and beauties, palaces that rear
Imperial domes within the painted atmosphere.
Princes on prancing steeds,
Heroic deeds
Unseen of man, whose eager hours are spent
In ways unseemly to the firmament.

Fever and fret are stranger to the trees
Riding among the stars in giant ease,
Dwelling amid an ecstasy of light. . . .
Such glory as would stun our smaller sight.
Trees are historians who strive to render,
Year upon year, the record of the sky's splendor.
Shedding their flaming stars for us to see,
Printing their new green pages, tirelessly. . . .
While we, who gather handfuls of their gold
See not it is the starlight that we hold!

GREEN LEAVES

By Basho

Ah, how sublime—
The green leaves, the young leaves,
In the light of the sun!

TAPESTRY TREES

By William Morris

Oak. I am the Roof-tree and the Keel:
I bridge the seas for woe and weal.

Fir. High o'er the lordly oak I stand,
And drive him on from land to land.

Ash. I heft my brother's iron bane;
I shaft the spear and build the wain.

Yew. Dark down the windy dale I grow,
The father of the fateful Bow.

Poplar. The war shaft and the milking-bowl
I make, and keep the hay-wain whole.

Olive. The King I bless; the lamps I trim;
In my warm wave do fishes swim.

Apple-tree. I bowed my head to Adam's will;
The cups of toiling men I fill.

Vine. I draw the blood from out the earth;
I store the sun for winter mirth.

Orange-tree. Amidst the greenness of my night
My odorous lamps hang round and bright.

Fig-tree. I who am little among trees
In honey-making mate the bees.

Mulberry-tree. Love's lack hath dyed my berries
    red:
For Love's attire my leaves are shed.

Pear-tree. High o'er the mead-flowers' hidden
    feet
I bear aloft my burden sweet.

Bay. Look on my leafy boughs, the Crown
Of living song and dead renown!

MY CATHEDRAL

By Henry Wadsworth Longfellow

Like two cathedral towers these stately pines
    Uplift their fretted summits tipped with cones;
    The arch beneath them is not built with stones,
Not Art but Nature traced these lovely lines,
And carved this graceful arabesque of vines;
    No organ but the wind here sighs and moans,
    No sepulchre conceals a martyr's bones,
No marble bishop on his tomb reclines.
Enter! the pavement, carpeted with leaves,
    Gives back a softened echo to thy tread!
Listen! the choir is singing; all the birds,
In leafy galleries beneath the eaves,
    Are singing! listen, ere the sound be fled,
And learn there may be worship without words.

TO THE FALLEN GUM-TREE ON
MT. BAW-BAW

By Douglas W. Sladen

Yes, you lie there in state unearthly-solemn,
As though you'd been a heaven-supporting column,
Not a dead tree, of bark and foliage stript,
    Gigantic Eucalypt!

Your brothers, standing still, look half-defiant,
Half in mute silence for the fallen giant:
I doubt if aught so great e'er fell so far
    Except a falling star.

How tall would you have grown in course of Nature?
How old are your five hundred feet of stature?
Can you remember Noah and the flood
    When you were yet a bud?

Standing beside your trunk, one almost fancies
That he beholds the Middle Age romances,
And that the stories travellers have told,
    In books despised and old,

May not have been without some slight foundation,
Though they, of course, lost nothing in narration:
Herodotus we dare not now ignore
    As Egypt we explore.

What have you witnessed in your long existence
On remote ranges in the Gippsland distance?
Have you seen savage empires rise and fall,
    And stories tragical?

Did some black Dido, flying from her lovers,
Found a new kingdom, happy in thy covers,
Until a Maori Æneas came
    And lit the cursed flame?

Or a dark Robin Hood devote his leisure
To stealing skulls, and take a savage pleasure
In making, what blacks have by way of, priests,
    Uneasy at their feasts?

Or saw you earlier and gentler races,
Of nobler instincts and with fairer faces,
Die out before the circling boomerang
    And the black serpent's fang?

You look like a great chip of the creation,
A relic of the former Dispensation,
When men were forced to spend nine hundred years
       Here in this vale of tears.

Yet to us, creatures of a day, it's soothing
To know that, as trees go, your years are nothing:
There's little in Australia but rocks
       Of old age orthodox.

Lie there in fallen majesty, I love you!
May you lie there till the last trump shall move you,
Magnificent as Cheops in his crypt,
       You dead king Eucalypt!

(This tree, lying in one of the gorges of Mt. Baw-Baw, Gippsland, Victoria, measured, as it lay 480 feet long, and where the top had been broken off, had a diameter of two feet. Our most eminent naturalist pronounces it to have been at least 40 feet longer, as it stood.)

THE LESSON OF A TREE

By Walt Whitman

I should not take either the biggest or the most picturesque tree to illustrate it. Here is one of my favorites now before me, a fine yellow poplar, quite straight, perhaps ninety feet high, and four feet thick at the butt. How strong, vital, enduring! how dumbly eloquent! What suggestions of imperturbability and *being*, as against the human trait of mere *seeming*. Then the qualities, almost emotional, palpably artistic, heroic, of a tree; so innocent and harmless, yet so savage. It *is*, yet says nothing. How it rebukes by its tough and equable serenity all weathers, this gusty-tempered little whiffet, man, that runs indoors at a mite of rain or snow. Science (or rather half-way science) scoffs at a reminiscence of dryad and hamadryad, and of trees speaking. But, if they don't, they do as well as most speaking, writing, poetry, sermons—or rather they do a great deal better. I should say indeed that those old dryad reminiscences are quite as true as any, and profounder than most reminiscences we get. ("Cut this out," as the quack mediciners say, and keep by you.) Go and sit in a grove or woods, with one or more of those voiceless companions, and read the foregoing, and think.

SONGS in MANY KEYS

Hast thou named all the birds without a gun?

Forbearance. RALPH WALDO EMERSON.

SONGS IN MANY KEYS

STUPIDITY STREET

By Ralph Hodgson

I saw with open eyes
    Singing birds sweet
Sold in the shops
    For the people to eat,
Sold in the shops of
    Stupidity Street.

I saw in vision
    The worm in the wheat,
And in the shops nothing
    For people to eat;
Nothing for sale in
    Stupidity Street.

THE BIRDS

By Jack Collins Squire

Within mankind's duration, so they say,
Khephren and Ninus lived but yesterday.
Asia had no name till man was old
And long had learned the use of iron and gold;
And æons had passed, when the first corn was planted,
Since first the use of syllables was granted.

43

Men were on earth while climates slowly swung,
Fanning wide zones to heat and cold, and long
Subsidence turned great continents to sea,
And seas dried up, dried up interminably,
Age after age; enormous seas were dried
Amid wastes of land.   And the last monsters died.

Earth wore another face.   O since that prime
Man with how many works has sprinkled time!
Hammering, hewing, digging tunnels, roads;
Building ships, temples, multiform abodes.
How, for his body's appetites, his toils
Have conquered all earth's products, all her soils;
And in what thousand thousand shapes of art
He has tried to find a language for his heart!

Never at rest, never content or tired:
Insatiate wanderer, marvellously fired,
Most grandly piling and piling into the air
Stones that will topple or arch he knows not where.
And yet did I, this spring, think it more strange,
More grand, more full of awe, than all that change,
And lovely and sweet and touching unto tears,
That through man's chronicled and unchronicled
        years,
And even into that unguessable beyond
The water-hen has nested by a pond,
Weaving dry flags into a beaten floor,
The one sure product of her only lore.
Low on a ledge above the shadowed water
Then, when she heard no men, as nature taught her,
Plashing around with busy scarlet bill
She built that nest, her nest, and builds it still.

O let your strong imagination turn
The great wheel backward, until Troy unburn,
And then unbuild, and seven Troys below
Rise out of death, and dwindle, and outflow,
Till all have passed, and none has yet been there:
Back, ever back. Our birds still crossed the air;
Beyond our myriad changing generations
Still built, unchanged, their known inhabitations.
A million years before Atlantis was
Our lark sprang from some hollow in the grass,
Some old soft hoof-print in a tussock's shade;
And the wood-pigeon's smooth snow-white eggs were
     laid,
High amid green pines' sunset-coloured shafts,
And rooks their villages of twiggy rafts
Set on the tops of elms, where elms grew then,
And still the thumbling tit and perky wren
Popped through the tiny doors of cosy balls
And the blackbird lined with moss his high-built walls;
A round mud cottage held the thrush's young,
And straws from the untidy sparrow's hung.
And, skimming forktailed in the evening air,
When man first was were not the martens there?
Did not those birds some human shelter crave,
And stow beneath the cornice of his cave
Their dry tight cups of clay? And from each door
Peeped on a morning wiseheads three or four.

Yes, daw and owl, curlew and crested hern,
Kingfisher, mallard, water-rail, and tern,
Chaffinch and greenfinch, wagtail, stonechat, ruff,
Pied warbler, robin, fly-catcher, and chough,

Missel-thrush, magpie, sparrow-hawk, and jay,
Built, those far ages gone, in this year's way.
And the first man who walked the cliffs of Rame,
As I this year, looked down and saw the same
Blotches of rusty red on ledge and cleft
With grey-green spots on them, while right and left
A dizzying tangle of gulls were floating and flying,
Wheeling and crossing and darting, crying and cry-
    ing,
Circling and crying, over and over and over,
Crying with swoop and hover and fall and recover.
And below on a rock against the grey sea fretted,
Pipe-necked and stationary and silhouetted,
Cormorants stood in a wise, black, equal row
Above the nests and long blue eggs we know.

O delicate chain over all the ages stretched,
O dumb tradition from what far darkness fetched:
Each little architect with its one design
Perpetual, fixed and right in stuff and line,
Each little ministrant who knows one thing,
One learnèd rite to celebrate the spring.
Whatever alters else on sea or shore,
These are unchanging: man must still explore.

PENSIONERS

By W. M. Letts

My Pensioners who daily
Come here to beg their fare,
For all their need dress gaily
And have a jaunty air.

With " Tira—lira—lira—
Now of your charity
Pray help the little brethren
Of noble poverty."

One shines in glossy sable,
One wears a russet coat,
And one who seeks my table
Has red about his throat.
With " Tira—lira—lira—"
Gay waistcoat, speckled vest,
Black cap and fine blue bonnet,
They all come bravely dressed.

To them I gladly scatter
In this their time of need,
Heap bread upon their platter
And ask not for my meed,
But in the jocund spring-time
Their songs give back to me
A thousand-fold—my brethren
Of noble poverty.

From " MAY-DAY "

By Ralph Waldo Emerson

O birds, your perfect virtues bring,
Your song, your forms, your rhythmic flight,
Your manners for the heart's delight,
Nestle in hedge, or barn, or roof,
Here weave your chamber weather-proof,

Forgive our harms, and condescend
To man, as to a lubber friend,
And, generous, teach his awkward race
Courage, and probity, and grace!

A HEALTH TO THE BIRDS

By Seumas MacManus

Here's a health to the birds one and all!
A health to the birds great and small!
The birds that from hill and hedge call,
Through the highlands and islands of grey
Donegal—
Here's a health to them,
Health to them,
Health to them all!

I

Here's a health to the mavis!
A health to the mavis that sits on the thorn,
And trolls a gay breastful to brighten the morn,
And lighten the load of the man in the corn!
May its breast ne'er be tuneless, its heart ne'er
forlorn—
A health to the mavis!

II

Here's a health to the leverock!
A health to the leverock that loves the blue sky!
No bog is too low, no hill is too high,
And the moor's not too poor, for the leverock to lie;
May its name, and its fame, and its song, never die!
A health to the leverock!

III

Here's a health to the linnet!
A health to the linnet that lilts on the tree,
The little green linnet so pretty to see,
The linnet whose tinkling tones gladden the lea—
High health, and heart-wealth, little linnet, to thee!
A health to the linnet!

IV

Here's a health to the blackbird!
A health to the blackbird who hides in the bush,
In the glen, far from men, where the dark rivers
rush,
And rolls a full soul in the round notes that gush
From his silver-toned throat at dawning's first
flush—
A health to the blackbird!

V

Here's a health to the wren!
Ay, a health to the wren, too, the devil's dear pet,
Though thousands of years he's owed a black debt,
And it's often we've made the vile thummikin
sweat—
But, away with old scores! forgive and forget!
Here's a health to the wren!

VI

Here's a health to the birds one and all!
A health to the birds great and small—
The birds that from hill and hedge call,

Through the highlands and islands of grey
    Donegal—
Here's a health to them,
    Health to them,
        Health to them all!

" SING ON, BLITHE BIRD "

By William Motherwell

I've plucked the berry from the bush, the brown nut
    from the tree,
But heart of happy little bird ne'er broken was by me.
I saw them in their curious nests, close couching, slyly
    peer
With their wild eyes, like glittering beads, to note if
    harm were near;
I passed them by, and blessed them all; I felt that it
    was good
To leave unmoved the creatures small whose home was
    in the wood.

And here, even now, above my head, a lusty rogue doth
    sing;
He pecks his swelling breast and neck, and trims his
    little wing.
He will not fly, he knows full well, while chirping on that
    spray,
I would not harm him for the world, or interrupt his lay.
Sing on, sing on, blithe bird! and fill my heart with
    summer gladness;
It has been aching many a day with measures full of
    sadness!

CHANTICLEER

By Katharine Tynan

Of all the birds from East to West
  That tuneful are and dear,
I love that farmyard bird the best,
  They call him Chanticleer.

Gold plume and copper plume,
  Comb of scarlet gay;
'Tis he that scatters night and gloom,
  And whistles back the day!

He is the sun's brave herald
  That, ringing his blithe horn,
Calls round a world dew-pearled
  The heavenly airs of morn.

O clear gold, shrill and bold!
  He calls through creeping mist
The mountains from the night and cold
  To rose and amethyst.

He sets the birds to singing,
  And calls the flowers to rise;
The morning cometh, bringing
  Sweet sleep to heavy eyes.

Gold plume and silver plume,
  Comb of coral gay;
'Tis he packs off the night and gloom,
  And summons home the day!

Black fear he sends it flying,
  Black care he drives afar;
And creeping shadows sighing
  Before the morning star.

The birds of all the forest
  Have dear and pleasant cheer,
But yet I hold the rarest
  The farmyard Chanticleer.

Red cock or black cock,
  Gold cock or white,
The flower of all the feathered flock,
  He whistles back the light!

A LITTLE BIRD

By Ellen M. Huntington Gates

I know a little bird that sings
  Its anthem from a slender tower,
Then from a cedar bough it swings
  And seems as fragile as a flower.

I long to hold it in my hand
  And tell it of my passing days;
I wish to make it understand
  How much I love its little ways.

But ah! the bird is wondrous wise;
  It sits superior in its place
Till something calls it, and it flies
  And flings its shadow in my face.

Up! up it goes! an atom fine
   That knows the secrets of the Blue,
And meets with no restraining line
   Among the clouds it passes through.

What thing is this that God has made
   And set between the earth and sky,
So blithe and small, yet unafraid
   Among His thunderbolts to fly?

THE BIRD MAN

By Lucy Branch Allen

Mr. Sylvanus McFarland of South Bristol, Maine, began at the age of seventy, carving and painting the birds of his locality. At the age of seventy-six, he had made and shipped to different parts of the world sixteen thousand birds. Over sixty varieties were represented.

His summer fled, but winter's chill
   Bred in him no deadening blight,
For underneath his cunning hand there thrill
   To life, and wing o'er distant hills their flight
Those little birds, those happy birds
     That sang along his morning way
       Of Beauty.

A robin in a mist of rain,
   A bluebird on a blossomy bough,
A veery fluting from some shadowy lane—
   His old remembering fingers mold them now—
Dawn's choristers, dawn's wingèd words
     Chanting at set of sun their lay
       Of Beauty.

O golden youth on the morning hill,
  With softly fluttering wings fair
Visions wait! With all things lovely fill
  Your soul; capture to-day life's glories rare,
Then set them free—late singing birds,
    Fulfillment of your yesterday
      Of Beauty.

THE MOTHER BIRD

By Walter de la Mare

Through the green twilight of a hedge
I peered, with cheek on the cool leaves pressed,
And spied a bird upon a nest:
Two eyes she had beseeching me
Meekly and brave, and her brown breast
Throbb'd hot and quick above her heart;
And then she oped her dagger bill,—
'Twas not a chirp, as sparrows pipe
At break of day; 'twas not a trill,
As falters through the quiet even;
But one sharp solitary note,
One desperate, fierce, and vivid cry
Of valiant tears, and hopeless joy,
One passionate note of victory:
Off, like a fool afraid, I sneaked,
Smiling the smile the fool smiles best,
At the mother bird in the secret hedge
Patient upon her lonely nest.

A BIRD IN THE HAND

By Norman Gale

Look at this ball of intractable fluff,
  Panting and staring with piteous eyes!
What a rebellion of heart! what a ruff
  Tickles my hand as the missel-thrush tries,
Pecking my hand with her termagant bill,
  How to escape (and I love her, the sweet!)
Back where the clustering oaks on the hill
  Climb to the blue with their branches, and meet!

Nay, polished beak, you are pecking a friend!
  Bird of the grassland, you bleed at the wing!
Stay with me, love; in captivity mend
  Wrong that was wrought by the boy and his
    sling.
Would that a Priest of the Birds might arise,
  Wonderful words on his lips to persuade
Reasoning creatures to leave to the skies
  Song at its purest, a-throb in the glade!

Bow, woodland heart, to the yoke for a while!
  Soon shall the lyrics of wind in the trees
Stir you to pipe in the green forest-aisle—
  God send me there with the grass to my knees!
Trusting to-day an affectionate breast
  Full of its duty to welcome and share,
Build from the twigs of my friendship a nest
  Not to be plundered, Delight of the air!

A MEADOW TRAGEDY

By Dora Sigerson Shorter

Here's a meadow full of sunshine,
    Ripe grasses lush and high;
There's a reaper on the roadway,
    And a lark hangs in the sky.

There's a nest of love enclosing
    Three little beaks that cry;
The reaper's in the meadow
    And a lark hangs in the sky.

Here's a mead all full of summer,
    And tragedy goes by
With a knife amongst the grasses,
    And a song up in the sky.

THE RAPE OF THE NEST

By Francis Adams

In early spring I watched two sparrows build,
And then their nest within the thickest hedge
Construct, two small dear mates within whose life
And love, foreshadowed and foreshadowing, I
Had some sweet underpart. And so at last
The little round blue eggs were laid, and her post
The mother brooding kept, while far and wide
He sought the food for both, or, weariness
Compelling her, he changed and kept his post
Within the nest, and she flew forth in turn.

One day, a schoolboy, or some other, came
And caught her, took the eggs, and tore the nest,
And went his way. Then, as I stood looking
Through gathering tears and sobs, all swiftly
    winged,
Food-bearing, came the lover back, and flew
Into the thickest hedge. How shall we say
How the sweet mate lost forever, the ruined home,
And the hope of young, with all life's life and light
Quenched at a moment forever, were to him?
For grief like this grows dumb, deeper than words,
And man and animal are only one.

MY THRUSH

By Mortimer Collins

All through the sultry hours of June,
From morning blithe to golden noon,
    And till the star of evening climbs
The gray-blue East, a world too soon,
    There sings a Thrush amid the limes.

God's poet, hid in foliage green,
Sings endless songs, himself unseen;
    Right seldom come his silent times.
Linger, ye summer hours serene!
    Sing on, dear Thrush, amid the limes!

Nor from these confines wander out,
Where the old gun, bucolic lout,
    Commits all day his murderous crimes:
Though cherries ripe are sweet, no doubt,
    Sweeter thy song amid the limes.

May I not dream God sends thee there,
Thou mellow angel of the air,
　　Even to rebuke my earthlier rhymes
With music's soul, all praise and prayer?
　　Is that thy lesson in the limes?

Closer to God art thou than I:
His minstrel thou, whose brown wings fly
　　Through silent ether's summer climes.
Ah, never may thy music die!
　　Sing on, dear Thrush, amid the limes!

THRUSHES

By Evelyn Underhill

I think the thrush's voice is more like God's
Than many a preacher's telling of the Word;
I think the mother-thrush, who turns the sods
To find fat earth-worms for her baby bird—
And, worn by her maternal toil,
With busy eye and mild
That marks each subtle movement of the soil
Patiently tends upon her greedy child—
　　She is the feathery image of that grace
　　Which spends itself to feed our thankless race.

THRUSHES

By Karle Wilson Baker

Through Tanglewood the thrushes trip,
As brown as any clod,
But in their spotted throats are hung
The vesper-bells of God.

And I know little secret truths,
And hidden things of good,
Since I have heard the thrushes sing
At dusk, in Tanglewood.

THE FIRST BLUEBIRDS

By Katharine Lee Bates

The poor earth was so winter-marred,
Harried by storm so long,
It seemed no spring could mend her,
No tardy sunshine render
Atonement for such wrong.
Snow after snow, and gale and hail,
Gaunt trees encased in icy mail,
The glittering drifts so hard
They took no trace
Of scared, wild feet,
No print of fox and hare
Driven by dearth
To forage for their meat
Even in dooryard bare
And frosty lawn
Under the peril of the human race;
And then one primrose dawn,
Sweet, sweet, O sweet,
And tender, tender,
The bluebirds woke the happy earth
With song.

BIRDS

By Katharine Morse

A bluebird in an apple-tree
A glad adventure is to me;

While, sudden glimpsed, the swallow's dart
Like laughter flicks across my heart;

Grey-shadowed gulls with wide blown wings
Wake in me vagrant hankerings;

A silver thrush at dusk of day
Calls from dim woods and then I pray.

THE ORIOLE

By Louise Helen Coburn

Hark! do you hear that note, sustained and clear?
Come, look into the top of yonder tree!
No, higher—higher yet! There, do you see?
It is the Oriole, that's lighted here
To bring a bit of tropic splendor near,—
A vision of the warmth and brilliancy
Of southern coloring to you and me.
Now he is stirring! There's a gleam of sheer
Translucent flame, and he has flown away.
We welcome, do we not, our timid guest;
Upon our tallest elm, if he will stay,
He and his mate shall hang their hammock nest,
Where the light zephyrs, that forever sway
The pendent leaves, shall rock their babes to rest.

TO SOME PHILADELPHIA SPARROWS

By Jeannette Marks

Men say unfriendly words of you, poor birds!
And I? I praise you for your saucy joy
On dusty streets; I love you for your twitter
In vines that cling to heated city walls;
Your noisy congregations on the trees;
Unchurchly ways of saying this and that
About your brother men; your gaieties
In parks near by a fountain's dripping brim.

Men say your manners are not fine. And, too,
They call you scavengers, they call you thief
And enemy to other prettier birds.
Perhaps we are one feather, you and I!
I would not hold it any grief to be
Your brother bird upon the city street.

I love you, chatterers! Yet I have heard
The lark in other lands, the thrush in this.
Dull many a day had been without your din,
Your wrangles under foot, your shameless ways.

Men say unfriendly words of you. Of me
They speak unkindly, too. Yet see how gay
We are! Ah, well, we are one feather, you
And I! We have the city streets for plunder,
The eaves for wonder, and above there is
    The sky!

THE SONG SPARROW

By Henry van Dyke

There is a bird I know so well,
   It seems as if he must have sung
    Beside my crib when I was young;
Before I knew the way to spell
   The name of even the smallest bird,
    His gentle-joyful song I heard.
Now see if you can tell, my dear,
What bird it is that, every year,
Sings " *Sweet—sweet—sweet—very merry cheer.*"

He comes in March, when winds are strong,
   And snow returns to hide the earth;
    But still he warms his heart with mirth,
And waits for May. He lingers long
   While flowers fade; and every day
    Repeats his small, contented lay;
As if to say, we need not fear
The season's change, if love is here
With " *Sweet—sweet—sweet—very merry cheer.*"

He does not wear a Joseph's-coat
   Of many colors, smart and gay;
    His suit is Quaker brown and gray,
With darker patches at his throat.
   'And yet of all the well-dressed throng
    Not one can sing so brave a song.
It makes the pride of looks appear
A vain and foolish thing, to hear
His " *Sweet—sweet—sweet—very merry cheer.*"

A lofty place he does not love,
    But sits by choice, and well at ease,
    In hedges, and in little trees
That stretch their slender arms above
    The meadow-brook; and there he sings
    Till all the field with pleasure rings;
And so he tells in every ear,
That lowly homes to heaven are near
In " *Sweet—sweet—sweet—very merry cheer.*"

I like the tune, I like the words;
    They seem so true, so free from art,
    So friendly, and so full of heart,
That if but one of all the birds
    Could be my comrade everywhere,
    My little brother of the air,
This is the one I'd choose, my dear,
Because he'd bless me, every year,
With " *Sweet—sweet—sweet—very merry cheer.*"

CHICKADEE

By Hilda Conkling
(Written at the age of six)

The chickadee in the apple-tree
Talks all the time very gently.
He makes me sleepy.
I rock away to the sea-lights.
Far off I hear him talking
The way smooth bright pebbles
Drop into water. . . .
Chick-a-*dee-dee-dee.* . . .

THE TITMOUSE

By Ralph Waldo Emerson

You shall not be overbold
When you deal with arctic cold,
As late I found my lukewarm blood
Chilled wading in the snow-choked wood.
How should I fight? my foeman fine
Has million arms to one of mine:
East, west, for aid I looked in vain,
East, west, north, south, are his domain.
Miles off, three dangerous miles, is home;
Must borrow his winds who there would come.
Up and away for life! be fleet!—
The frost-king ties my fumbling feet,
Sings in my ears, my hands are stones,
Curdles the blood to the marble bones,
Tugs at the heart-strings, numbs the sense,
And hems in life with narrowing fence.
Well, in this broad bed lie and sleep,—
The punctual stars will vigil keep,—
Embalmed by purifying cold;
The winds shall sing their dead-march old,
The snow is no ignoble shroud,
The moon thy mourner, and the cloud.

Softly,—but this way fate was pointing,
'Twas coming fast to such anointing,
When piped a tiny voice hard by,
Gay and polite, a cheerful cry,
Chic-chicadeedee! saucy note
Out of sound heart and merry throat,

As if it said, " Good day, good sir!
Fine afternoon, old passenger!
Happy to meet you in these places,
Where January brings few faces."

This poet, though he live apart,
Moved by his hospitable heart,
Sped, when I passed his sylvan fort,
To do the honors of his court,
As fits a feathered lord of land;
Flew near, with soft wing grazed my hand,
Hopped on the bough, then, darting low,
Prints his small impress on the snow,
Show feats of his gymnastic play,
Head downward, clinging to the spray.

Here was this atom in full breath,
Hurling defiance at vast death;
This scrap of valor just for play
Fronts the north-wind in waistcoat gray,
As if to shame my weak behavior;
I greeted loud my little savior,
" You pet! what dost here? and what for?
In these woods, thy small Labrador,
At this pinch, wee San Salvador!
What fire burns in that little chest
So frolic, stout and self-possest?
Henceforth I wear no stripe but thine;
Ashes and jet all hues outshine.
Why are not diamonds black and gray,
To ape thy dare-devil array?
And I affirm, the spacious North
Exists to draw thy virtue forth.

I think no virtue goes with size;
The reason of all cowardice
Is, that men are overgrown,
And, to be valiant, must come down
To the titmouse dimension."

'Tis good-will makes intelligence,
And I began to catch the sense
Of my bird's song: " Live out of doors
In the great woods, on prairie floors.
I dine in the sun; when he sinks in the sea,
I too have a hole in a hollow tree;
And I like less when Summer beats
With stifling beams on these retreats,
Than noontide twilights which snow makes
With tempest of the blinding flakes.
For well the soul, if stout within,
Can arm impregnably the skin;
And polar frost my frame defied,
Made of the air that blows outside."

With glad remembrance of my debt,
I homeward turn; farewell, my pet!
When here again thy pilgrim comes,
He shall bring store of seeds and crumbs.
Doubt not, so long as earth has bread,
Thou first and foremost shalt be fed;
The Providence that is most large
Takes hearts like thine in special charge,
Helps who for their own need are strong,
And the sky doats on cheerful song.
Henceforth I prize thy wiry chant
O'er all that mass and minster vaunt;

For men mis-hear thy call in Spring,
As 'twould accost some frivolous wing,
Crying out of the hazel copse, *Phe-be!*
And, in winter, *Chic-a-dee-dee!*
I think old Cæsar must have heard
In northern Gaul my dauntless bird,
And, echoed in some frosty wold,
Borrowed thy battle-numbers bold.
And I will write our annals new,
And thank thee for a better clew,
I, who dreamed not when I came here
To find the antidote of fear,
Now hear thee say in Roman key,
Paean! Veni, vidi, vici.

TITMOUSE

By Walter de la Mare

If you would happy company win,
Dangle a palm-nut from a tree,
Idly in green to sway and spin,
Its snow-pulped kernel for bait; and see,
    A nimble titmouse enter in.

Out of earth's vast unknown of air,
Out of all summer, from wave to wave,
He'll perch, and prank his feathers fair,
Jangle a glass-clear wildering stave,
    And take his commons there—

This tiny son of life; this spright,
By momentary Human sought,
Plume will his wing in the dappling light,
Clash timbrel shrill and gay—
And into time's enormous nought,
  Sweet-fed, will flit away.

BOB WHITE

By Edgar A. Guest

Out near the links where I go to play
My favorite game from day to day,
There's a friend of mine that I've never met,
Walked with or broken bread with, yet
I've talked to him oft and he's talked to me
Whenever I've been where he's chanced to be;
He's a cheery old chap who keeps out of sight,
A gay little fellow whose name's Bob White.

Bob White! Bob White! I can hear him call
As I follow the trail to my little ball—
Bob White! Bob White! with a note of cheer
That was just designed for a mortal ear;
Then I drift far off from the world of men
An' stand an' answer him back right then,
An' we whistle away to each other there,
Glad of the life which is ours to share.

Bob White! Bob White! May you live to be
The head of a numerous family!
May you boldly call to your friends out here,
With never an enemy's gun to fear;

I'm a better man as I pass along,
For your cheery call and your bit of song;
May your food be plenty and skies be bright
To the end of your days, good friend, Bob White!

PARTRIDGES

By Alonzo Teall Worden

Under the alders, along the brooks,
Under the hemlocks, along the hill,
Spreading their plumage with furtive looks,
Daintily pecking the leaves at will;
Whir! and they flit from the startled sight,—
And the forest is silent, the air is still.

Crushing the leaves 'neath our careless feet,
Snapping the twigs with a heavy tread,
Dreamy October is late and sweet,
And stooping we gather a blossom dead;
Boom! and our heart has a thunderous beat
As the gray apparition flits overhead.

Up from the path with a thunderous roar
That startles the dreamer amid his dreams,
Till he peers into vistas that open before
For the flash of the plumage with silver gleams:
Why, modest brown hermit, thus fearful of him
Who would share in the secrets of forest and
    streams?

I lie on windrows of leaves and gaze
At thy innocent preening of serrate wing,
Or watch where the last crimson colors blaze,
And the red autumn leaves to the maple cling,—
Too fond of this life myself, to destroy
The motion and life I am worshiping.

THE LIBRARY DOVE

By John Russell Hayes

Columba, O Columba, come again,
And murmur softly at my window-pane!

One day a dove in at our window flew,
A comely dove with neck of iris hue.
He seemed bewildered, far from home, and lost,
As if on some wild wind he had been tossed,
Then in the after-lull had drifted down
And sought a refuge in our friendly town;—
I know not,—but for weeks he lingered near,
And every day I heard his murmur clear
And soft as music from a fairy flute
Or far-heard throb of mandolin or lute,
So gently would he murmur.

                        He was tame,
And every morning to the window came
To eat the oats and corn I scattered there;
Then would he croon, and preen his feathers fair
And entertain me with his murmur sweet,
While sideways on the sill with dainty feet

He stepped, with air most solemn and sedate
And head aslant, as pondering the fate
That kept folks bound to books through such long
    hours
While all outdoors was bright with sun and flowers!

At last, in late October, off he flew.
Alas, the lovely creature never knew
How much I miss my little fairy friend,
And how I hope a kindly fate will send
This darling dove some day again to cheer
Our dusty hours with murmured music clear.

Columba, with your lovely Latin name,
Come back again as long ago you came,
And croon your pensive songs upon the sill;
Tap on the window with your little bill
And tell us how the sunshine and the flowers
Rebuke us for our long and bookish hours.
Columba, O Columba, come again,
And murmur gently at my window-pane.

THE BELFRY PIGEON

By N. P. Willis

On the cross-beams, under the Old South bell,
The nest of a pigeon is builded well;
In summer and winter that bird is there,
Out and in with the morning air.
I love to see him track the street,
With his wary eye and active feet;
And I often watch him as he springs,
Circling the steeple with easy wings,

Till across the dial his shade has passed,
And the belfry edge is gained at last.
'Tis a bird I love with its brooding note,
And the trembling throb in its mottled throat;
I often stop with the fear I feel,
He runs so close to the rabbit wheel.
Whatever is rung on that noisy bell—
Chime of the hour or funeral knell—
The dove in the belfry must hear it well.
When the tongue swings out to the midnight
    moon,
When the sexton cheerily rings for noon;
When the clock strikes clear at morning light,
When the child is waked with " Nine at night,"
When the chimes play soft in the Sabbath air,
Filling the spirit with tones of prayer—
Whatever tale in the bell is heard,
He broods on his folded feet unstirred;
Or, rising half in his rounded nest,
He takes the time to smooth his breast,
Then drops again with filmed eyes,
And sleeps as the last vibration dies.
Sweet bird! I would that I could be
A hermit in the crowd like thee!

THE WILD DUCK'S NEST

By William Wordsworth

The imperial Consort of the Fairy-King
Owns not a sylvan bower, or gorgeous cell
With emerald floored, and with purpureal shell

Ceilinged and roofed, that is so fair a thing
As this low structure, for the tasks of Spring
Prepared by one who loves the buoyant swell
Of the brisk waves, yet here consents to dwell;
And spreads in steadfast peace her brooding wing.
Words cannot paint the o'ershadowing yew-tree
    bough,
And dimly-gleaming nest—a hollow crown
Of golden leaves inlaid with silver down,
Fine as the mother's softest plumes allow:
I gazed—and self-accused while gazing, sighed
For human-kind, weak slaves of cumbrous pride!

WAGTAIL AND BABY

By Thomas Hardy

A baby watched a ford, whereto
    A wagtail came for drinking;
A blaring bull went wading through,
    The wagtail showed no shrinking.

A stallion splashed his way across,
    The birdie nearly sinking;
He gave his plumes a twitch and toss,
    And held his own unblinking.

Next saw the baby round the spot
    A mongrel slowly slinking;
The wagtail gazed, but faltered not
    In dip and sip and prinking.

A perfect gentleman then neared;
    The wagtail, in a winking
With terror rose and disappeared;
    The baby fell a-thinking.

THE OWLS

By Helen Granville-Barker

Three little feathery owls flew overhead
As I walked down the frozen garden path;
One on the chestnut lit, one chose the pine,
And one a twisted pear-tree, bare and brown.

There in the garden it was still as death;
Beyond the wintry meadows glowed the west,
Rose that receded swiftly into gray;
The little owls and I seemed all that lived.

Softly I tiptoed near the chestnut-tree,
Two little, shining, curious eyes looked out;
And from the pear-tree two, and from the pine.
I fancied for the moment we were friends.

THE SANDPIPER

By Celia Thaxter

Across the narrow beach we flit,
    One little sandpiper and I;
And fast I gather, bit by bit,
    The scattered driftwood, bleached and dry.

The wild waves reach their hands for it,
The wild wind raves, the tide runs high,
As up and down the beach we flit,—
One little sandpiper and I.

Above our heads the sullen clouds
Scud black and swift across the sky;
Like silent ghosts in misty shrouds
Stand out the white lighthouses high.
Almost as far as eye can reach
I see the close-reefed vessels fly,
As fast we flit along the beach,—
One little sandpiper and I.

I watch him as he skims along,
Uttering his sweet and mournful cry;
He starts not at my fitful song,
Or flash of fluttering drapery.
He has no thought of any wrong;
He scans me with a fearless eye;
Stanch friends are we, well tried and strong,
The little sandpiper and I.

Comrade, where wilt thou be to-night
When the loosed storm breaks furiously?
My driftwood fire will burn so bright!
To what warm shelter canst thou fly?
I do not fear for thee, though wroth
The tempest rushes through the sky;
For are we not God's children both,
Thou, little sandpiper, and I?

TO A WATERFOWL

By William Cullen Bryant

Whither, midst falling dew,
While glow the heavens with the last steps of day,
Far, through their rosy depths, dost thou pursue
    Thy solitary way?

Vainly the fowler's eye
Might mark thy distant flight to do thee wrong,
As, darkly painted on the crimson sky,
    Thy figure floats along.

Seek'st thou the plashy brink
Of weedy lake, or marge of river wide,
Or where the rocking billows rise and sink
    On the chafed ocean-side?

There is a Power whose care
Teaches thy way along that pathless coast,—
The desert and illimitable air,—
    Lone wandering, but not lost.

All day thy wings have fanned
At that far height, the cold, thin atmosphere,
Yet stoop not, weary, to the welcome land,
    Though the dark night is near.

And soon that toil shall end;
Soon shalt thou find a summer home, and rest,
And scream among thy fellows; reeds shall bend,
    Soon, o'er thy sheltered nest.

Thou'rt gone, the abyss of heaven
Hath swallowed up thy form; yet, on my heart
Deeply hath sunk the lesson thou hast given,
    And shall not soon depart.

He who, from zone to zone,
Guides through the boundless sky thy certain flight,
In the long way that I must tread alone,
    Will lead my steps aright.

ON SCARING SOME WATERFOWL IN LOCH-TURIT

By Robert Burns

Why, ye tenants of the lake,
For me your watery haunt forsake?
Tell me, fellow creatures, why
At my presence thus you fly?
Why disturb your social joys,
Parent, filial, kindred ties?
Common friend to you and me,
Nature's gifts to all are free:
Peaceful keep your dimpling wave,
Busy feed, or wanton lave;
Or, beneath the sheltering rock,
Bide the surging billow's shock.

Conscious, blushing for our race,
Soon, too soon, your fears I trace.
Man, your proud usurping foe,
Would be lord of all below:
Plumes himself in Freedom's pride,
Tyrant stern to all beside.

The eagle, from the cliffy brow,
Marking you his prey below,
In his breast no pity dwells,
Strong necessity compels,
But man, to whom alone is given
A ray direct from pitying Heaven,
Glories in his heart humane—
And creatures for his pleasure slain.

In these savage, liquid plains,
Only known to wand'ring swains,
Where the mossy riv'let strays;
Far from human haunts and ways;
All on Nature you depend,
And life's poor season peaceful spend.

Or, if man's superior might,
Dare invade your native right,
On the lofty ether borne,
Man with all his powers you scorn;
Swiftly seek, on clanging wings,
Other lakes and other springs;
And the foe you cannot brave,
Scorn at least to be his slave.

WILD GEESE

By Frederick Peterson

How oft against the sunset sky or moon
    I watched that moving zigzag of spread wings
In unforgotten Autumns gone too soon,
    In unforgotten Springs!

Creatures of desolation, far they fly
  Above all lands bound by the curling foam;
In misty fens, wild moors and trackless sky
  These wild things have their home.
They know the tundra of Siberian coasts,
  And tropic marshes by the Indian seas;
They know the clouds and night and starry hosts
  From Crux to Pleiades.
Dark flying rune against the western glow—
  It tells the sweep and loneliness of things,
Symbol of Autumns vanished long ago.
  Symbol of coming Springs!

THE WOUNDED GULL

By Edmund Gosse

Along a grim and granite shore
  With children and with wife I went,
And in our face the stiff breeze bore
  Salt savours and a samphire scent.

So wild the place and desolate,
  That on a rock before us stood—
All upright, silent and sedate—
  Of slate-gray gulls a multitude.

The children could not choose but shout
  To see these lovely birds so near,
Whereat they spread their pinions out,
  Yet rather in surprise than fear.

They rose and wheeled around the cape,
    They shrieked and vanished in a flock—
But lo! one solitary shape
    Still sentinelled the lonely rock.

The children laughed, and called it tame!
    But ah! one dark and shrivell'd wing
Hung by its side; the gull was lame,
    A suffering and deserted thing.

With painful care it downward crept;
    Its eye was on the rolling sea;
Close to our very feet, it stept
    Upon the wave, and then—was free.

Right out into the east it went,
    Too proud, we thought, to flap or shriek;
Slowly it steered, in wonderment
    To find its enemies so meek.

Calmly it steered, and mortal dread
    Disturbed nor crest nor glossy plume;
It could but die, and being dead,
    The open sea should be its tomb.

We watched it till we saw it float
    Almost beyond our furthest view;
It flickered like a paper boat,
    Then faded in the dazzling blue.

It could but touch an English heart,
    To find an English bird so brave;
Our life-blood glowed to see it start
    Thus boldly on the leaguered wave;

And we shall hold, till life departs,
  For flagging days when hope grows dull,
Fresh as a spring within our hearts,
  The courage of the wounded gull.

SEA-GULLS OF MANHATTAN

By Henry van Dyke

Children of the elemental mother,
  Born upon some lonely island shore
Where the wrinkled ripples run and whisper,
  Where the crested billows plunge and roar;
Long-winged, tireless roamers and adventurers,
  Fearless breasters of the wind and sea,
In the far-off solitary places
  I have seen you floating wild and free!

Here the high-built cities rise around you;
  Here the cliffs that tower east and west,
Honeycombed with human habitations,
  Have no hiding for the sea-bird's nest:
Here the river flows begrimed and troubled;
  Here the hurrying, panting vessels fume,
Restless, up and down the watery highway,
  While a thousand chimneys vomit gloom.

Toil and tumult, conflict and confusion,
  Clank and clamour of the vast machine
Human hands have built for human bondage—
  Yet amid it all you float serene;

Circling, soaring, sailing, swooping lightly
   Down to glean your harvest from the wave;
In your heritage of air and water,
   You have kept the freedom Nature gave.

Even so the wild-woods of Manhattan
   Saw your wheeling flocks of white and gray;
Even so you fluttered, followed, floated,
   Round the *Half-Moon* creeping up the bay;
Even so your voices creaked and chattered,
   Laughing shrilly o'er the tidal rips,
While your black and beady eyes were glistening
   Round the sullen British prison-ships.

Children of the elemental mother,
   Fearless floaters 'mid the double blue,
From the crowded boats that cross the ferries
   Many a longing heart goes out to you.
Though the cities climb and close around us,
   Something tells us that our souls are free,
While the sea-gulls fly above the harbour,
   While the river flows to meet the sea!

THE SEA-MEW

By Elizabeth Barrett Browning

How joyously the young sea-mew
Lay dreaming on the waters blue
Whereon our little bark had thrown
A little shade, the only one,
But shadows ever man pursue.

Familiar with the waves and free
As if their own white foam were he,
His heart upon the heart of ocean
Lay learning all its mystic motion,
And throbbing to the throbbing sea.

And such a brightness in his eye
As if the ocean and the sky
Within him had lit up and nurst
A soul God gave him not at first,
To comprehend their majesty.

We were not cruel, yet did sunder
His white wing from the blue waves under,
And bound it, while his fearless eyes
Shone up to ours in calm surprise,
As deeming us some ocean wonder.

We bore our ocean bird unto
A grassy place where he might view
The flowers that curtsey to the bees,
The waving of the tall green trees,
The falling of the silver dew.

But flowers of earth were pale to him
Who had seen the rainbow fishes swim;
And when earth's dew around him lay
He thought of ocean's wingèd spray,
And his eyes waxèd sad and dim.

The green trees round him only made
A prison with their darksome shade;
And drooped his wing, and mournèd he
For his own boundless glittering sea—
Albeit he knew not they could fade.

Then One her gladsome face did bring,
Her gentle voice's murmuring,
In ocean's stead his heart to move
And teach him what was human love:
He thought it a strange, mournful thing.

He lay down in his grief to die,
(First looking to the sea-like sky
That hath no waves) because, alas!
Our human touch did on him pass,
And, with our touch, our agony.

THE EAGLE

By Alfred, Lord Tennyson

He clasps the crag with hookèd hands;
Close to the sun in lonely lands,
Ring'd with the azure world, he stands.

The wrinkled sea beneath him crawls;
He watches from his mountain walls;
And like a thunderbolt he falls.

THE LOON

By Amelia Josephine Burr

Where shaken shallows multiply the moon,
Alone amid the silence laughs the Loon.
Heard far away across the night, he seems
Some happy wood-god laughing in his dreams.

THE BLACK VULTURE

By George Sterling

Aloof upon the day's immeasured dome,
    He holds unshared the silence of the sky.
    Far down his bleak, relentless eyes descry
The eagle's empire and the falcon's home—
Far down, the galleons of sunset roam;
    His hazards on the sea of morning lie;
    Serene, he hears the broken tempest sigh
Where cold sierras gleam like scattered foam.
And least of all he holds the human swarm—
    Unwitting now that envious men prepare
    To make their dream and its fulfillment one,
When, poised above the caldrons of the storm,
    Their hearts, contemptuous of death, shall dare
    His roads between the thunder and the sun.

THE
HORSE

A righteous man regardeth the life of his beast: but the tender mercies of the wicked are cruel.

PROVERBS 12:10.

THE HORSE

THE OLD PLOUGH-HORSE

By Mahlon Leonard Fisher

Worn-out and useless, lone, he stands and dreams,
  Day after day, the long sweet summer through:
  The last turf-ridge upturned, what is to do
Save watch the crow-hordes, or a hawk that screams
High o'er his master's dooryard, till it seems
The world was made a place for dreaming in?
Around him, daisy-wheels ecstatic spin,
  And cattle splash, knee-deep, through cooling streams;
But he, inert, thought-wrapt, oblivious, drifts,
  Dream-drawn, a-browse, towards other fields than these,
  Where first he felt the Spring's quick kiss, and seas
Of green about him swam. . . . His bent head lifts . . .
Like some sweet message caught from far-off lands,
He hears his mother whinny, where he stands!

THE ARAB'S FAREWELL TO HIS STEED

By Caroline Norton

My beautiful, my beautiful, that standest meekly by,
With thy proudly arched and glossy neck, and dark and
    fiery eye!
Fret not to roam the desert now with all thy winged
    speed,
I may not mount on thee again—thou'rt sold, my Arab
    steed!

89

Fret not with that impatient hoof—snuff not the breezy
wind;
The farther that thou fliest now, so far am I behind!
The stranger hath thy bridle-rein, thy master hath his
gold—
Fleet-limbed and beautiful, farewell—thou'rt sold, my
steed, thou'rt sold!

Farewell! those free, untired limbs full many a mile must
roam,
To reach the chill and wintry clime that clouds the
stranger's home;
Some other hand, less kind, must now thy corn and bed
prepare;
The silk mane that I braided once must be another's
care.

The morning sun shall dawn again—but nevermore
with thee
Shall I gallop o'er the desert paths where we were wont
to be;
Evening shall darken on the earth, and o'er the sandy
plain
Some other steed with slower pace shall bear me home
again.

Only in sleep shall I behold that dark eye glancing
bright—
Only in sleep shall hear again that step so firm and
light;
And when I raise my dreaming arms to check or cheer
thy speed,
Then must I startling wake to feel thou'rt sold, my
Arab steed!

Ah, rudely then, unseen by me, some cruel hand may
    chide,
Till foam-wreaths lie, like crested waves, along thy
    panting side,
And the rich blood that's in thee swells in thy indignant
    pain,
Till careless eyes that on thee gaze may count each
    starting vein.

Will they ill-use thee? if I thought—but no, it can-
    not be;
Thou art so swift, yet easy curbed; so gentle, yet so
    free.
And yet if haply when thou'rt gone this lonely heart
    should yearn,
Can the hand that casts thee from it now command
    thee to return?

" Return! " alas, my Arab steed! what will thy master
    do,
When thou that wast his all of joy hast vanished from
    his view?
When the dim distance greets mine eyes, and through
    the gathering tears
Thy bright form for a moment like the false mirage
    appears?

Slow and unmounted will I roam with wearied foot
    alone,
Where, with fleet step and joyous bound, thou oft hast
    borne me on,

And sitting down by the green well, I'll pause, and
sadly think,
" 'Twas here he bowed his glossy neck when last I saw
him drink."

When last I saw thee drink?—Away! the fevered dream
is o'er!
I could not live a day and know that we should meet no
more;
They tempted me, my beautiful—for hunger's power is
strong—
They tempted me, my beautiful—but I have loved too
long—

Who said that I had given thee up? Who said that
thou wert sold?
'Tis false, 'tis false, my Arab steed! I fling them back
their gold!
Thus—thus I leap upon thy back, and scour the distant plains!
Away! who overtakes us now shall claim thee for his
pains.

THE BLOOD HORSE

By Bryan Waller Procter

Gamarra is a dainty steed,
Strong, black, and of a noble breed,
Full of fire, and full of bone,
With all his line of fathers known;

Fine his nose, his nostrils thin,
But blown abroad by the pride within!
His mane is like a river flowing,
And his eyes like embers glowing
In the darkness of the night,
And his pace as swift as light.

Look,—how round his straining throat
Grace and shifting beauty float;
Sinewy strength is in his reins,
And the red blood gallops through his veins:
Richer, redder, never ran
Through the boasting heart of man.
He can trace his lineage higher
Than the Bourbon dare aspire,—
Douglas, Guzman, or the Guelph,
Or O'Brien's blood itself!

He, who hath no peer, was born
Here, upon a red March morn.
But his famous fathers dead
Were Arabs all, and Arab-bred,
And the last of that great line
Trod like one of a race divine!
And yet,—he was but friend to one
Who fed him at the set of sun
By some lone fountain fringed with green;
With him, a roving Bedouin,
He lived (none else would he obey
Through all the hot Arabian day),
And died untamed upon the sands
Where Balkh amidst the desert stands.

HASSAN TO HIS MARE

By Bayard Taylor

Come, my beauty! come, my desert darling!
  On my shoulder lay thy glossy head!
Fear not, though the barley-sack be empty,
  Here's the half of Hassan's scanty bread.

Thou shalt have thy share of dates, my beauty!
  And thou know'st my water-skin is free:
Drink and welcome, for the wells are distant,
  And my strength and safety lie in thee.

Bend thy forehead now, to take my kisses!
  Lift in love thy dark and splendid eye:
Thou art glad when Hassan mounts the saddle,—
  Thou art proud he owns thee: so am I.

Let the Sultan bring his boasted horses,
  Prancing with their diamond-studded reins;
They, my darling, shall not match thy fleetness
  When they course with thee the desert-plains!

Let the Sultan bring his famous horses,
  Let him bring his golden swords to me,—
Bring his slaves, his eunuchs, and his harem;
  He would offer them in vain for thee.

We have seen Damascus, O my beauty!
  And the splendor of the Pashas there:
What's their pomp and riches? Why, I would not
  Take them for a handful of thy hair!

●   ●   ●   ●   ●   ●   ●   ●

ON THE PASSING OF THE LAST FIRE HORSE FROM MANHATTAN ISLAND

By Kenneth Slade Alling

I remember the cleared streets, the strange suspense,
  As if a thunder-storm were under way;
Magnificently furious, hurrying thence,
  The fire-eyed horses racing to the fray;
Out of old Homer where the heroes are,
  Beating upon the whirlwind thunderous hoofs,
Wild horses and plumed Ajax in his car:
  Oh, in those days we still possessed the proofs
Men battled shouting by the gates of Troy,
  With shields of triple brass and spears of flame.
With what distended nostrils; what fierce joy;
  What ring on stone and steel; those horses came;
Like horses of gods that whirl to the dawn's burning,
  They came, and they are gone, and unreturning.

DIALOGUE OF THE HORSES

(The Festival of Industry)

By Will Carleton

First Horse

We are the pets of men—
  The pampered pets of men!
There is naught for us too gentle and good
In the graceful days of our babyhood;
We frisk and caper in childish glee—
Oh, none so pretty and proud as we!

They cheer and cherish us in our play—
Oh, none so smilingly sweet as they!
And when a little our lives have grown,
Each has a table and room his own,
A waiter to fill his bill of fare,
A barber to clean and comb his hair.
    Yes, we are the pets of men—
    The pampered pets of men!
They show us, gayly dressed and proud,
To the eager eyes of the clamorous crowd;
They champion us in the rattling race,
They praise our beauty and cheer our pace;
They keep for us our family trees—
They trumpet our names beyond the seas;
They hang our portraits on their walls,
And paint and garnish and gild our stalls.
    Yes, we are the pets of men—
    The pampered pets of men!

SECOND HORSE

We are the slaves of men—
The menial slaves of men!
They lash us over the dusty roads,
They bend us down with murderous loads;
They fling vile insults on our track,
And know that we cannot answer back;
In the winds of Winter, or Summer sun,
The tread of our toil is never done;
And when we are weak, and old, and lame,
And labor-stiffened, and bowed with shame
And hard of hearing, and blind of eye,
They drive us out in the world to die.

Yes, we are the slaves of men—
The slaves of selfish men!
They draft us into their bloody spites,
They spur us, bleeding, into their fights;
They poison our souls with their senseless ire
And curse us into a storm of fire.
And when to death we are bowed and bent,
And take the ball that for them was meant,
Alone they leave us to groan and bleed,
And dash their spurs in another steed!
Yes, we are the slaves of men—
The slaves of brutish men!

DAT OL' MARE O' MINE

By Paul Laurence Dunbar

Want to trade me, do you, mistah? Oh, well, now, I
reckon not,
W'y you couldn't buy my Sukey fu' a thousan' on de
spot.
Dat ol' mare o' mine?
Yes, huh coat ah long an' shaggy, an' she ain't no
shakes to see;
Dat's a ring-bone, yes, you right, suh, an' she got a
on'ry knee,
But dey ain't no use in talkin', she de only hoss fu' me,
Dat ol' mare o' mine.

Co'se, I knows dat Suke's contra'y, an' she moughty
ap' to vex;
But you got to mek erlowance fu' de nature of huh sex;
Dat ol' mare o' mine.

Ef you pull her on de lef' han'; she plum 'termined to
  go right,
A cannon couldn't skeer huh, but she boun' to tek a
  fright
At a piece o' common paper, or anyt'ing whut's white,
  Dat ol' mare o' mine.

W'en my eyes commence to fail me, dough, I trus'es to
  huh sight,
An' she'll tote me safe an' hones' on de ve'y da'kes'
  night,
  Dat ol' mare o' mine.
Ef I whup huh, she jes' switch huh tail, an' settle to a
  walk,
Ef I whup huh mo', she shek huh haid, an' lak ez not,
  she balk.
But huh sense ain't no ways lackin', she do evah t'ing
  but talk,
  Dat ol' mare o' mine.

But she gentle ez a lady w'en she know huh beau kin
  see.
An' she sholy got mo' gumption any day den you or me,
  Dat ol' mare o' mine.
She's a leetle slow a-goin', an' she moughty ha'd to sta't,
But we's gittin' ol' togathah, an' she's closah to my
  hea't,
An' I doesn't reckon, mistah, dat she'd sca'cely keer to
  pa't;
  Dat ol' mare o' mine.

  .   .   .   .

POLO PONIES

By Eleanor Baldwin

Has Pegasus, then, visited the earth,
Borne on great pinions lyrical with thunder,
And these his foals,—this breed of racing wonder,
Fearless and free, and sensible of worth?
With flash of eye and silver gleam of girth.
They charge, now neck to neck, now wheeled
    asunder,
With shining sides, small feet that scorn to blunder,
Dark nostrils trembling in their pride of birth.
Sired from the skies, they eddy down the plain,
Chestnut and black and the fast-flying dun,
And swift and strong they crowd, and tense and
    fain,
Eager as fire though the last goal is won,
These wilding creatures gentled to the rein,
These little brothers of the wind and sun.

"MY DOG and I"

He was a gash and faithfu' tyke
As ever lapt a sheugh or dyke.

Lauth.   ROBERT BURNS.

"MY DOG AND I"

THE ROAD TO VAGABONDIA

By Dana Burnet

He was sitting on the doorstep as I went strolling by;
A lonely little beggar with a wistful, homesick eye—
And he wasn't what you'd borrow, and he wasn't what
  you'd steal,
But I guessed his heart was breaking, so I whistled him
  to heel.

They had stoned him through the city streets, and
  naught the city cared,
But I was heading outward, and the roads are sweeter
  shared,
So I took him for a comrade, and I whistled him away—
On the road to Vagabondia, that lies across the day!

Yellow dog he was; but bless you—he was just the chap
  for me!
For I'd rather have an inch of dog than miles of pedigree.
So we stole away together, on the road that has no end,
With a new-coined day to fling away and all the stars
  to spend!

Oh, to walk the road at morning, when the wind is blowing clean,
And the yellow daisies fling their gold across a world of
  green—

103

For the wind it heals the heartache, and the sun it dries
    the scars,
On the road to Vagabondia that lies beneath the stars.

'Twas the wonder of our going cast a spell about our
    feet—
And we walked because the world was young, because
    the way was sweet;
And we slept in wild-rose meadows by the little wayside
    farms,
Till the Dawn came up the highroad with the dead moon
    in her arms.

Oh, the Dawn it went before us through a shining lane
    of skies,
And the Dream was at our heartstrings, and the Light
    was in our eyes,
And we made no boast of glory and we made no boast
    of birth,
On the road to Vagabondia that lies across the earth!

MY DOG

By William Griffith

To-day hell chuckled at another lie,
    That gave no human being any pain,
    Except one temporary soul. Nor Cain
Was more heart-heavy when he came to die.

I branded him a cur that by-and-bye
    Would go the way of mongrels and be slain,
    By man nor God regretted; clear and plain
Were the reproaches written in his eye.

He bridled slightly ere he slunk away
  An hour ago and perished in a bog,
Saving two children who had gone astray:
  Since when the sirens sounding through the fog
Are Gabriel horns that thunder me to pray,
  Or to be damned for slandering my dog.

"IS THY SERVANT A DOG?"

By John B. Tabb

So *must* he be who, in the crowded street,
Where shameless Sin and flaunting Pleasure meet,
Amid the noisome footprints finds the sweet
Faint vestige of Thy feet.

BISHOP DOANE'S TRIBUTE
TO HIS DOG CLUNY

I am quite sure he thinks that I am God—
Since He is God on whom each one depends
For life, and all things that His bounty sends—
My dear old dog, most constant of all friends;
Not quick to mind, but quicker far than I
To Him whom God I know and own; his eye
Deep brown and liquid, watches for my nod;
He is more patient underneath the rod
Than I, when God His wise corrections sends.
He looks love at me, deep as words e'er spake;
And from me never crumb or sup will take
But he wags thanks with his most vocal tail;

And when some crashing noise wakes all his fear
He is content and quiet if I'm near,
Secure that my protection will prevail;
So, faithful, mindful, thankful, trustful, he
Tells me what I unto my God should be.

MY DOG

By John Kendrick Bangs

I have no dog, but it must be
Somewhere there's one belongs to me—
A little chap with wagging tail,
And dark brown eyes that never quail,
But look you through, and through, and
  through,
With love unspeakable, but true.

Somewhere it must be, I opine,
There is a little dog of mine
With cold black nose that sniffs around
In search of what things may be found
In pocket, or some nook hard by
Where I have hid them from his eye.

Somewhere my doggie pulls and tugs
The fringes of rebellious rugs,
Or with the mischief of the pup
Chews all my shoes and slippers up,
And when he's done it to the core,
With eyes all eager pleads for more.

Somewhere upon his hinder legs
My little doggie sits and begs,
And in a wistful minor tone
Pleads for the pleasures of the bone—
I pray it be his owner's whim
To yield, and grant the same to him.

Somewhere a little dog doth wait,
It may be by some garden-gate.
With eyes alert and tail attent—
You know the kind of tail that's meant—
With stores of yelps of glad delight
To bid me welcome home at night.

Somewhere a little dog is seen,
His nose two shaggy paws between,
Flat on his stomach, one eye shut
Held fast in dreamy slumber, but
The other open, ready for
His master coming through the door.

FOR A LITTLE BROWN DOG

Anonymous

For a Little Brown Dog, who " sees " me down
The hill to the car when I go to town,
And carries my bag with an air of pride,
As he trots sedately by my side,
And waits to see that I'm on all right,
And watches the car till it's out of sight—
    I thank thee.

For the way he tears down the hill to meet
That car at night on his mad little feet—
The car that will bring me, he knows, from town—
And the joyous greeting, as I step down,
A greeting the passengers hear, and see,
Every one of them envying me,
      I thank thee.

For the great true heart that is in his eyes,
Tender, and patient, and brave, and wise,
That makes him know when I'm sick, or sad,
And, knowing, love me the more—dear lad—
With a love unquestioning, high and fine—
For all of that Little Brown Dog of mine,
      I thank thee.

MY DOG AND I

By Norah M. Holland

My dog and I, the hills we know
Where the first faint wild roses blow,
  We know the shadowy paths and cool
That wind across the woodland dim,
'And where the water beetles swim
  Upon the surface of the pool.

My dog and I, our feet brush through
Full oft the fragrant morning dew,
  Or when the summer sun is high
We linger where the river flows,
Chattering and chuckling as it goes,
  Two happy tramps, my dog and I.

Or, when the winter snows are deep,
Into some fire-lit nook we creep
    And, while the north wind howls outside,
See castles in the dancing blaze,
Or, dozing, dream of summer days
    And woodland stretches, wild and wide.

My dog and I are friends till death,
And when the chill, dark angel's breath
    Shall call him from me, still I know
Somewhere within the shadowy land
Waiting his master he will stand
    Until my summons comes to go.

And, in that life so strange and new,
We'll tramp the fields of heaven through,
    Loiter the crystal river by,
Together walk the hills of God
As when the hills of earth we trod,
    Forever friends, my dog and I.

DA PUP EEN DA SNOW

By T. A. Daly

Deed you evra see Joy
    Gona wild weeth delight,
Jus' so lika small boy
W'en som' brighta new toy
    Mak's heem crazy excite',
You would know w'at I mean
Eef you jus' coulda seen—

Not so long time ago—
How my leetla fat pup
Ees first play een da snow.

O! I scream an' I roar
  An' so shaka weeth laughtra,
Dat my sides dey are sore
  For mos' three-four days aftra.
An' how mooch I would try,
  I no speak weeth sooch skeell
I could put een your eye
  W'at ees fresh een mine steell:
How dat leetla pup romp
  All aroun' da whole place,
How he bark, how he jomp
  An' fall down on hees face;
How he fight, how he bite
  An' ees tumble aroun',
Teel hees cover' weeth white
  Lik a leetla fat clown;
W'at su'prise fill hees eyes
  W'en he see da flakes sail,
How he bark at da skies,
  How he chasa hees tail.

O! I weesh I could show
  How ees looka, dat pup,
How he puff an' he blow
W'en hees leecked by da snow
  An' ees gotta geeve up.
An' I sposa, no doubt,
  You would say I am fibbin'

W'en I say hees tongue's out
   Lika yarda peenk ribbon—
O! how mooch I would try,
   I no speak weeth sooch skeell
I could put een your eye
   W'at's so fresh een mine steell.

But I weesh you had been
Where you, too, coulda seen
   W'at delighta me so—
How my leetla fat pup
   Ees first play een da snow!

WE MEET AT MORN

By Hardwicke Drummond Rawnsley

Still half in dream, upon the stair I hear
A patter coming nearer and more near,
And then upon my chamber door
A gentle tapping,
For dogs, though proud, are poor,
And if a tail will do to give command
Why use a hand?
And after that a cry, half sneeze, half yapping,
And next a scuffle on the passage floor,
And then I know the creature lies to watch
Until the noiseless maid will lift the latch,
And like a spring
That gains its power by being tightly stayed,
The impatient thing
Into the room
Its whole glad heart doth fling,
And where the gloom

Melts into light, and window blinds are rolled,
I hear a bounce upon the bed,
I feel a creeping toward me—a soft head,
And on my face
A tender nose, and cold—
This is the way, you know, that dogs embrace—
And on my hand, like sun-warmed rose-leaves
    flung,
The least faint flicker of the warmest tongue
—And so my dog and I have met and sworn
Fresh love and fealty for another morn.

DREAMS

By S. Virginia Sherwood

I sing of a dog, the dearest dog
   That ever teased a shoe;
His ears were straight, and his eyes were bright,
And filled with an impish heathen light;
   I loved him, and he loved me true.

We played together, Dreams and I,
   We ran at a leaping pace,
We laughed and barked in the summer sun,
And I slept on the hill when the play was done
   And Dreams had won the race.

And after the breeze had cooled my cheek,
   And the summer sounds had sung
And hummed and rustled a lullaby,
I woke with a yawn and a happy sigh
   At the touch of a rough warm tongue.

Ah, Dreams, you were ever so real to me,
  And I was glad and sad
To look down into the eyes of you—
So deep, so deep, for the size of you,
  Dear dog that I never had.

LAUTH

By Robert Burns

He was a gash and faithfu' tyke
As ever lapt a sheugh or dyke.
His honest, sawnsie, bawsint face
Aye gat him friends in ilka place.
His breast was white, his towsie back
Weel clad wi' coat o' glossy black.
His gawcie tail, wi' upward curl,
Hung ower his hurdies wi' a swurl.

THE IRISH WOLF-HOUND

(From " The Foray of Con O'Donnell ")
By Denis Florence McCarthy

His stature tall, his body long,
  His back like night, his breast like snow,
His fore leg pillar-like and strong,
  His hind leg like a bended bow;
Rough curling hair, head long and thin,
  His ear a leaf so small and round;
Not Bran, the favourite dog of Finn,
  Could rival John MacDonnell's hound.

As fly the shadows o'er the grass,
   He flies with step as light and sure,
He hunts the wolf through Tostan pass,
   And starts the deer by Lisanoure.
The music of the Sabbath bells,
   O Con! has not a sweeter sound
Than when along the valley swells
   The cry of John MacDonnell's hound.

AT THE DOG SHOW

To an Irish Wolf Hound

By Christopher Morley

Long and grey and gaunt he lies,
A Lincoln among dogs; his eyes,
Deep and clear of sight, appraise
The meaningless and shuffling ways
Of human folk that stop to stare.
One witless woman seeing there
How tired, how contemptuous
He is of all the smell and fuss
Asks him, " Poor fellow, are you sick? "

Yea, sick, and weary to the quick
Of heat and noise from dawn to dark.
He will not even stoop to bark
His protest, like the lesser bred.
Would he might know, one gazer read
The wistful longing in his face,
The thirst for wind and open space
And stretch of limbs to him begrudged.

There came a little dapper, fat
And bustling man, with cane and spat
And pearl-grey vest and derby hat—
Such were the judger and the judged!

IN A SHOP WINDOW

By Margaret E. Sangster

He was such a little puppy, in a window of a shop,
And his wistful eyes looked at me, and they begged me
please to stop
And buy him—for a window's awful lonely, and folk
pass
And they make strange, ugly faces and rap sharply on
the glass!

He was such a cunning beggar, and his paws were soft
and wide,
And he had a way of standing with his head held on
one side,
And his mouth just slightly open, and he always
seemed to cry:
" Take me from this horrid window, 'cause I'm ready,
most to die! "

He got tangled in my heart-strings, made me want to
break away
From the lease I signed so gladly—was it only yesterday?
Said that dogs were not admitted. . . . He was not
a dog, not yet!
Only just a tiny puppy—and his nose was black and
wet.

Did you ever speak unkindly of the friend you hold
    most dear?
Did you ever call out crossly, so that bystanders could
    hear?
Did you ever pull a curtain to shut out the smiling
    day?
That's how I felt—but more so—as I turned and
    walked away!

THE PUP

By Edgar A. Guest

He tore the curtains yesterday,
    And scratched the paper on the wall;
Ma's rubbers, too, have gone astray—
    She says she left them in the hall;
He tugged the table cloth and broke
    A fancy saucer and a cup;
Though Bud and I think it a joke
    Ma scolds a lot about the pup.

The sofa pillows are a sight,
    The rugs are looking somewhat frayed,
And there is ruin, left and right,
    That little Boston bull has made.
He slept on Buddy's counterpane—
    Ma found him there when she woke up.
I think it needless to explain
    She scolds a lot about the pup.

And yet he comes and licks her hand
    And sometimes climbs into her lap
And there, Bud lets me understand,
    He very often takes his nap.

And Bud and I have learned to know
She wouldn't give the rascal up:
She's really fond of him, although
She scolds a lot about the pup.

THE YELLOW DOG

By Edgar A. Guest

It was a little yellow dog, a wistful thing to see,
A homely, skinny, battered pup, as dirty as could be;
His ribs were showing through his hide, his coat was
thick with mud,
And yet the way he wagged his tail completely cap-
tured Bud.

He had been kicked from door to door and stoned upon
his way,
" Begone! " was all he'd ever heard, 'twas all that folks
would say;
And yet this miserable cur, forever doomed to roam,
Struck up a comradeship with Bud, who proudly
brought him home.

I've never seen so poor a dog in all my stretch of
years,
The burrs were thick upon his tail and thick upon his
ears;
He'd had to fight his way through life and carried many
a scar,
But still Bud brought him home and cried, " Say, can
I keep him, Ma? "

I think the homeless terrier knows that age is harsh and
  stern,
And from the shabby things of life in scorn is quick
  to turn;
And when some scrubby yellow dog needs sympathy and
  joy,
He's certain of a friend in need, if he can find a boy.

A BOY AND HIS DOG

By Edgar A. Guest

A boy and his dog make a glorious pair:
No better friendship is found anywhere,
For they talk and they walk and they run and they
  play,
And they have their deep secrets for many a day;
And that boy has a comrade who thinks and who feels,
Who walks down the road with a dog at his heels.

He may go where he will and his dog will be there,
May revel in mud and his dog will not care;
Faithful he'll stay for the slightest command
And bark with delight at the touch of his hand;
Oh, he owns a treasure which nobody steals,
Who walks down the road with a dog at his heels.

No other can lure him away from his side;
He's proof against riches and station and pride;
Fine dress does not charm him, and flattery's breath
Is lost on the dog, for he's faithful to death;
He sees the great soul which the body conceals—
Oh, it's great to be young with a dog at your heels!

A BOY AND A PUP

By Arthur Guiterman

The Boy wears a grin,
A scratch on his chin,
A wind-rumpled thatch,
A visible patch,
A cheek like a rose,
A frecklesome nose.

The Pup, though he may
Be tawny as hay,
Is blithe as a song;
He gambols along
And waves to each friend
A wagglesome end.

With whistle and bark
They're off for a lark;
According to whim,
A hunt or a swim,
A tramp or a run
Or any old fun.

They don't care a jot
If school keeps or not,
When anything's up,
The Boy and the Pup,—
That duo of joy,
A Pup and a Boy!

LITTLE LOST PUP

By Arthur Guiterman

He was lost!—not a shade of doubt of that;
For he never barked at a slinking cat,
But stood in the square where the wind blew raw,
With a drooping ear and a trembling paw
And a mournful look in his pleading eye
And a plaintive sniff at the passer-by
That begged as plain as a tongue could sue,
"O Mister, please may I follow you?"
A lorn, wee waif of a tawny brown
Adrift in the roar of a heedless town—
Oh, the saddest of sights in a world of sin
Is a little lost pup with his tail tucked in!

Well, he won my heart (for I set great store
On my own red Bute—who is here no more)
So I whistled clear, and he trotted up,
And who so glad as that small lost pup!
Now he shares my board, and he owns my bed,
And he fairly shouts when he hears my tread;
Then, if things go wrong, as they sometimes do,
And the world is cold and I'm feeling blue,
He asserts his right to assuage my woes
With a warm, red tongue and a nice, cold nose
And a silky head on my arm or knee
And a paw as soft as a paw can be.

When we rove the woods for a league about
He's as full of pranks as a school let out;

For he romps and frisks like a three-months' colt,
And he runs me down like a thunder-bolt.
Oh, the blithest of sights in the world so fair
Is a gay little pup with his tail in the air!

THE DOG

By George Sterling

"The dog!" a friend exclaimed; and hearing
there
  The swift contempt expressed,
I wondered how an angel might compare
  The planet's worst and best.

Fidelity and love we value most:
  Of all the hearts that live,
What one fidelity like his can boast,
  Or such affection give?

Love absolute, undoubting and untaught!
  How grudging seems our own,
Compared to his, the changeless and unbought,
  From so scant nurture grown—

The careless word, the cold hand's hurried touch,
  The cast-off bone or crust!
What squandering of all we value much
  Shall buy that perfect trust?

O true, deep eyes! O heart that so delights
　　To be the grateful slave!
O poor, dumb lips that kiss the hand that smites,
　　And mourn above its grave!

If truer soul be known, proclaim who can!
　　Nor would my tongue deny,
If heavenly tongue should praise a blameless man,
　　" The dog! " it well could cry.

THE OUTCAST

By Henry Herbert Knibbs

With thrill of birds adown the dawn there came
　　A golden arrow through the eastern pass,
And in the gold were eyes of amber flame
　　That burned upon me from the dewy grass.

A wolf-dog, from some distant rancho strayed,
　　Had made his bed beneath the pepper-tree;
A great, gray ghost, sore-wounded, lone, afraid,
　　He growled deep-throated as he glared at me.

With kindly word I lured him from his bed
　　To proffer food and drink and nearer drew,
But in his eyes I saw affection dead;
　　'Twas only hate and hunger that he knew.

Poor brute, once brave and fearless as the best,
　　Faithful to some lost master's kindly hand,
I grieved that I had so disturbed his rest,
　　As trembling in the sun I saw him stand,

Fearful, and yet assured that in my voice
    A friend he knew. He quivered, turned, and then,
As though he had made choice against his choice,
    Betook him, limping, to the road again.

Slowly I followed, coaxing, calling, till
    The very act of fleeing lent him fear,
Swiftly he climbed the long, low, eastern hill,
    Gazed back an instant; turned to disappear;

And still I followed, sick at heart for him,
    Sad for the strong, brave brute he once had been,
As in the morning sun my eyes grew dim
    To see him stretched again amid the green,

Resting his battered head upon his paws,
    Licking his wounds, then glancing wildly round;
Ah, pity that his fear was without cause;
    I turned and left him stretched upon the ground

An outcast; but if human love for beast
    Has any worth, I prayed that night would send
An easy death. Ah, could he know at least
    How much, how much I would have been his friend!

THE CAT

Please, friends, now have the grace
To plead the cause of my ill-treated race!

Pussy's Plea.   HENRY COYLE.

THE CAT

IN HONOUR OF TAFFY TOPAZ

By Christopher Morley

Taffy, the topaz-coloured cat,
Thinks now of this and now of that,
But chiefly of his meals.
Asparagus, and cream, and fish,
Are objects of his Freudian wish;
What you don't give, he steals.

His gallant heart is strongly stirred
By clink of plate or flight of bird,
He has a plumy tail;
At night he treads on stealthy pad
As merry as Sir Galahad
A-seeking of the Grail.

His amiable amber eyes
Are very friendly, very wise;
Like Buddha, grave and fat,
He sits, regardless of applause,
And thinking, as he kneads his paws,
What fun to be a cat!

THE GARDENER'S CAT

By Patrick R. Chalmers

The gardener's cat's called Mignonette,
She hates the cold, she hates the wet,
She sits among the hothouse flowers
And sleeps for hours and hours and hours.

127

She dreams she is a tiger fierce
With great majestic claws that pierce,
She sits by the hot-water pipes
And dreams about a coat of stripes;

And in her slumbers she will go
And stalk the sullen buffalo,
And when he roars across the brake
She does not wink, she does not wake.

It must be perfectly immense
To dream with such magnificence,
And pass the most inclement day
In this indeed stupendous way.

She dreams of India's sunny clime,
And only wakes at dinner-time,
And even then she does not stir
But waits till milk is brought to her.

How nice to be the gardener's cat,
She troubles not for mouse or rat,
But, when it's coming down in streams,
She sits among the flowers and dreams.

The gardener's cat would be the thing,
Her dreams are so encouraging;
She dreams that she's a tiger, yet
She's just a cat called Mignonette!
. . . .
The moral's this, my little man—
Sleep 'neath life's hailstones when you can,
And if you're humble in estate,
Dream splendidly, at any rate!

TO MY CAT

By Rosamund Marriott Watson

Half loving-kindliness and half disdain,
Thou comest to my call serenely suave,
With humming speech and gracious gestures grave,
In salutation courtly and urbane;
Yet must I humble me thy grace to gain,
For wiles may win thee though no arts enslave,
And nowhere gladly thou abidest save
Where naught disturbs the concord of thy reign.
Sphinx of my quiet hearth! who deign'st to dwell
Friend of my toil, companion of mine ease,
Thine is the lore of Ra and Rameses;
That men forget dost thou remember well,
Beholden still in blinking reveries
With sombre, sea-green gaze inscrutable.

TO MY CAT

By John G. Neihardt

I watch you basking sleepy in the light,
Majestic dreamer, humorously stern.
Your little scratch-scarred nose betrays you quite,
Yet how I long to know your thoughts, to learn
What magic dreams beget themselves and burn
Throughout your subtle nerves; for once I saw
A cat's form graven on an antique urn,
And round their god Egyptians knelt in awe.
Was once thy hiss a blight, was once thy purr a law?

Perhaps through sentient chains of linkèd ages
Your soul has fled; yet like a haunting dream
Can recollect the prayers of swarthy sages,
Can hear the wash of Nilus' mystic stream!
It seems I see you basking in the gleam
Of desert dawns. Majestical you gaze
Into the eye of Ra, and dream a dream.
Vast multitudes wait breathless in amaze
For your oraculous purr to set their hearts ablaze!

Perhaps you think " How stupid grows the world,"
And pine for godhood, till you come to be
A broken spirit, like a war flag furled,
Or drought-drained river sighing for the sea!
What potent utterance do you waste on me
When I am kind and stroke your glossy fur?
What do you gaze on that I cannot see?
Perhaps if men could know the things that were,
Their petted faiths should quake and tremble at
      your purr!

TO A CAT

By Algernon Charles Swinburne

I

Stately, kindly, lordly friend,
      Condescend
Here to sit by me, and turn
Glorious eyes that smile and burn,
Golden eyes, love's lustrous meed,
On the golden page I read.

All your wondrous wealth of hair,
    Dark and fair,
Silken-shaggy, soft and bright
As the clouds and beams of night,
Pays my reverent hand's caress
Back with friendlier gentleness.

Dogs may fawn on all and some
    As they come;
You, a friend of loftier mind,
Answer friends alone in kind.
Just your foot upon my hand
Softly bids it understand.

Morning round this silent sweet
    Garden-seat
Sheds its wealth of gathering light,
Thrills the gradual clouds with might,
Changes woodland, orchard, heath,
Lawn, and garden there beneath.

Fair and dim they gleamed below:
    Now they glow
Deep as even your sunbright eyes,
Fair as even the wakening skies.
Can it not or can it be
Now that you give thanks to see?

May not you rejoice as I,
    Seeing the sky
Change to heaven revealed, and bid
Earth reveal the heaven it hid
All night long from stars and moon,
Now the sun sets all in tune?

What within you wakes with day
    Who can say?
All too little may we tell,
Friends who like each other well,
What might haply, if we might,
Bid us read our lives aright.

II

Wild on woodland ways your sires
    Flashed like fires;
Fair as flame and fierce and fleet
As with wings on wingless feet
Shone and sprang your mother, free,
Bright and brave as wind or sea.

Free and proud and glad as they,
    Here to-day
Rests or roams their radiant child,
Vanquished not, but reconciled,
Free from curb of aught above
Save the lovely curb of love.

Love through dreams of souls divine
    Fain would shine
Round a dawn whose light and song
Then should right our mutual wrong—
Speak, and seal the love-lit law
Sweet Assisi's seer foresaw.

Dreams were theirs; yet haply may
    Dawn a day
When such friends and fellows born,
Seeing our earth as fair at morn,
May for wiser love's sake see
More of heaven's deep heart than we.

PUSSY'S PLEA

By Henry Coyle

Now is the winter of my discontent:
  When summer comes, and all the world is gay
  With Nature's smile, my mistress hies away
To shore and woodlands green, while I am pent
In backyards lone and empty. Weak and spent
  From lack of food, I prowl by night and day
  O'er fence and gate, and howl my doleful lay,
But there are none to heed a cat's lament.
Sad is my lot! why was I born a cat?
  My lady's ugly poodle takes his nap
  On some hotel veranda in her lap.
Without a care he feasts and waxes fat
  The summer long. Please, friends, now have the
    grace
  To plead the cause of my ill-treated race!

"DOOMED"

Anonymous

One day a statistician great
  Computed that the pussies ate
Six million, thirteen birds a year,
  And called upon the clubs to hear
His figures that were truly strange,
  And showed a quite stupendous range
Of most laborious observation,
  Coupled with fine imagination.

He told how pussies in the spring
  Made mince meat of the birds that sing.
Descanted on this shame of shames,
  While many gatherings of dames
With aviaries on their hats
  Wept at the perfidy of cats,
And cried, " Our birds destroyed?   No, no,
  The cat is doomed and he must go."

BURDEN-BEARERS

And the Lord opened the mouth of the ass, and she said unto Balaam, What have I done unto thee, that thou hast smitten me these three times?

NUMBERS 22:28.

BURDEN-BEARERS

THE DONKEY

By G. K. Chesterton

When fishes flew and forests walked
 And figs grew upon thorn,
Some moment when the moon was blood
 Then surely I was born;

With monstrous head and sickening cry
 And ears like errant wings,
The devil's walking parody
 On all four-footed things.

The tattered outlaw of the earth,
 Of ancient crooked will;
Starve, scourge, deride me: I am dumb,
 I keep my secret still.

Fools! For I also had my hour;
 One far fierce hour and sweet:
There was a shout about my ears,
 And palms before my feet.

A FRIEND IN NEED

By Jack Burroughs

There is a public garden in Bordeaux,
 Where, carved in true, compelling lines of stone,
 Rosa Bonheur, calm visaged and alone,
Looks ever down upon the endless flow

Of life in the less rugged flesh. A slow,
  Ungainly little donkey, as, wind-blown,
  A weed into a garden drifts, unknown,
Stole in one day to feed where flowers grow.

A keeper, shocked that this dull beast should browse
  Before the statue of the mighty dead,
Rushed up, with blows the sinner to arouse.
  He stops, club poised above the shaggy head;
Calm eyes seem watching him; his head he bows,
  And leads the dumb brute gently forth instead.

I AM THE MULE

By Will Chamberlain

I am the mule, from ears which catch the gale
To that unresting terminus, my tail;
From downcast head and eye upon the soil,
Where burdens chain me to the post of toil,
To my one quick defense, the nimble heel,
Which lashing tyrants sometimes justly feel.
I climb the mountains where the eagles rule
And tramp the dingy mine-path—I, the mule.

I am the mule—the butt of countless jokes—
But since time was my neck has known the yokes
Of labor merciless, of crushing tasks which tell
Of human cruelty which breeds a human hell.
But as for me, without a sigh or tear,
Heat, cold or storm, I get my hell right here—
On city street, in miry, rustic pool;
My prayer a bray for pity on the mule.

I am the mule—where snows eternal cling,
Or where tropics flaunt perpetual Spring;
On trains which hide behind the mask of night,
Where cotton bales are stacked and blackskins fight,
Where bleak Alaska binds a pack of dust
Upon the spine—the spoils of human lust—
Or where for heartless Cubans I'm the tool
To pull the ponderous cane-carts—I, the mule.

I am the mule, and when men madly fly
To belching guns and paint a war-red sky,
And cities tumble and armadas sink,
I drag the cannons while the cowards slink.
And when are ended all the blood-wet days
Who ever hears for me a note of praise—
I who have triumphs fashioned in the school
Of world events—your humble slave—the mule?

THE BURTHEN OF THE ASS

By John B. Tabb

On Christmas night at Bethlehem
When Shepherds came, I watched with them
 The Mother and the Child,
Who, warned from Herod's wrath to flee,
Were into Egypt borne by me,
 Beyond the desert wild.

And back again, at Herod's death,
I brought them home to Nazareth;
 And when unto His own,
With loud Hosannas to His Name
As King the Son of David came,
 My shoulders were His throne.

NICHOLAS NYE

By Walter de la Mare

Thistle and darnel and dock grew there,
　And a bush, in the corner, of may,
On the orchard wall I used to sprawl,
　In the blazing heat of the day;
Half asleep and half awake,
　While the birds went twittering by,
And nobody there my lone to share
　But Nicholas Nye.

Nicholas Nye was lean and grey,
　Lame of a leg and old,
More than a score of donkey's years
　He had seen since he was foaled;
He munched the thistles, purple and spiked,
　Would sometimes stoop and sigh,
And turn to his head, as if he said,
　" Poor Nicholas Nye! "

Alone with his shadow he'd browse in the meadow,
　Lazily swinging his tail,
At break of day he used to bray,—
　Not much too hearty and hale;
But a wonderful gumption was under his skin,
　And a clear calm light in his eye,
And once in a while he'd smile:—
　Would Nicholas Nye.

Seemed to be smiling at me, he would,
　From his bush, in the corner, of may,—
Bony and ownerless, widowed and worn,
　Knobble-kneed, lonely and grey;
And over the grass would seem to pass
　'Neath the deep dark blue of the sky,
Something much better than words between **me**
　And Nicholas Nye.

But dusk would come in the apple boughs,
　The green of the glow-worm shine,
The birds in nest would crouch to rest,
　And home I'd trudge to mine;
And there, in the moonlight, dark with dew,
　Asking not wherefore nor why,
Would brood like a ghost, and as still as a post,
　Old Nicholas Nye.

SMALL CREATURES

I would not enter on my list of friends
(Though graced with polish'd manners and fine
    sense,
Yet wanting sensibility) the man
Who needlessly sets foot upon a worm.

The Task.   WILLIAM COWPER.

SMALL CREATURES

SNAKE

By D. H. Lawrence

A snake came to my water-trough
On a hot, hot day, and I in pyjamas for the heat,
To drink there.

In the deep, strange-scented shade of the great dark
      carob tree
I came down the steps with my pitcher
And must wait, must stand and wait, for there he was
    at the trough before me.

He reached down from a fissure in the earth-wall in the
      gloom
And trailed his yellow-brown slackness soft-bellied down,
    over the edge of the stone trough
And rested his throat upon the stone bottom,
And where the water had dripped from the tap, in a
    small clearness,
He sipped with his straight mouth,
Softly drank through his straight gums, into his slack
    long body,
Silently.

Some one was before me at my water-trough,
And I, like a second-comer, waiting.

He lifted his head from his drinking, as cattle do,
And looked at me vaguely, as drinking cattle do,

And flickered his two-forked tongue from his lips, and
    mused a moment,
And stooped and drank a little more,
Being earth-brown, earth-golden from the burning
    bowels of the earth
On the day of Sicilian July, with Etna smoking.

The voice of my education said to me
He must be killed,
For in Sicily the black, black snakes are innocent, the
    gold are venomous.

And voices in me said, If you were a man
You would take a stick and break him now, and finish
    him off.

But must I confess how I liked him,
How glad I was he had come like a guest in quiet, to
    drink at my water-trough
And depart peaceful, pacified, and thankless,
Into the burning bowels of this earth?

Was it cowardice, that I dared not kill him?
Was it perversity, that I longed to talk to him?
Was it humility, to feel honoured?
I felt so honoured.

And yet those voices:
If you were not afraid you would kill him.

And truly I was afraid, I was most afraid,
But even so, honoured still more
That he should seek my hospitality
From out the dark door of the secret earth.

He drank enough
And lifted his head, dreamily, as one who has drunken,
And flickered his tongue like a forked night on the air,
    so black,
Seeming to lick his lips,
And looked around like a god, unseeing, into the air,
And slowly turned his head,
And slowly, very slowly, as if thrice adream,
Proceeded to draw his slow length curving round
And climb again the broken bank of my wall-face.

And as he put his head into that dreadful hole,
And as he slowly drew up, snake-easing his shoulders,
    and entered further,
A sort of horror, a sort of protest against his with-
    drawing into that horrid black hole,
Deliberately going into the blackness, and slowly draw-
    ing himself after,
Overcame me now his back was turned.

I looked round, I put down my pitcher,
I picked up a clumsy log
And threw it at the water-trough with a clatter.

I think it did not hit him,
But suddenly that part of him that was left behind
    convulsed in undignified haste,
Writhed like lightning, and was gone
Into the black hole, the earth-lipped fissure in the
    wall-front,
At which, in the intense still noon, I stared with
    fascination.

And immediately I regretted it.
I thought how paltry, how vulgar, what a mean act!
I despised myself and the voices of my accursèd human
    education.

And I thought of the albatross,
And I wished he would come back, my snake.
For he seemed to me again like a king,
Like a king in exile, uncrowned in the underworld,
Now due to be crowned again.

And so, I missed my chance with one of the lords
Of life,
And I have something to expiate:
A pettiness.

THE LIZARD

By Edwin Markham

I sit among the hoary trees
With Aristotle on my knees,
And turn with serious hand the pages,
Lost in the cobweb-hush of ages;
When suddenly with no more sound
Than any sunbeam on the ground,
The little hermit of the place
Is peering up into my face—
The slim gray hermit of the rocks,
With bright inquisitive, quick eyes,
His life a round of harks and shocks,
A little ripple of surprise.

Now lifted up, intense and still,
Sprung from the silence of the hill
He hangs upon the ledge a-glisten,
And his whole body seems to listen!
My pages give a little start,
And he is gone! to be a part
Of the old cedar's crumpled bark,
A mottled scar, a weather-mark!

How halt am I, how mean of birth,
Beside this darting pulse of earth!
I only have the wit to look
Into a big presumptuous book,
To find some sage's rigid plan
To tell me how to be a man.
Tradition lays its dead hand cold
Upon our youth—and we are old.
But this wise hermit, this gray friar,
He has no law but heart's desire.
He somehow touches higher truth,
The circle of eternal youth.

TO A TREE-FROG

By Amélie Rives

Little enchanted leaf,
    Apart from the tree yet of it,
The magic of water made you
    That so you love it;
The brook gave you a voice,
    Dew drops your eyes,
Your little watery soul
    From a mist did rise;

And so you're ever trilling,
  While rain is rilling,
    For sheer delight
    In its wetness bright,—
And so you're ever crooning
  With muted glee
While the wind his harp is tuning
  To a higher key,
    For well you know
    When he doth so,
Full soon he'll strike the chord of power
  That brings a shower,
And while the rain is rilling
  Again you will be trilling;—

  " Tree! Tree! Tree!
    Dr-rink! Dr-rink!
  Creek! Creek! Creek!
    Br-rim a-br-rink!
  Dr-r-r-ops in millions,
    Billions, tr-r-rillions! "

  It is ecstasy to be
  A little green frog on a tree
    When rain is rilling,
When summer showers are shrilling.

THE TOAD

By Arthur C. Benson

Old fellow-loiterer, whither wouldst thou go?
  The lonely eve is ours.
When tides of richer fragrance ooze and flow
  From heavy-lidded flowers.

With solemn hampered pace proceeding by
    The dewy garden-bed,
Like some old priest in antique finery,
    Stiff cope and jewelled head;

Thy sanctuary lamps are lit at dusk,
    Where leafy aisles are dim;
The bat's shrill piccolo, the swinging musk
    Blend with the beetle's hymn.

Aye something paramount and priestly too,
    Some cynic mystery,
Lurks in the dull skin with its dismal hue,
    The bright ascetic eye;

Thou seem'st the heir of centuries, hatched out
    With æons on thy track;
The dust of ages compasses about
    Thy lean and shrivelled back.

Thy heaving throat, thy sick repulsive glance
    Still awes thy foes around;
The eager hound starts back and looks askance,
    And whining paws the ground.

Yet thou hast forfeited thy ancient ban,
    Thy mystical control;
We know thee now to be the friend of man,
    A simple homely soul;

And when we deemed thee curiously wise,
    Still chewing venomed paste,
Thou didst but crush the limbs of juicy flies
    With calm and critic taste.

By tne grey stone half sunk in mossy mold,
    Beside the stiff boxhedge,
Thou slumberest, when the dawn with fingers cold
    Plucks at the low cloud's edge.

O royal life! in some cool cave all day,
    Dreaming old dreams, to lie,
Or peering up to see the larkspur sway
    Above thee in the sky;

Or wandering when the sunset airs are cool
    Beside the elm-tree's foot,
To splash and sink in some sequestered pool,
    Amid the cresses' root.

Abhorred, despised, the sad wind o'er thee sings;
    Thou hast no friend to fear,
Yet fashioned in the secret mint of things
    And bidden to be here.

Man dreams of loveliness, and bids it be;
    To truth his eye is dim.
Thou wert, because the spirit dreamed of thee,
    And thou art born of him.

THE WOODMOUSE

By Mary Howitt

Do you know the little woodmouse,
    That pretty little thing,
That sits among the forest leaves,
    Or by the forest spring?

Its fur is red like the chestnut,
  And it is small and slim,
It leads a life most innocent,
  Within the forest dim.

It makes a bed of the soft, dry moss,
  In a hole that's deep and strong,
And there it sleeps secure and warm,
  The dreary winter long;
And though it keeps no calendar,
  It knows when flowers are springing,
And it waketh to its summer life,
  When nightingales are singing.

TO A FIELD MOUSE

By Robert Burns

Wee, sleekit, cow'rin', tim'rous beastie,
O what a panic's in thy breastie!
Thou need na start away sae hasty,
  Wi' bickering brattle!
I wad be laith to rin and chase thee
  Wi' murd'ring pattle!

I'm truly sorry man's dominion
Has broken Nature's social union,
And justifies that ill opinion
  Which makes thee startle
At me, thy poor earth-born companion,
  And fellow-mortal!

I doubt na, whyles, but thou may thieve;
What then? poor beastie, thou maun live!
A daimen icker in a thrave
　　's a sma' request:
I'll get a blessin' wi' the lave,
　　And never miss't!

Thy wee bit housie, too, in ruin!
Its silly wa's the win's are strewin':
And naething, now, to big a new ane,
　　O' foggage green!
And bleak December's winds ensuin',
　　Baith snell and keen!

Thou saw the fields laid bare and waste,
And weary winter coming fast;
And cozie here, beneath the blast,
　　Thou thought to dwell,
Till, crash! the cruel coulter past
　　Out thro' thy cell.

That wee bit heap o' leaves and stibble
Has cost thee mony a weary nibble!
Now thou's turn'd out for a' thy trouble
　　But house or hald,
To thole the winter's sleety dribble
　　And cranreuch cauld!

But, Mousie, thou are no thy lane
In proving foresight may be vain:
The best laid schemes o' mice and men
　　Gang aft a-gley,
And lea'e us nought but grief and pain,
　　For promised joy.

Still thou art blest, compared wi' me!
The present only toucheth thee:
But, och! I backward cast my e'e
    On prospects drear!
And forward, tho' I canna see,
    I guess and fear.

TO A WOOD-RAT

Whose home was destroyed by a class in Zoology

By James Leo Duff

Och, it pulls at me heart to see you afflicted,
    You with th' great, sobbin' eyes of ye there;
Could the Irish stand by to see one evicted
    An' say, " I don't care? "

You that have labored your home to be earnin',
    You've toiled in th' buildin' be day an' be night.
Now they've pulled it apart for th' sake of their
    learnin'—
God send thim light!

REMORSE ON KILLING A SQUIRREL IN A GARDEN

By William Ray

Rash was the hand, and foul the deed,
    That gave thee, thus, to death a prey;
Oh! I could weep to see thee bleed
    And pant thy gasping life away.

What hast thou done to merit death,
　But gather for a future day,
Just to prolong thy little breath?
　And yet I took thy life away.

For thou no wealth or fame didst crave,
　No costly food, or clothing gay;
But only sought thy life to save;
　And yet I took thy life away.

Poor little thing; how hard it strove
　To shun the blow, as hid it lay:
But all could not my pity move,
　I took its trembling life away.

Oh! how inhospitably vile!
　It came, a stranger, here to stay;
To eat and drink, and live awhile,
　But I have taken its life away.

Too late, I now repent the blow,
　'Tis stiff, alas! and cold as clay!
Its life to me it did not owe,
　And yet I took its life away.

The *power* which gave all nature law,
　Whose summons we must all obey,
Gave thee thy vital breath to draw,
　And yet I took that breath away.

Whether thou hast a mate to moan,
　Or offspring dear, ah! who can say?
No harm to me thou e'er hast done,
　And yet I took thy life away.

What millions do mankind destroy,
  Of their own race, for power or pay!
Some would have kept thee for a toy,
  But I have toyed thy life away.

A NEIGHBOUR

By Norman Gale

The Lord Almighty chose to give
This hedgehog room enough to live
Upon the world where you and I
Look up to praise Him in the sky.

The hedgehog clearly understands
The weakness of the little hands
That seem, when he considers all
His work and dangers, very small.

He steadily and strongly grows
A bunch of thorns, to prick the nose
Of any dog that dares attack
The fortress on his rounded back.

If threatened, he applies the rule
They taught him at his Infant School:
He makes a ball of back and chest,
And keeps on hoping for the best.

The Lord Almighty chose to give
The hedgehog room enough to live
Upon the world. I want to add
That I, for one, am very glad.

"UPON a THOUSAND HILLS"

For every beast of the forest is mine, and the cattle upon a thousand hills.

PSALM 50:10.

" UPON A THOUSAND HILLS "

A COW AT SULLINGTON

By Charles Dalmon

She leaves the puddle where she drinks,
    And comes toward the roadway bar
And looks into our eyes, and thinks
    What curious animals we are!

THE OLD BRINDLE COW

By Thomas O'Hagan

Of all old memories that cluster round my heart,
    With their root in my boyhood days,
The quaintest is linked to the old brindle cow
    With sly and mysterious ways.
She'd linger round the lot near the old potato patch,
    A sentinel by night and by day,
Watching for the hour when all eyes were asleep,
    To start on her predatory way.

The old brush fence she would scorn in her course,
    With turnips and cabbage just beyond,
And corn that was blooming through the halo of the
      night—
    What a banquet so choice and so fond!
But when the stars of morn were paling in the sky
    The old brindle cow would take the cue,
And dressing up her line she'd retreat beyond the fence,
    For the old cow knew just what to do.

What breed did you say? Why the very best blood
    That could flow in a democratic cow;
No herd-book could tell of the glory in her horns
    Or whence came her pedigree or how:
She was Jersey in her milk and Durham in her build,
    And Ayrshire when she happened in a row,
But when it came to storming the old " slash " fence
    She was simply the old brindle cow.

It seems but a day since I drove her to the gate
    To yield up her rich and creamy prize;
For her theft at midnight hour she would yield a double
      dower,
    With peace of conscience lurking in her eyes.
But she's gone—disappeared with the ripened years of
      time,
    Whose memories my heart enthrall e'en now;
And I never hear a bell tinkling through the forest dell
    But I think of that old brindle cow.

THE KERRY COW

By W. M. Letts

It's in Connacht in Munster that yourself might travel
    wide,
And be asking all the herds you'd meet along the
    country-side,
But you'd never meet a one could show the likes of her
    till now,
Where she's grazing in a Leinster field—my little Kerry
    cow.

If herself went to the cattle fairs she'd put all cows to
    shame,
For the finest poets of the land would meet to sing her
    fame;
And the young girls would be asking leave to stroke her
    satin coat,
They'd be praising and caressing her, and calling her
    a dote.

If the King of Spain gets news of her, he'll fill his purse
    with gold,
And set sail to ask the English King where she is to
    be sold.
But the King of Spain may come to me, a crown upon
    his brow.
It is he may keep his golden purse—and I my Kerry
    cow.

The priest maybe will tell her fame to the Holy Pope
    of Rome,
And the Cardinals' College send for her to leave her
    Irish home;
But it's heart-broke she would be itself to cross the
    Irish sea,
'Twould be best they'd send a blessing to my Kerry
    cow and me.

When the Ulster men hear tell of her, they'll come with
    swords an' pikes,
For it's civil war there'll be no less if they should see
    her likes,
And you'll read it on the paper of the bloody fight
    there's been,
An' the Orangemen they're burying in fields of Leinster
    green.

There are red cows that's contrary, and there's white
    cows quare and wild,
But my Kerry cow is biddable, an' gentle as a child.
You may rare up kings and heroes on the lovely milk
    she yields,
For she's fit to foster generals to fight our battlefields.

In the histories they'll be making they've a right to put
    her name
With the horse of Troy and Oisin's hounds and other
    beasts of fame.
And the painters will be painting her beneath the haw-
    thorn bough
Where she's grazing on the good green grass—my little
    Kerry cow.

CATTLE BEFORE THE STORM

By Glenn Ward Dresbach

About the water hole, half dried,
The restless cattle weary eyed,
Watching dark omens in the skies,
Stir up the choking dust that settles
Upon them with the flies
That sting like nettles.

No shelter lifts where they may go.
Far hazy hills in ragged row
Are out where trails on distance break;
And cattle group and mill together
With rumps now hunched to take
The lashing weather.

Sparse pasture cannot lure them back
Along the plain while lightnings crack
Long whips of flame the clouds writhe from.
Though something tells them to beware it,
The cattle tense and dumb
Must stay and bear it.

FEEDIN' THE STOCK

By Holman F. Day

Hear the chorus in that tie-up, runch, gerrunch, and
    runch and runch!
—There's a row of honest critters! Does me good to
    hear 'em munch.
When the barn is gettin' dusky and the sun's behind the
    drifts,
—Touchin' last the gable winder where the dancin'
    hay-dust sifts,
When the coaxin' from the tie-up kind o' hints it's five
    o'clock—
Wal, I've got a job that suits me—that's the chore of
    feedin' stock.

We've got patches down to our house—honest patches,
    though, and neat,
But we'd rather have the patches than to skinch on
    what we eat.
Lots of work, and grub to back ye—that's a mighty
    wholesome creed.
—Critters fust, s'r, that's my motto—give the critters
    all they need.

And the way we do at our house, marm and me take
  what is left,
And—wal,—we ain't goin' hungry, as you'll notice by
  our heft.
Drat the man that's calculatin' when he measures out
  his hay,
Groanin' ev'ry time he pitches ary forkful out the bay;
Drat the man who feeds out ruff-scuff, wood and wire
  from the swale,
'Cause he wants to press his herds'-grass, send his clover
  off for sale.

Down to our house we wear patches, but it ain't nobody's biz
Jest as long as them 'ere critters git the best of hay
  there is.
When the cobwebs on the rafters drip with winter's
  early dusk
And the rows of critters' noses, damp with breath as
  sweet as musk,
Toss and tease me from the tie-up—ain't a job that
  suits me more
Than the feedin' of the cattle—that's the reg'lar wind-
  up chore.

When I grain 'em or I meal 'em—wal, there's plenty in
  the bin,
And I give 'em Quaker measure ev'ry time I dip down
  in;
And the hay, wal, now I've cut it, and I own it and
  it's mine
And I jab that blamed old fork in, till you'd think I'd
  bust a tine.

I ain't doin' it for praises—no one sees me but the pup,
—And I get his apperbation, 'cause he pounds his tail,
rup, rup!
No, I do it 'cause I want to; 'cause I couldn't sleep a
wink,
If I thought them poor dumb critters lacked for fodder
or for drink.
And to have the scufflin' barnful give a jolly little blat
When you open up o' mornin's, ah, there's comfort,
friend, in that!
And you've prob'ly sometimes noticed, when his cattle
hate a man,
That it's pretty sure his neighbors size him up on that
same plan.

But I'm solid in my tie-up; when I've finished up that
chore,
I enjoy it standin' list'nin' for a minit at the door.
And the rustle of the fodder and the nuzzlin' in the
meal
And the runchin's of their feedin' make this humble
feller feel
That there ain't no greater comfort than this 'ere—to
understand
That a dozen faithful critters owe their comfort to my
hand.

Oh, the dim old barn seems homelike, with its overhang-
ing mows,
With its warm and battened tie-up, full of well-fed sheep
and cows.

Then I shet the door behind me, drop the bar and drive
    the pin
And, with Jeff a-waggin' after, lug the foamin' milk-
    pails in.

That's the style of things to our house—marm and me
    we don't pull up
Until ev'ry critter's eatin', from the cattle to the pup.
Then the biskits and the spare-rib and plum preserves
    taste good,
For we're feelin', me and mother, that we're actin'
    'bout's we should.
Like as can be, after supper mother sews another patch
And she says the duds look trampy, 'cause she ain't got
    goods to match.
Fust of all, though, comes the mealbins and the hay-
    mows; after those
If there's any extry dollars, wal, we'll see about new
    clothes.
But to-night, why, bless ye, mother, pull the rug acrost
    the door;
—Warmth and food and peace and comfort—let's not
    pester God for more.

THE STOCK IN THE TIE-UP

By Holman F. Day

I'm workin' this week in the wood-lot; a hearty old job,
    you can bet;
I finish my chores with a larntern, and marm has the
    table all set

By the time I get in with the milkin'; and after I wash
  at the sink,
And marm sets a saucer o' strainin's for the cat and
  the kittens to drink,
Your uncle is ready for supper, with an appetite whet
  to an edge
That'll cut like a bush-scythe in swale-grass, and
  couldn't be dulled on a ledge.
And marm, she slats open the oven, and pulls out a
  heapin'-full tin
Of the rippin'est cream-tartar biskit a man ever pushed
  at his chin.
We pile some more wood on the fire, and open the
  damper full blare,
And pull up and pitch into supper—and comfort—and
  taste good—wal, there!
And the wind swooshes over the chimbly, and scrapes at
  the shingles cross-grain,
But good double winders and bankin' are mighty good
  friends here in Maine.
I look 'crost the table to mother, and marm she looks
  over at me,
And passes another hot biskit and says, " Won't ye
  have some more tea? "
And while I am stirrin' the sugar, I relish the sound of
  the storm.
For, thank the good Lord, we are cosy, and the stock
  in the tie-up is warm.

I tell ye, the song o' the fire and the chirruping hiss o'
  the tea,
The roar of the wind in the chimbly, they sound dreadful cheerful to me.

But they'd harrer me, plague me, and fret me, unless as
    I set here I knew
That the critters arc munchin' their fodder and bedded
    and comf'table, too.
These biskits are light as a feather, but, boy, they'd be
    heavier'n lead
If I thought that my hosses was shiv'rin', if I thought
    that my cattle warn't fed.
There's men in the neighborhood 'round me who pray
    som'w'at louder than me,
They wear better clothes, sir, on Sunday—chip in for
    the heathen Chinee,
But the cracks in the sides o' their tie-ups are wide as
    the door o' their pew,
And the winter comes in there a-howlin', with the sleet
    and the snow peltin' through.

Step in there, sir, ary a mornin' and look at their
    critters! 'Twould seem
As if they were bilers or engines, and all o' them chock-
    full o' steam.
I've got an old-fashioned religion that calkalates Sun-
    days for rest,
But if there warn't time, sir, on week days to batten a
    tie-up, I'm blest
I'd use up a Sunday or such-like, and let the durned
    heathen folks go
While I fastened some boards on the lintel to keep out
    the frost and the snow.
I'd stand all the frowns of the parson before I'd have
    courage to face
The dumb holler eyes o' the critters hooked up in a
    frosty old place.

And I'll bet ye that in the Hereafter the men who have
    stayed on their knees
And let some poor, fuzzy old cattle stand out in a tie-up
    and freeze,
Will find that the heat o' the Hot Place is keyed to an
    extra degree
For the men who forgot to consider that critters have
    feelin's same's we.

I dasn't go thinkin' o' tie-ups where winter goes whistlin'
    through.
Where cattle are humped at their stanchions with
    scarcely the gumption to moo.
But I'm glad for the sake of Hereafter that mine ain't
    the sin and the guilt,
And I tell you I relish my feelin's when I pull up the
    big patchwork quilt.
I can laugh at the pelt o' the snowflakes, and grin at
    the slat o' the storm,
And thank the good Lord I can sleep now, the stock in
    the tie-up is warm.

I'VE GOT THEM CALVES TO VEAL

By Holman F. Day

It's a jolly sort of season, is the spring—is the spring,
And there isn't any reason for not feeling like a king.
The sun has got flirtatious and he kisses Mistress Maine,
And she pouts her lips, a-saying, " Mister, can't you
    come again? "
The hens are all a-laying, the potatoes sprouting well,

And fodder spent so nicely that I'll have some hay to
sell.
But when I get to feeling just as well as I can feel,
All to once it comes across me that I've got them calves
to veal.

Oh! I can't go in the stanchion, look them mothers in
the eye,
For I'm meditatin' murder; planning how their calves
must die.
Every time them little shavers grab a teat, it wrings
my heart,
—Hate to see 'em all so happy, for them cows and
calves must part.
That's the reason I'm so mournful; that's the reason
in the spring
I go feeling just like Nero or some other wicked thing,
For I have to slash and slaughter; have to set an iron
heel
On the feelings of them mothers; I have got them calves
to veal.

Spring is happy for the poet and the lover and the girl,
But the farmer has to do things that will make his
harslet curl.
And the thing that hits me hardest is to stand the lonesome moos
Of that stanchion full of critters when they find they're
going to lose
Little Spark-face, Little Brindle—when the time has
come to part,
And the calves go off a-blatting in a butcher's rattling
cart.

Though the cash the butcher pays me sort of smooths
    things up and salves
All the really rawest feeling when I sell them little
    calves,
Still I'm mournful in the springtime; knocks me off my
    even keel,
Seeing suffering around me when I have them calves to
    veal.

THE LITTLE RED BULLOCK

By Herbert Tremaine

" Colleen, under the thorn-tree
    Wit' the sunbeams filtering through
—Is it dreaming you are, sweet colleen,
    An' all the milking to do? "
. . . " I'm thinking of my little red bullock
    That they're killing at Ballinasloe.

" 'Twas myself that watched by his mother
    All night in the old tarred shed;
An' as soon as her pain was over
    The creature put down her head,
An' she licked him as clean as a sixpence
    —An' she no better than dead!

" That's his field on the edge of the bogland
    Where there's bushes of wild sweet-gale. . . .
Do you see where the wall is broken? . . .
    I usety come wit' my pail. . . .
I think I can feel him sucking
    An' see him whisking his tail. . . .

" Agh, I'd reared him so big an' so lovely
    In the sun an' the green an' the blue!
. . . I'm a fool to be sitting here crying,
    An' all the milking to do.
. . . But it seemed like killing my baby
    When they tuk him to Ballinasloe."

THE CATTLE TRAIN

By Charlotte Perkins Gilman

Below my window goes the cattle train,
    And stands for hours along the river park,
Fear, Cold, Exhaustion, Hunger, Thirst, and Pain;
    Dumb brutes we call them—Hark!

The bleat of frightened mother-calling young,
    Deep-throated agony, shrill frantic cries,
Hoarse murmur of the thirst-distended tongue,
    Up to my window rise.

Bleak lies the shore to northern wind and sleet,
    In open-slatted cars they stand and freeze;
Beside the broad blue river in the heat
    All waterless go these.

Hot, fevered, frightened, trampled, bruised, and
        torn;
    Frozen to death before the ax descends;
We kill these weary creatures, sore and worn,
    And eat them—with our friends.

SHEEP

By William H. Davies

When I was once in Baltimore
    A man came up to me and cried,
" Come, I have eighteen hundred sheep,
    And we will sail on Tuesday's tide.

" If you will sail with me, young man,
    I'll pay you fifty shillings down;
These eighteen hundred sheep I take
    From Baltimore to Glasgow town."

He paid me fifty shillings down,
    I sailed with eighteen hundred sheep;
We soon had cleared the harbour's mouth,
    We soon were in the salt sea deep.

The first night we were out at sea
    Those sheep were quiet in their mind;
The second night they cried with fear—
    They smelt no pastures in the wind.

They sniffed, poor things, for their green fields,
    They cried so loud I could not sleep:
For fifty thousand shillings down
    I would not sail again with sheep.

A CHILD'S PET

By William H. Davies

When I sailed out of Baltimore,
  With twice a thousand head of sheep,
They would not eat, they would not drink,
  But bleated o'er the deep.

Inside the pens we crawled each day,
  To sort the living from the dead;
And when we reached the Mersey's mouth,
  Had lost five hundred head.

Yet every night and day one sheep,
  That had no fear of man or sea,
Stuck through the bars its pleading face,
  And it was stroked by me.

And to the sheep-men standing near,
  " You see," I said, " this one tame sheep?
It seems a child has lost her pet,
  And cried herself to sleep."

So every time we passed it by,
  Sailing to England's slaughter-house,
Eight ragged sheep-men—tramps and thieves—
  Would stroke that sheep's black nose.

THE CALF

By Eleanor Baldwin

In a pasture toward the sun, O my brothers,
I have seen him leap and run with the others.
I have watched him as he fed,
Nuzzling with his curly head,
And his baby coat was red
Like his mother's.

They have penned him in the train with the others,
And that distant low of pain is his mother's.
For they seized him as he nursed—
Hot his hunger and his thirst
In this groaning place accursed,
O my brothers.

He is goaded from the car, and he smothers
Where the wheels and pulleys are, O my brothers!
For his fear has found its proof:
By his hind and cloven hoof
He is swung twixt floor and roof
With the others.

Now the knife has crossed his throat—like the
others.
Redder glows his little coat than his mother's.
(Far the pastures toward the south!)
Bitter drink for bitter drouth
Is the dark blood in his mouth,
O my brothers!

OXEN

And the plain ox,
That harmless, honest, guileless animal,
In what has he offended? he whose toil,
Patient and ever ready, clothes the land
With all the pomp of harvest.

The Seasons.   JAMES THOMSON.

OXEN

OXEN

By Mahlon Leonard Fisher

Weary, they plod the ploughlands of the World.
  Wherever turf is turned their hooves have pressed.
  Gladly the great Earth-mother gives her breast
For them to trample—her pure bosom, pearled
With dews of innumerable mornings. Where were
    furled
  Slit pitiful flags, their passing stills dismay:
  Yoke-ridden, mute, Peace binds on them her bay.—
For this the goad, the lash, the curse age-hurled!
Patient (Ah, theirs the patient eyes of Christ!),
  They tread the centuries. Behind them flows
  The furrowed glebe, and hath since Egypt rose,
Starlike, above the Nile. They bide the tryst
  Man hath appointed; till he dig their graves,
  Serve him, complaintless, who hath made them
    slaves.

THE OX

From the " Poesie."

I love thee, pious ox; a gentle feeling
  Of vigor and of peace thou giv'st my heart.
  How solemn, like a monument, thou art!
Over wide fertile fields thy calm gaze stealing,
Unto the yoke with grave contentment kneeling,
  To man's quick work thou dost thy strength impart.
  He shouts and goads, and answering thy smart,

181

Thou turn'st on him thy patient eyes appealing.
From thy broad nostrils, black and wet, arise
   Thy breath's soft fumes; and on the still air swells,
Like happy hymn, thy lowing's mellow strain.
In the grave sweetness of thy tranquil eyes
   Of emerald, broad and still reflected dwells
All the divine green silence of the plain.

               From the Italian of Giosué Carducci.
                  Translation of Frank Sewall.

A YOKE OF STEERS

By DuBose Heyward

A heave of mighty shoulders to the yoke,
Square patient heads, and flaring sweep of horn;
The darkness swirling down beneath their feet
Where sleeping valleys stir and feel the dawn;
Uncouth and primal, on and up they sway,
Taking the summit in a drench of day.
The night-winds volley upward bitter-sweet,
And the dew shatters to a rainbow spray
Under the slow-moving cloven feet.

There is a power here that grips the mind—
A force repressed and inarticulate,
Slow as the swing of centuries, as blind
As Destiny, and as deliberate.

They will arrive in their appointed hour
Unhurried by the goad of lesser wills,
Bearing vast burdens on.
              They are the great
Unconquerable spirit of these hills.

CROSSING THE PLAINS

By Joaquin Miller

What great yoked brutes with briskets low;
With wrinkled necks like buffalo,
With round, brown, liquid, pleading eyes,
That turned so slow and sad to you,
That shone like love's eyes soft with tears,
That seemed to plead, and make replies,
The while they bowed their necks and drew
The creaking load; and looked at you.
Their sable briskets swept the ground,
Their cloven feet kept solemn sound.

Two sullen bullocks led the line,
Their great eyes shining bright like wine;
Two sullen captive kings were they,
That had in time held herds at bay,
And even now they crushed the sod
With stolid sense of majesty,
And stately stepped and stately trod,
As if 'twere something still to be
Kings even in captivity.

Permission to use this poem granted by Harr Wagner
Publishing Company, San Francisco, California, publishers of
Joaquin Miller's Complete Poems.

" The LAST and LEAST of THINGS "

O'er folded blooms
  On swirls of mush,
The beetle booms adown the glooms
  And bumps along the dusk.

The Beetle.   JAMES WHITCOMB RILEY.

————

The spider's touch, how exquisitely fine!
Feels at each thread, and lives along the line.

Essay on Man, Epistle I.   ALEXANDER POPE.

————

His labor is a chant,
  His idleness a tune;
Oh, for a bee's experience
  Of clovers and of noon!

The Bee.   EMILY DICKINSON.

————

What more felicitie can fall to creature
Than to enjoy delight with libertie,
And to be lord of all the workes of Nature,
To raine in th' aire from earth to highest skie,
To feed on flowres and weeds of glorious feature.

Muiopotmos: or, The Fate of the Butterflie.
                          EDMUND SPENSER.

————

Go to the ant, thou sluggard; consider her ways, and
be wise.

                          PROVERBS 6:6.

186

"THE LAST AND LEAST OF THINGS"

ALL THINGS WAIT UPON THEE

By Christina G. Rossetti

Innocent eyes not ours
And made to look on flowers,
Eyes of small birds, and insects small;
Morn after summer morn
The sweet rose on her thorn
Opens her bosom to them all.
The last and least of things,
That soar on quivering wings,
Or crawl among the grass blades out of sight,
Have just as clear a right
To their appointed portion of delight
As queens or kings.

THE BEE IN CHURCH

By Alfred Noyes

The nestling church at Ovingdean
Was fragrant as a hive in May;
And there was nobody within
To preach, or praise, or pray.

The sunlight slanted through the door,
And through the panes of painted glass,
When I stole in, alone, once more
To feel the ages pass.

Then, through the dim grey hush there droned
   An echoing plain-song on the air,
As if some ghostly priest intoned
   An old Gregorian there.

Saint Chrysostom could never lend
   More honey to the heavenly Spring
Than seemed to murmur and ascend
   On that invisible wing.

So small he was, I scarce could see
   My girdled brown hierophant;
But only a Franciscan bee
   In such a bass could chant.

His golden Latin rolled and boomed.
   It swayed the altar flowers anew,
Till all that hive of worship bloomed
   With dreams of sun and dew.

Ah, sweet Franciscan of the May,
   Dear chaplain of the fairy queen,
You sent a singing heart away
   That day, from Ovingdean.

A BEE SETS SAIL

By Katharine Morse

The wind blows east, the wind blows storm,
And yet this very hour
I saw a bumblebee embark
In frigate of a flower;

An admiral in epaulets,
He strode the scented deck
And in the teeth of tossing gales
He rode without a wreck.

More valorous adventurer
I never hope to see,—
Though mariners be gallant men, —
Than that same bumblebee.

THE HUMBLE-BEE

By Ralph Waldo Emerson

Burly, dozing humble-bee,
Where thou art is clime for me.
Let them sail for Porto Rique,
Far-off heats through seas to seek;
I will follow thee alone,
Thou animated torrid-zone!
Zigzag steerer, desert cheerer,
Let me chase thy waving lines;
Keep me nearer, me thy hearer,
Singing over shrubs and vines.

Insect lover of the sun,
Joy of thy dominion!
Sailor of the atmosphere;
Swimmer through the waves of air;
Voyager of light and noon;
Epicurean of June;
Wait, I prithee, till I come
Within earshot of thy hum,—
All without is martyrdom.

When the south wind, in May days,
With a net of shining haze
Silvers the horizon wall,
And, with softness touching all,
Tints the human countenance
With a color of romance,
And, infusing subtle heats,
Turns the sod to violets,
Thou, in sunny solitudes,
Rover of the underwoods,
The green silence dost displace
With thy mellow, breezy bass.

Hot midsummer's petted crone,
Sweet to me thy drowsy tone
Tells of countless sunny hours,
Long days, and solid banks of flowers;
Of gulfs of sweetness without bound
In Indian wildernesses found;
Of Syrian peace, immortal leisure,
Firmest cheer, and bird-like pleasure.

Aught unsavory or unclean
Hath my insect never seen;
But violets and bilberry bells,
Maple-sap and daffodels,
Grass with green flag half-mast high,
Succory to match the sky,
Columbine with horn of honey,
Scented fern, and agrimony,
Clover, catchfly, adder's-tongue
And brier-roses, dwelt among;
All besides was unknown waste,
All was picture as he passed.

Wiser far than human seer,
Yellow-breeched philosopher!
Seeing only what is fair,
Sipping only what is sweet,
Thou dost mock at fate and care,
Leave the chaff, and take the wheat
When the fierce northwestern blast
Cools sea and land so far and fast,
Thou already slumberest deep;
Woe and want thou canst outsleep;
Want and woe, which torture us,
Thy sleep makes ridiculous.

INDIFFERENCE

By Louise Driscoll

Over my garden
    An airplane flew,
But nothing there
    Either cared or knew.

Cabbage butterflies
    Chased each other.
A young wren cried
    Seeking his mother.

Gay zinnias
    With heavy heads
Flaunted yellows
    And mauves and reds.

A humming-bird
  On the late larkspur
Never knew what
  Went over her.

Crickets chirped
  And a blinking toad
Watched for flies
  On the gravel road.

They don't care
  How smart men are—
To go through Heaven
  In a flying car!

To a yellow bee
  On a marigold
The adventure seems
  A trifle old.

THE DRAGON FLY

By Jessie B. Rittenhouse

The day was set to a beautiful theme
  By the blue of a dragon-fly
That poised with his airy wings agleam
  On a flower, as I passed by.

So frail and so lovely—a touch would destroy;
  He seemed but a fancy, a whim;
Yet this gossamer thing is a breath of God's joy,
  And Life is made perfect in him!

A CATERPILLAR'S APOLOGY FOR EATING A FAVORITE GLADIOLUS

By Charles Dalmon

Confuse me not with impious things;
But wait for the appointed hour
When you shall see your vanished flower
Reborn resplendent in my wings!

THE CAPTIVE BUTTERFLY

By Helen Granville-Barker

If I lie quite still in their net
  Good fortune may befall—
They may think it was only a moth they
      caught—
  No butterfly at all!

But if once they learn of the blue
  And purple of my wings,
And their flash, when the rays of the
      noonday sun
  Light all their golden rings;

If once they know me the love
  Of the rose that sheltered me,
And the playmate of all the garden
      flowers,—
  They will never set me free.

BÊTE HUMAINE

By Francis Brett Young

Riding through Ruwu swamp, about sunrise,
I saw the world awake; and as the ray
Touched the tall grasses where they dream till
    day,
Lo, the bright air alive with dragonflies,
With brittle wings aquiver, and great eyes
Piloting crimson bodies, slender and gay.
I aimed at one, and struck it, and it lay
Broken and lifeless, with fast-fading dyes. . . .
Then my soul sickened with a sudden pain
And horror, at my own careless cruelty,
That where all things are cruel I had slain
A creature whose sweet life it is to fly:
Like beasts that prey with bloody claw. . . .
      Nay, they
Must slay to live, but what excuse had I?

A CRICKET SINGING IN THE MARKET-PLACE

By Louella C. Poole

Down in the city's market-place,
  To-day, as I passed by,
Above the tumult and the din
  I heard a cricket cry.
Poor little straying vagabond,
  Wee singer of the street,
Trilling in that mad wilderness
  His song so blithely sweet!

I halted in that busy mart,
  Amongst the produce there,
For suddenly I seemed to see
  A vista wondrous fair—
Of God's great open country,
  Horizons dim and far,
And that same call at even-fall,
  When rose the first pale star.

I saw a brooklet edged with ferns,
  Where tiny minnows play,
Above the glittering golden sands,
  At hide-and-seek all day;
And rustling cornfields, meadows brown,
  A-spangled with the dew;
The hills with Indian summer haze
  Ethereal and blue.

I heard the tinkling cow-bells,
  And smelt the breath of kine,
The scent of ripening orchards,
  Grapes purpling on the vine.
O vision fair, revealing
  Such range of time and space!
Moved nigh to tears, in softened mood
  I left the market-place.

Ah, minstrel gay, wee troubadour
  With voice so shrilly sweet,
You little know what power you had
  To spur my lagging feet,
And bear my spirit far away
  From all that rush and roar,
To God's own blessed country
  And happy days of yore!

THE GRASSHOPPER

By W. R. Childe

Upon a viol of carven jade,
  With crystal stops and silver strings,
Unvexed, untiring, unafraid,
  He strums and sings, he strums and sings.
Ah, what a music he imparts,
  While every rich hill-meadow flames;
He is a wizard of wise arts,
  He is a minstrel of sweet names.
Through the hot noonday's breathless hours
  His delicate secret joy he tells,
Amid wind-murmuring azure flowers,
  Wild crimson buds and golden bells.
Beneath the cold marmoreal horns,
  Beside the river's gray-green foam,
He lifts his song to hail the morns,
  And leads the coloured evenings home.
The peaks shine towering in the sun,
  The waters leap, the sweet winds stir;
His faery praise he ne'er hath done,
  That emerald lad the grasshopper.

THE ANTS

By John Clare

What wonder strikes the curious, while he views
  The black ant's city, by a rotten tree,
Or woodland bank! In ignorance we muse:
  Pausing, annoyed,—we know not what we see,
Such government and thought there seem to be;

Some looking on, and urging some to toil,
Dragging their loads of bent-stalks slavishly:
And what's more wonderful, when big loads foil
One ant or two to carry, quickly then
A swarm flock round to help their fellow-men.
Surely they speak a language whisperingly,
Too fine for us to hear; and sure their ways
Prove they have kings and laws, and that they be
Deformed remnants of the Fairy-days.

THE GARDEN SPIDER

By Charles Mackay

I

Though fear'd by many, scorn'd by all,
Poor spider on my garden wall,
Accused as ugly, cruel, sly,
And seen with an averted eye;
Thou shalt not lack one friend to claim
Some merit for thy injured name,
If I have strength to right the wrong,
Or in men's memory lives my song.

II

Men call thee ugly;—did they look
With closer eyes on Nature's book,
They might behold in seeing thee
A creature robed in brilliancy;
They might admire thy speckled back
Begemm'd with purple, gold, and black;
Thy hundred eyes, with diamond rims;
Thy supple and resplendent limbs.

III

They call thee cruel; but forget,
Although thy skilful trap be set
To capture the unwary prey,
That thou must eat as well as they.
No pamper'd appetites hast thou;
What kindly Nature's laws allow
Thou takest for thy daily food,
And kindly Nature owns it good.

IV

Fie on us! we who hunt and kill,
Voracious, but unsated still;
Who ransack earth, and sea, and air,
And slay all creatures for our fare,
Complain of thee, whose instinct leads,
Unerring, to supply thy needs,
Because thou takest now and then
A fly, thy mutton, to thy den.

V

And then we call thee sly, forsooth,
As if from earliest dawn of youth
We did not lay our artful snares
For rabbits, woodcocks, larks, and hares,
Or lurk all day by running brooks
To capture fish with cruel hooks,
And with a patient, deep, deceit
Betray them with a counterfeit.

VI

So let the thoughtless sneer or laugh ;
I'll raise my voice in thy behalf.
The life thou livest, Nature meant—
It cannot be but innocent ;
She gave thee instinct to obey,
Her faultless hand design'd thy prey ;
And if thou killest, well we know
'Tis need, not sport, compels the blow.

VII

And while I plead thy simple case
Against the slanderers of thy race,
And think thy skilful web alone
Might for some venial faults atone,
I will not pass unnoticed by
Thy patience in calamity,
Thy courage to endure or wait,
Thy self-reliance strong as Fate.

VIII

Should stormy wind or thunder-shower
Assail thy web in evil hour ;
Should ruthless hand of lynx-eyed boy,
Or the prim gardener's rake, destroy
The clever mathematic maze
Thou spreadest in our garden ways,
No vain repinings mar thy rest,
No idle sorrows fill thy breast.

IX

Thou mayst perchance deplore thy lot,
Or sigh that fortune loves thee not;
But never dost thou sulk and mope,
Or lie and groan, forgetting hope;
Still with a patience, calm and true,
Thou workest all thy work anew,
As if thou felt that Heaven is just
To every creature of the dust,

X

And that the Providence whose plan
Gives life to spiders as to man,
Will ne'er accord its aid divine
To those who lazily repine;
But that all strength to those is given
Who help themselves, and trust in Heaven.
Poor insect! to that faith I cling—
I learn thy lesson while I sing.

IN STREAM and SEA

In a cool curving world he lies
And ripples with dark ecstasies.

The Fish.   RUPERT BROOKE.

IN STREAM AND SEA

"LUKANNON"

(Song of the Seal-Rookeries, Aleutian Islands)

By Rudyard Kipling

I met my mates in the morning (and oh, but I am old!)
Where roaring on the ledges the summer ground-swell
rolled.
I heard them lift the chorus that drowned the breakers'
song—
The Beaches of Lukannon—two million voices strong!

The song of pleasant stations beside the salt lagoons,
The song of blowing squadrons that shuffled down the
dunes,
The song of midnight dances that churned the sea to
flame—
The Beaches of Lukannon—before the sealers came!

I met my mates in the morning (I'll never meet them
more!);
They came and went in legions that darkened all the
shore.
And through the foam-flecked offing as far as voice
could reach
We hailed the landing-parties and we sang them up the
beach.

The Beaches of Lukannon—the winter-wheat so tall—
The dripping, crinkled lichens, and the sea-fog drench-
ing all!

The platforms of our playground, all shining smooth and worn!
The beaches of Lukannon—the home where we were born!

I meet my mates in the morning, a broken, scattered band.
Men shoot us in the water and club us on the land;
Men drive us to the Salt House like silly sheep and tame,
And still we sing Lukannon—before the sealers came.

Wheel down, wheel down to southward! Oh, Gooverooska go!
And tell the Deep-Sea Viceroys the story of our woe;
Ere, empty as the shark's egg the tempest flings ashore,
The Beaches of Lukannon shall know their sons no more!

MINNOWS

By John Keats

How silent comes the water round that bend;
Not the minutest whisper does it send
To the o'erhanging sallows; blades of grass
Slowly across the chequer'd shadows pass,—
Why, you might read two sonnets, ere they reach
To where the hurrying freshnesses aye preach
A natural sermon o'er their pebbly beds;
Where swarms of minnows show their little heads,
Staying their wavy bodies 'gainst the streams,
To taste the luxury of sunny beams
Tempered with coolness. How they ever wrestle
With their own sweet delight, and ever nestle

Their silver bellies on the pebbly sand.
If you but scantily hold out the hand,
That very instant not one will remain;
But turn your eye, and they are there again.
The ripples seem right glad to reach those cresses,
And cool themselves among the em'rald tresses;
The while they cool themselves, they freshness give,
And moisture, that the bowery green may live.

"THOU LITTLE GOD WITHIN THE BROOK"

By Philip Henry Savage

Thou little god within the brook
That dwellest, friend of man,
I oft have heard the simple prayer
Thou tellest unto Pan:

That he who comes with rod and line
And robs thy life to-day,
May yet by the great god be taught
To come some other way.

THE FISH

By Rupert Brooke

In a cool curving world he lies
And ripples with dark ecstasies.
The kind luxurious lapse and steal
Shapes all his universe to feel
And know and be; the clinging stream
Closes his memory, glooms his dream,

Who lips the roots o' the shore, and glides
Superb on unreturning tides.
Those silent waters weave for him
A fluctuant mutable world and dim,
Where wavering masses bulge and gape
Mysterious, and shape to shape
Dies momently through whorl and hollow,
And form and line and solid follow
Solid and line and form to dream
Fantastic down the eternal stream;
An obscure world, a shifting world,
Bulbous, or pulled to thin, or curled,
Or serpentine, or driving arrows,
Or serene sliding, or March narrows,
There slipping wave and shore are one,
And weed and mud. No ray of sun,
But glow to glow fades down the deep
(As dream to unknown dream in sleep) ;
Shaken translucency illumes
The hyaline of drifting glooms;
The strange soft-handed depth subdues
Drowned colour there, but black to hues,
As death to living, decomposes—
Red darkness of the heart of roses,
Blue brilliant from dead starless skies,
And gold that lies behind the eyes,
The unknown unnameable sightless white
That is the essential flame of night,
Lusterless purple, hooded green,
The myriad hues that lie between
Darkness and darkness! . . .

And all's one,
Gentle, embracing, quiet, dun,
The world he rests in, world he knows,
Perpetual curving. Only—grows
And eddy in that ordered falling
A knowledge from the gloom, a calling
Weed in the wave, gleam in the mud—
The dark fire leaps along his blood;
Dateless and deathless, blind and still,
The intricate impulse works its will;
His woven world drops back; and he,
Sans providence, sans memory,
Unconscious and directly driven
Fades to some dank sufficient heaven.

O world of lips, O world of laughter,
Where hope is fleet and thought flies after,
Of lights in the clear night, of cries
That drift along the wave and rise
Thin to the glittering stars above,
You know the hands, the eyes of love!
The strife of limbs, the sightless clinging,
The infinite distance, and the singing
Blown by the wind, a flame of sound,
The gleam, the flowers, and vast around
The horizon, and the heights above—
You know the sigh, the song of love!

But there the night is close, and there
Darkness is cold and strange and bare;
And the secret deeps are whisperless;
And rhythm is all deliciousness;

And joy is in the throbbing tide,
Whose intricate fingers treat and glide
In felt bewildering harmonies
Of trembling touch; and music is
The exquisite knocking of the blood.
Space is no more, under the mud;
His bliss is older than the sun.
Silent and straight the waters run.
The lights, the cries, the willows dim,
And the dark tide are one with him.

WESTERN TRAILS

The war-lord, yea, of a countless host,
　　But gone is your kingly sway;
For never again will you head the herd
　　In the spring when the young calves play.

To a Buffalo Skull.　　　　　　Robert V. Carr.

WESTERN TRAILS

THE BRONCHO THAT WOULD NOT BE BROKEN

By Vachel Lindsay

A little colt—broncho, loaned to the farm
To be broken in time without fury or harm,
Yet black crows flew past you, shouting alarm,
Calling " Beware," with lugubrious singing .   .   .
The butterflies there in the bush were romancing,
The smell of the grass caught your soul in a trance,
So why be a-fearing the spurs and the traces,
O broncho that would not be broken of dancing?

You were born with the pride of the lords great and
    olden
Who danced, through the ages, in corridors golden.
In all the wide farm-place the person most human.
You spoke out so plainly with squealing and capering,
With whinnying, snorting, contorting and prancing,
As you dodged your pursuers, looking askance,
With Greek-footed figures, and Parthenon paces,
O broncho that would not be broken of dancing.

The grasshoppers cheered. " Keep whirling," they said.
The insolent sparrows called from the shed
"If men will not laugh, make them wish they were
    dead."
But arch were your thoughts, all malice displacing,
Though the horse-killers came, with snake-whips advanc-
    ing.

You bantered and cantered away your last chance.
And they scourged you; with Hell in their speech and
their faces,
O broncho that would not be broken of dancing.

"Nobody cares for you," rattled the crows,
As you dragged the whole reaper next day down the
rows.
The three mules held back, yet you danced on your toes.
You pulled like a racer, and kept the mules chasing.
You tangled the harness with bright eyes side-glancing,
While the drunk driver bled you—a pole for a lance—
And the giant mules bit at you—keeping their places.
O broncho that would not be broken of dancing.

In that last afternoon your boyish heart broke.
The hot wind came down like a sledge-hammer stroke.
The blood-sucking flies to a rare feast awoke.
And they searched out your wounds, your death-
warrant tracing.
And the merciful men, their religion enhancing,
Stopped the red reaper to give you a chance.
Then you died on the prairie, and scorned all disgraces,
O broncho that would not be broken of dancing.

THE MEETING

By Arthur Chapman

When walkin' down a city street,
    Two thousand miles from home,
The pavestones hurtin' of the feet
    That never ought to roam,

A pony just reached to one side
   And grabbed me by the clothes;
He smelled the sagebrush, durn his hide!
   You bet a pony knows!

I stopped and petted him, and seen
   A brand upon his side;
I'll bet, across the prairie green,
   He useter hit his stride;
Some puncher of the gentle cow
   Had owned him—that I knows;
Which same is why he jest says: " How!
   There's sagebrush in your clothes."

He knowed the smell—no doubt it waked
   Him out of some bright dream;
In some far stream his thirst is slaked—
   He sees the mountains gleam;
He bears his rider far and fast,
   And real the hull thing grows
When I come sorter driftin' past
   With sagebrush in my clothes.

Poor little hoss! It's tough to be
   Away from that fair land—
Away from that wide prairie sea
   With all its vistas grand;
I feel for you, old hoss, I do—
   It's hard, the way life goes;
I'd like to travel back with you—
   Back where that sagebrush grows!

A COYOTE PROWLED

By Annie Elizabeth Cheney

A coyote came one night to the sea,
And howled at the waves and howled at me,
And the white-maned monster roared and mumbled
At the dog that prowled and starved and grumbled.
Thin and lank and ruffled and grey,
He stalked and stalked in search of prey,
And snarled and snapped and wailed at fate
That dealt him dust and the dregs of hate.
I gave him a bone and words and sighs,
And he showed me his teeth and he showed me his eyes;
And his teeth were clean and strong and white,
And his eyes were fine as a frosty night.

GRIZZLY

By Bret Harte

Coward,—of heroic size,
In whose lazy muscles lies
Strength we fear and yet despise;
Savage,—whose relentless tusks
Are content with acorn husks;
Robber,—whose exploits ne'er soared
O'er the bee's or squirrel's hoard;
Whiskered chin and feeble nose,
Claws of steel on baby toes,—
Here, in solitude and shade,
Shambling, shuffling plantigrade,
Be thy courses undismayed!

Here, where Nature makes thy bed,
Let thy rude, half-human tread
  Point to hidden Indian springs,
Lost in ferns and fragrant grasses,
  Hovered o'er by timid wings,
Where the wood-duck lightly passes,
Where the wild bee bolds her sweets,—
Epicurean retreats,
Fit for thee, and better than
Fearful spoils of dangerous man.
In thy fat-jowled deviltry
Friar Tuck shall live in thee;
Thou mayst levy tithe and dole;
  Thou shalt spread the woodland cheer,
From the pilgrim taking toll;
  Match thy cunning with his fear;
Eat, and drink, and have thy fill;
Yet remain an outlaw still!

THE LAST ANTELOPE

By Edwin Ford Piper

Behind the board fence at the banker's house
The slender, tawn-gray creature starves and thirsts
In agony of fear. A dog may growl,
It cowers; the cockcrow shakes it with alarm.

White frost lay heavy on the buffalo grass
That winter morning when three graceful shapes
Slipped by the saddle-back across the ridge
Along the rutted pathway to the creek.
In former years the track was bare, and worn
With feet of upland creatures every day.

A boy spied these three outlaws. Two hours' chase,
Fifty pursuers, and the ways all stopped,—
Guns, dogs, and fences. Torn by the barbed wire,
Drilled by a dozen buckshot, one; the next,
O'erheaped by snapping jaws, cried piteously
An instant; but the last on treacherous ice
Crashed through, a captive.

             Ropes—the jolting wagon—
Its heart was audible as you touched its fur.

Behind the board fence at the banker's house,—
Oh, once it capered wild on dewy grass
In grace and glee of dancing, arrowy bounds!—
At the banker's house, behind the high board fence
The last slim pronghorn perishes of fear.

TO A BUFFALO SKULL

By Robert V. Carr

On the sable wall your great skull gleams,
   A regal ornament;
A relic of weathered bone and horn,
   Once lord of a continent.

The war-lord, yea, of a countless host,
   But gone is your kingly sway;
For never again will you head the herd
   In the spring when the young calves play.

All bleached with the merciless sun and rain
   Of many and many a day,
You're all that is left to tell the tale
   How the black lines passed this way.

TO A RATTLESNAKE

By Robert V. Carr

You try your best to slip away
  Across the sun-baked alkali;
And failing, rattle warning fair,
  While I decree that you must die.
My gun roars out, I ride away,
  I've killed a rattlesnake, that's all;
No more o'er sun-baked alkali
  Will that dread shape in hatred crawl.

" In hatred crawl? " Speak I the truth?
  I take your life as if I knew
I had the right; yet I cannot
  Return that which I took from you.
A baby has been known to lay
  Its little hands on you in glee,
And you struck not. Perhaps my hate
  Is what stirs hate in you for me.

A BISON-KING

By Joaquin Miller

Once, morn by morn, when snowy mountains flam'd
With sudden shafts of light, that shot a flood
Into the vale like fiery arrows aim'd
At night from mighty battlements, there stood
Upon a cliff, high-limn'd against Mount Hood,
A matchless bull fresh forth from sable wold,
And standing so seem'd grander 'gainst the wood

Than wingèd bull, that stood with tips of gold
Beside the brazen gates of Nineveh of old.

A time he toss'd the dewy turf, and then
Stretch'd forth his wrinkled neck, and long and loud
He call'd above the far abodes of men
Until his breath became a curling cloud
And wreathed about his neck a misty shroud.

Permission to use this poem granted by Harr Wagner Publishing Company, San Francisco, California, publishers of Joaquin Miller's Complete Poems.

FROM the JUNGLE

I will remember what I was, I am sick of rope and
chain—
I will remember my old strength and all my forest-
affairs.

Toomai of the Elephants.   RUDYARD KIPLING.

FROM THE JUNGLE

THE TIGER

By William Blake

Tiger! Tiger! burning bright,
In the forests of the night,
What immortal hand or eye
Could frame thy fearful symmetry?

In what distant deeps or skies
Burnt the fire of thine eyes?
On what wings dare he aspire?
What the hand dare seize the fire?

And what shoulder, and what art,
Could twist the sinews of thy heart?
And when thy heart began to beat,
What dread hand and what dread feet?

What the hammer? what the chain?
In what furnace was thy brain?
What the anvil? what dread grasp
Dare its deadly terrors clasp?

When the stars threw down their spears,
And watered heaven with their tears,
Did He smile His work to see?
Did He who made the Lamb, make thee?

Tiger! Tiger! burning bright,
In the forests of the night,
What immortal hand or eye
Dare frame thy fearful symmetry?

THE PANTHER

By Edwin Markham

The moon shears up on Tahoe now:
A panther leaps to a tamarack bough.
She crouches, hugging the crookèd limb:
She hears the nearing steps of him
Who sent the little puff of smoke
That stretched her mate beneath the oak.

Her eyes burn beryl, two yellow balls,
As Fate counts out his last footfalls,
A sudden spring, a demon cry,
Carnivorous laughter to the sky.
Her teeth are fastened in his throat
(The moon rides in her silver boat)
And now one scream of long delight
Across the caverns of the night!

TOOMAI OF THE ELEPHANTS

By Rudyard Kipling

I will remember what I was, I am sick of rope and
    chain—
  I will remember my old strength and all my forest-
    affairs.
I will not sell my back to man for a bundle of sugar-
    cane.
  I will go out to my own kind, and the wood-folk in
    their lairs.

I will go out until the day, until the morning break,
  Out to the winds' untainted kiss, the waters' clean
    caress.
I will forget my ankle-ring and snap my picket-stake.
  I will revisit my lost loves, and playmates masterless!

BEAST AND MAN IN INDIA

By John Lockwood Kipling

They killed a child to please the Gods
In earth's young penitence,
And I have bled in that Babe's stead
Because of innocence.

I bear the sins of sinful men
That have no sin of my own,
They drive me forth to Heaven's wrath
Unpastured and alone.

I am the meat of sacrifice,
The ransom of man's guilt,
For they give my life to the altar-knife
Wherever shrine is built.
          The Goat.

Between the waving tufts of jungle-grass,
Up from the river as the twilight falls,
Across the dust-beclouded plain they pass
On to the village walls.

Great is the sword and mighty is the pen,
But over all the labouring ploughman's blade—
For on its oxen and its husbandmen
An Empire's strength is laid.

The Oxen.

The torn boughs trailing o'er the tusks aslant,
The saplings reeling in the path he trod,
Declare his might—our lord the Elephant,
Chief of the ways of God.

The black bulk heaving where the oxen pant,
The bowed head toiling where the guns careen,
Declare our might—our slave the Elephant
And servant of the Queen.

The Elephant.

Dark children of the mere and marsh,
Wallow and waste and lea,
Outcaste they wait at the village gate
With folk of low degree.

Their pasture is in no man's land,
Their food the cattle's scorn,
Their rest is mire and their desire
The thicket and the thorn.

But woe to those that break their sleep,
And woe to those that dare
To rouse the herd-bull from his keep,
The wild boar from his lair!

Pigs and Buffaloes.

The beasts are very wise,
Their mouths are clean of lies,
They talk one to the other,
Bullock to bullock's brother
Resting after their labours,
Each in stall with his neighbours.
But man with goad and whip,
Breaks up their fellowship,
Shouts in their silky ears
Filling their soul with fears.
When he has ploughed the land,
He says: "They understand."
But the beasts in stall together,
Freed from the yoke and tether,
Say as the torn flanks smoke:
"Nay, 'twas the whip that spoke."

THE MONKEY

By Nancy Campbell

I saw you hunched and shivering on the stones,
The bleak wind piercing to your fragile bones,
Your shabby scarlet all inadequate:
A little ape that had such human eyes
They seemed to hide behind their miseries—
Their dumb and hopeless bowing down to fate—
Some puzzled wonder. Was your monkey soul
Sickening with memories of gorgeous days,
Of tropic playfellows and forest ways,
Where, agile, you could swing from bole to bole
In an enchanted twilight with great flowers
For stars; or on a bough the long night hours

Sit out in rows, and chatter at the moon?
Shuffling you went, your tiny chilly hand
Outstretched for what you did not understand;
Your puckered mournful face begging a boon
That but enslaved you more. They who passed by
Saw nothing sorrowful; gave laugh or stare,
Unheeding that the little antic there
Played in the gutter such a tragedy.

IN
WAR SERVICE

And he shall judge among the nations, and shall rebuke many people: and they shall beat their swords into plowshares, and their spears into pruninghooks: nation shall not lift up sword against nation, neither shall they learn war any more.

ISAIAH 2:4.

IN WAR SERVICE

A MASCOT

By Arthur Guiterman

In the glow of their youth they have come, and they
    pass
With the flare of the steel and the blare of the brass;
And the brave little dog, with a brisk little wag
To his stump of a tail, trots along by the flag,
At his post in the ranks like the rest of the corps,
For the brave little dog is away to the war.

"They will go! They will go!" throbs a drum as it
    nears;
There's the fall of a wail in the roar of our cheers.
But the brave little dog is as gay as a lark;
There is joy, there is heart in his brave little bark
As he gambols behind or he frolics before,
For the brave little dog is away to the war.

He's away to the war. There'll be need of him there—
Of the stanch little tyke that's the foe of despair;
For there's none that's so old in the world, or so wise,
But may find a new faith in the depth of his eyes,
And his tongue is a balm to the heart that is sore;
So the brave little dog is away to the war.

May the powers be good to the glad little elf,
Who is first for his friends and is last for himself;
May there still be a bone for his hunger to find,
And a pat on the head from a hand that is kind;
May the heaven of men keep a wide-open door
For the brave little dog that's away to the war.

THE FUSILIERS' DOG

(Run over, after having gone through the Crimean Campaign)

By Francis Doyle

Go lift him gently from the wheels,
   And soothe his dying pain,
For love and care e'en yet he feels
   Though love and care be vain;
'Tis sad that, after all these years,
   Our comrade and our friend,
The brave dog of the Fusiliers,
   Should meet with such an end.

Up Alma's hill, among the vines,
   We laughed to see him trot,
Then frisk along the silent lines,
   To chase the rolling shot:
And, when the work waxed hard by day,
   And hard and cold by night;
When that November morning lay
   Upon us, like a blight,

And eyes were strained, and ears were bent,
   Against the muttering north,
Till the grey mist took shape, and sent
   Grey scores of Russians forth—
Beneath that slaughter wild and grim,
   Nor man nor dog would run;
He stood by us, and we by him,
   Till the great fight was done.

And right throughout the snow and frost
  He faced both shot and shell;
Though unrelieved, he kept his post,
  And did his duty well.
By death on death the time was stained,
  By want, disease, despair;
Like autumn leaves our army waned,
  But still the dog was there:

He cheered us through those hours of gloom;
  We fed him in our dearth;
Through him the trench's living tomb
  Rang loud with reckless mirth;
And thus, when peace returned once more,
  After the city's fall,
That veteran home in pride we bore,
  And loved him, one and all.

With ranks refilled, our hearts were sick,
  And to old memories clung;
The grim ravines we left glared thick
  With death-stones of the young.
Hands which had patted him lay chill,
  Voices which called were dumb,
And footsteps that he watched for still
  Never again could come.

Never again; this world of woe
  Still hurries on so fast;
They come not back, 'tis he must go
  To join them in the past:

There, with brave names and deeds entwined,
    Which Time may not forget,
Young Fusiliers unborn shall find
    The legend of our pet.

Whilst o'er fresh years, and other life
    Yet in God's mystic urn,
The picture of the mighty strife
    Arises sad and stern—
Blood all in front, behind far shrines
    With women weeping low,
For whom each lost one's fane but shines,
    As shines the moon on snow—

Marked by the medal, his of right,
    And by his kind keen face,
Under that visionary light
    Poor Bob shall keep his place;
And never may our honoured Queen
    For love and service pay,
Less brave, less patient, or more mean
    Than his we mourn to-day!

THE TURKISH TRENCH DOG

By Geoffrey Dearmer

Night held me as I crawled and scrambled near
The Turkish lines. Above, the mocking stars
Silvered the curving parapet, and clear
Cloud-latticed beams o'erflecked the land with bars
I, crouching, lay between
Tense-listening armies peering through the night,
Twin giants bound by tentacles unseen.

Here in dim-shadowed light
I saw him, as a sudden movement turned
His eyes towards me, glowing eyes that burned
A moment ere his snuffling muzzle found
My trail; and then as serpents mesmerize
He chained me with those unrelenting eyes,
That muscle-sliding rhythm, knit and bound
In spare-limbed symmetry, those perfect jaws
And soft-approaching pitter-patter paws.
Nearer and nearer like a wolf he crept—
That moment had my swift revolver leapt—
But terror seized me, terror born of shame
Brought flooding revelation. For he came
As one who offers comradeship deserved,
An open ally of the human race,
And sniffling at my prostrate form unnerved
He licked my face!

THE DOGS OF WAR

By Nora Archibald Smith

Time was, and not so long ago, as men count time,
When dogs were symbols of uncleanliness,
Wretched, abhorred, ranked with the scum of earth.
No taunt, no insult deeper could be thought,
When taunts were needed, than the old, old phrase:
" Dog that thou art! Thou shameless and impenitent!"

Dogs such as these have had their evil day;
No more they crawl and fawn, abased and suffering;
No more they slink in gutters, feed from offal heaps.

Theirs is the post of pow'r, the warlike field,
And man, who once abused them, trusts to-day
In doggish fortitude, in doggish constancy.

Oh, wondrous change! Beasts that were scorned of all
Sit by their masters now, as loaded wains
Creep o'er the country with their freight of war.
The soldier drives, one arm about his friend,
And half his comfort in the endless days
Is the warm heart beside him, doglike answering.

Pariahs once, now mascots dearly prized;
Fugitives once, now messengers of war;
No creature's place so changed in common estimate.
Like beasts bewitched, in fairy tales of old,
Some magic touch laid on their shaggy heads
Has turned them all to kings, to four-foot potentates.

THE WAR-HORSE BUYERS

By Arthur Chapman

Twenty of us ridin' bronks, headed for the war;
Twenty top-hand saddlemen, up in bustin' lore;
Off the ranges fast they come, hosses black and gray,
Hosses roan and calico, hosses brown and bay;
Saddle, bridle, cinch and ride—buck, you big hoss, buck!
You will be the captain's choice—'bye, old nag—good
    luck!

'Tillery and cavalry, 'tillery and cavalry,
That's the way they pick 'em when the judges are at
    work;

'Tillery and cavalry, 'tillery and cavalry,
Farewell, Western mountain hoss, and don't you ever
shirk;
Steel and lead and powder smoke, there acrost the
way—
If it wasn't I'm a neutral I'd be off with you to-day.

All the range is bein' combed of the strong and fit;
Bring more in, you wrangler men—let 'em taste the bit;
Let the busters show each pace, 'neath the captain's
eyes;
Good-bye, all of you to-day, to these Western skies;
Twice around the ring you go—saddle off and stand
While the captain tallies you for the fightin' band.

'Tillery and cavalry, 'tillery and cavalry,
That's the way they pick and choose for the game of
war;
'Tillery and cavalry, 'tillery and cavalry,
Little difference where you go—fightin' is in store;
Little difference where you show—most of you must die;
Western hosses, do your best—good luck, and good-bye!

THE ARMY HORSE

By McLandburgh Wilson

Once they ploughed the fruitful field,
Helped the reaper gain his yield,
Came to eve with sweet content,
Browsing when the day was spent.
Now they lie with mangled hide,
Fallen in the carnage tide.

What to them the sounding phrase
Which explains the bloody ways?
Honour, place or racial stem,
Slav or Teuton, what to them?
Torn and dead or death denied,
Fallen in the carnage tide.

Now they wage the battle hot,
Plunging under shell and shot,
Charging in the cannon's breath
Bearing dealers of the death,
Till in agony they bide,
Fallen in the carnage tide.

Theirs was not the chance to say
Words of peace to save the day.
They who could not hush the drum,
Whose Creator made them dumb,
Yet are one with those who ride,
Fallen in the carnage tide.

THE HORSES

By Katharine Lee Bates

" Thus far 80,000 horses have been shipped from the
United States to the European belligerents."

What was our share in the sinning,
    That we must share the doom?
Sweet was our life's beginning
    In the spicy meadow-bloom,
With children's hands to pet us
    And kindly tones to call.
To-day the red spurs fret us
    Against the bayonet wall.

What had we done, our masters,
  That you sold us into hell?
Our terrors and disasters
  Have filled your pockets well.
You feast on our starvation;
  Your laughter is our groan.
Have horses then no nation,
  No country of their own?

What are we, we your horses,
  So loyal where we serve,
Fashioned of noble forces
  All sensitive with nerve?
Torn, agonized, we wallow
  On the blood-bemired sod;
And still the shiploads follow.
  Have horses then no God?

"GOOD-BYE, OLD FRIEND!"

Anonymous

*(An actual incident on the road to a battery position in
Southern Flanders)*

Only a dying horse! Pull off the gear
  And slip the needless bit from frothing jaws.
Drag it aside there—leave the roadway clear—
  The battery thunders on with scarce a pause.

Prone by the shell swept highway there it lies
  With quivering limbs, as fast the life tide fails.
Dark films are closing o'er the faithful eyes
  That mutely plead for aid where none avails.

Onward the battery rolls—but one there speeds,
  Heedless of comrade's voice or bursting shell—
Back to a wounded friend who lonely bleeds
  Beside the stony highway where it fell.

Only a dying horse! He swiftly kneels,
  Lifts the limp head and hears the shivering sigh,
Kisses the horse while down his cheek there steals
  Sweet Pity's tear—" Good-bye, old man, good-
    bye! "

No honors wait him, medal, badge or star,
  Though scarce could war a kindlier deed unfold;
He bears within his breast, more precious far
  Beyond the gift of kings, a heart of gold.

THE HORSE

By Ella Wheeler Wilcox

(Dedicated to the American Red Star Animal Relief)

The man who goes into the fight,
With the heart of a volunteer,
Has the high ideal of doing right,
To conquer his pain and fear,
And the man who is forced to go
Has his pride, and his will, and his faith,
To help him over the road of woe
To the goal of a crutch, or death.

But the steed that is dragged from his stall
To be plunged in the hell of war—
Why what does he know of the country's call,
Or the cause he is suffering for?

But I think when he lies in his pain,
Tortured and torn by the fray,
He must long for the touch of a hand on his mane
And the fields where he used to play.

The world as we see it now
Is only half man-made;
As the horse recedes with a parting bow
We know the part he has played.
For the wonderful brain of man,
However mighty its force,
Had never achieved its lordly plan
Without the aid of the horse.

The forests felled by hand
By the horse were carried away:
And furrow and field were made to yield
By his willing toil each day.
He helped bring true in this age,
The visions our forebears saw;
And oft was given a grudging wage,
Scant fare and a bundle of straw.

The horse has no passion to kill
Like man and the tiger and bear;
Yet slave of a murderous will
To the front of the fight he must fare
Now the heart of a horse has love
For the master and home it knew:
And the mind of a horse can prove
That memory dwells there, too.

Oh, I think on the blood red sod
Each wounded man prays to God:

And I think from the heart of a steed
There must rise in his hour of need
A cry for his master who seems
A god in his equine dreams.

GUN-TEAMS

By Gilbert Frankau, R. S. A.

Their rugs are sodden, their heads are down, their tails
    are turned to the storm.
  (Would you know them, you that groomed them in
    the sleek fat days of peace,—
When the tiles rang to their pawings in the lighted stalls
    and warm,—
  Now the foul clay cakes on breeching-strap and clogs
    the quick-release?)

The blown rain stings, there is never a star, the tracks
    are rivers of slime.
  (You must harness up by guesswork with a failing
    torch for light,
Instep-deep in unmade standings, for it's active-service
    time,
  And our resting weeks are over, and we move the guns
    to-night.)

The iron tires slither, the traces sag; their blind hooves
    stumble and slide;
  They are war-worn, they are weary, soaked with
    sweat and sopped with rain.

(You must hold them, you must help them, swing your
   lead and centre wide
   Where the greasy granite pavé peters out to squelch-
      ing drain.)

There is shrapnel bursting a mile in front on the road
      that the guns must take;
   (You are nervous, you are thoughtful, you are shift-
      ing in your seat,
As you watch the ragged feathers flicker orange flame
      and break)—
   But the teams are pulling steady down the battered
      village street.

You have shod them cold, and their coats are long, and
      their bellies gray with the mud;
   They have done with gloss and polish, but the fight-
      ing heart's unbroke.
We, who saw them hobbling after us down white roads
      flecked with blood,
   Patient, wondering why we left them, till we lost them
      in the smoke;

Who have felt them shiver between our knees, when the
      shells rain black from the skies,
   When the bursting terrors find us and the lines
      stampede as one;
Who have watched the pierced limbs quiver and the pain
      in the stricken eyes,
   Know the worth of humble servants, foolish-faithful
      to their gun!

" BAY BILLY "

By F. H. Gassaway

'Twas the last fight at Fredericksburg—
    Perhaps the day you reck—
Our boys, the Twenty-second Maine,
    Kept Early's men in check.
Just where Wade Hampton boomed away
    The fight went neck and neck.

All day we held the weaker wing,
    And held it with a will;
Five several stubborn times we charged
    The battery on the hill,
And five times beaten back, re-formed,
    And kept our columns still.

At last from out the center fight
    Spurred up a general's aid.
" That battery *must* silenced be ! "
    He cried, as past he sped.
Our colonel simply touched his cap,
    And then, with measured tread,
To lead the crouching line once more
    The grand old fellow came.
No wounded man but raised his head
    And strove to gasp his name,
And those who could not speak nor stir
    " God blessed him " just the same.

For he was all the world to us,
    That hero gray and grim;

Right well he knew that fearful slope
  We'd climb with none but him,
Though while his white head led the way
  We'd charge Hell's portals in.

This time we were not half-way up,
  When, 'midst the storm of shell,
Our leader, with his sword upraised,
  Beneath our bay'nets fell;
And, as we bore him back, the foe
  Set up a joyous yell.

Our hearts went with him. Back we swept
  And when the bugle said,
" Up, charge, again! " no man was there
  But hung his dogged head.
" We've no one left to lead us now,"
  The sullen soldiers said.

Just then, before the laggard line,
  The colonel's horse we spied—
Bay Billy, with his trappings on,
  His nostril swelling wide,
As though still on his gallant back
  The master sat astride.

Right royally he took the place
  That was of old his wont,
And with a neigh, that seemed to say,
  Above the battle's brunt,
" How can the Twenty-second charge
  If I am not in front? "

Like statues we stood rooted there,
    And gazed a little space;
Above that floating mane we missed
    The dear familiar face;
But we saw Bay Billy's eye of fire,
    And it gave us heart of grace.

No bugle-call could rouse us all
    As that brave sight had done;
Down all the battered line we felt
    A lightning impulse run;
Up, up the hill we followed Bill,
    And captured every gun!

And when upon the conquered height
    Died out the battle's hum,
Vainly 'mid living and the dead
    We sought our leader dumb;
It seemed as if a specter steed
    To win that day had come.

At last the morning broke.   The lark
    Sang in the merry skies,
As if to e'en the sleepers there
    It bade awake! arise!—
Though naught but that last trump of al
    Could ope their heavy eyes.

And then once more, with banners gay,
    Stretched out the long brigade;
Trimly upon the furrowed field
    The troops stood on parade,
And bravely 'mid the ranks were closed
    The gaps the fight had made.

Not half the Twenty-second's men
  Were in their place that morn,
And Corp'ral Dick, who yester-morn
  Stood six brave fellows on,
Now touched my elbow in the ranks,
  For all between were gone.

Ah! who forgets that dreary hour
  When, as with misty eyes,
To call the old familiar roll
  The solemn sergeant tries—
One feels that thumping of the heart
  As no prompt voice replies.

And as in falt'ring tone and slow
  The last few names were said,
Across the field some missing horse
  Toiled up with weary tread.
It caught the sergeant's eye, and quick
  Bay Billy's name was read.

Yes! there the old bay hero stood,
  All safe from battle's harms,
And ere an order could be heard,
  Or the bugle's quick alarms,
Down all the front, from end to end,
  The troops presented arms!

Not all the shoulder-straps on earth
  Could still our mighty cheer.
And ever from that famous day,
  When rang the roll-call clear,
Bay Billy's name was read, and then
  The whole line answered, " Here! "

SHERIDAN'S RIDE

By Thomas Buchanan Read

Up from the South, at break of day,
Bringing to Winchester fresh dismay,
The affrighted air with a shudder bore,
Like a herald in haste, to the chieftain's door,
The terrible grumble, and rumble, and roar,
Telling the battle was on once more,
  And Sheridan twenty miles away.

And wider still those billows of war
Thundered along the horizon's bar;
And louder yet into Winchester rolled
The roar of that red sea uncontrolled,
Making the blood of the listener cold,
As he thought of the stake in that fiery fray,
  And Sheridan twenty miles away.

But there is a road from Winchester town,
A good, broad highway leading down:
And there, through the flush of the morning light,
A steed as black as the steeds of night
Was seen to pass, as with eagle flight;
As if he knew the terrible need,
He stretched away with his utmost speed;
Hills rose and fell, but his heart was gay,
  With Sheridan fifteen miles away.

Still sprang from those swift hoofs, thundering
  south,
The dust, like smoke from the cannon's mouth,

Or the trail of a comet, sweeping faster and faster,
Foreboding to traitors the doom of disaster.
The heart of the steed and the heart of the master
Were beating like prisoners assaulting their walls,
Impatient to be where the battle-field calls;
Every nerve of the charger was strained to full play,
    With Sheridan only ten miles away.

Under the spurning feet, the road
Like an arrowy Alpine river flowed,
And the landscape sped away behind
Like an ocean flying before the wind;
And the steed, like a bark fed with furnace ire,
Swept on, with his wild eye full of fire;
But, lo! he is nearing his heart's desire;
He is snuffing the smoke of the roaring fray,
    With Sheridan only five miles away.

The first that the general saw were the groups
Of stragglers, and then the retreating troops;
What was done? what to do? a glance told him
    both,
Then, striking his spurs, with a terrible oath,
He dashed down the line, 'mid a storm of huzzas,
And the wave of retreat checked its course there,
    because
The sight of the master compelled it to pause.
With foam and with dust the black charger was
    gray;
By the flash of his eye, and the red nostril's play,
He seemed to the whole great army to say:
" I have brought you Sheridan all the way
    From Winchester town to save the day! "

Hurrah! hurrah for Sheridan!
Hurrah! hurrah for horse and man!
And when their statues are placed on high,
Under the dome of the Union sky,
The American soldier's Temple of Fame,
There, with the glorious general's name,
Be it said, in letters both bold and bright:
" Here is the steed that saved the day
By carrying Sheridan into the fight,
    From Winchester—twenty miles away! "

MILES KEOGH'S HORSE

By John Hay

On the bluff of the Little Big-Horn,
  At the close of a woful day,
Custer and his Three Hundred
  In death and silence lay.

Three hundred to three thousand!
  They had bravely fought and bled;
For such is the will of Congress
  When the White man meets the Red.

The White men are ten millions,
  The thriftiest under the sun;
The Reds are fifty thousand,
  And warriors every one.

So Custer and all his fighting men
  Lay under the evening skies,
Staring up at the tranquil heaven
  With wide, accusing eyes.

And of all that stood at noonday
 In that fiery scorpion ring,
Miles Keogh's horse at evening
 Was the only living thing.

Alone from that field of slaughter,
 Where lay the three hundred slain,
The horse Comanche wandered,
 With Keogh's blood on his mane.

And Sturgis issued this order,
 Which future times shall read,
While the love and honor of comrades
 Are the soul of the comrade's creed.

He said:
        Let the horse Comanche,
 Henceforth till he shall die,
Be kindly cherished and cared for
 By the Seventh Cavalry.

He shall do no labor; he never shall know
 The touch of spur or rein;
Nor shall his back be ever crossed
 By living rider again.
And at regimental formation
 Of the Seventh Cavalry,
Comanche, draped in mourning, and
 By a trooper of Company I,
Shall parade with the regiment!

                Thus it was
 Commanded, and thus done,
By the order of General Sturgis, signed
 By Adjutant Garlington.

Even as the sword of Custer,
  In his disastrous fall,
Flashed out a blaze that charmed the world
  And glorified his pall,

This order, issued amid the gloom
  That shrouds our army's name,
When all foul beasts are free to rend
  And tear its honest fame,

Shall prove to a callous people
  That the sense of a soldier's worth,
That the love of comrades, the honor of arms,
  Have not perished from earth.

ONLY MULES

By Katharine Lee Bates

" The submarine was quite within its rights in sinking the cargo of the *Armenian,*—1,422 mules valued at $191,400."

No matter; we are only mules
  And slow to understand
We drown according to the rules
  Of war, we contraband.

War reckons us as shot and shell,
  As so much metal lost,
And mourns the dollars gone to swell
  The monstrous bill of cost.

Would that we had been wrought of steel
  And not of quivering flesh!
Of iron, not of nerves that feel
  And maddened limbs that thresh

The sucking seas in stubborn strife
  For that dim right of ours
To what no factory fashions, life,
  No Edison endowers.

Our last wild screams are choked; you know
  It does not matter, for
We're only mules that suffered so,
  And contraband of war.

THE LARK

By Robert W. Service

From wrath-red dawn to wrath-red dawn,
The guns have brayed without abate;
And now the sick sun looks upon
The bleared, blood-boltered fields of hate
As if it loathed to rise again.
How strange the hush! Yet sudden, hark!
From yon down-trodden gold of grain,
The leaping rapture of a lark.

A fusillade of melody,
That sprays us from yon trench of sky;
A new amazing enemy
We cannot silence though we try;
A battery on radiant wings,
That from yon gap of golden fleece
Hurls at us hopes of such strange things
As joy and home and love and peace.

Pure heart of song! do you not know
That we are making earth a hell?
Or is it that you try to show
Life still is joy and all is well?
Brave little wings! Ah, not in vain
You beat into that bit of blue:
Lo! we who pant in war's red rain
Lift shining eyes, see Heaven too.

THE NIGHTINGALES OF FLANDERS

By Grace Hazard Conkling

"Le rossignol n'est pas mobilisé."

A FRENCH SOLDIER.

The nightingales of Flanders,
  They have not gone to war.
A soldier heard them singing
  Where they had sung before.

The earth was torn and quaking,
  The sky about to fall.
The nightingales of Flanders,
  They minded not at all.

At intervals he heard them
  Between the guns, he said,
Making a thrilling music
  Above the listening dead.

Of woodland and of orchard
  And roadside tree bereft,
The nightingales of Flanders
  Were singing, *France is left!*

IN LEGEND

I cannot tell how the truth may be;
I say the tale as 'twas said to me.

Lay of the Last Minstrel. Sir Walter Scott.

IN LEGEND

THE HOMAGE OF BEASTS
A Persian Fable
By Augusta Larned

King Solomon, as I have heard,
The language knew of every bird.
He reigned alike o'er man and beast,
And bade them to his marriage feast.

Slow filing past his ivory throne
The animals came, one by one,
And humbly made obeisance there
For all their sovereign's gentle care.

The elephant, with mighty tread,
This strange procession fitly led;
And close behind the lion stalked,
And all with due decorum walked.

Such gifts they brought to please the bride,
As nature's richest stores supplied,
And Solomon rejoiced to prove
His subjects' loyalty and love.

Now far behind the stately train
An ant came toiling o'er the plain,
And in his mouth he dragged along
A single grass-blade through the throng.

Nor him did Solomon contemn,
Nor this poor offering condemn;
The ant he welcomed to the feast,
E'en though the very last and least.

By honoring both great and small,
By scorning none and loving all,
Was Solomon the wisest king
In those old days whereof I sing.

"HOW THEY BROUGHT THE GOOD NEWS FROM GHENT TO AIX"

By Robert Browning

I sprang to the stirrup, and Joris, and he;
I galloped, Dirck galloped, we galloped all three;
"Good speed!" cried the watch, as the gate-bolts un-
    drew;
"Speed!" echoed the wall to us galloping through;
Behind shut the postern, the lights sank to rest,
And into the midnight we galloped abreast.

Not a word to each other; we kept the great pace
Neck by neck, stride by stride, never changing our
    place;
I turned in my saddle and made its girths tight,
Then shortened each stirrup, and set the pique right,
Rebuckled the cheek-strap, chained slacker the bit,
Nor galloped less steadily Roland a whit.

'Twas the moonset at starting; but while we drew near
Lokeren, the cocks crew and twilight dawned clear;
At Boom, a great yellow star came out to see;
At Düffield, 'twas morning as plain as could be;
And from Mecheln church-steeple we heard the half-
    chime
So Joris broke silence with, " Yet there is time! "

At Aershot, up leaped of a sudden the sun,
And against him the cattle stood black every one,
To stare through the mist at us galloping past,
And I saw my stout galloper Roland at last,
With resolute shoulders, each butting away
The haze, as some bluff river headland its spray:

And his low head and crest, just one sharp ear bent
    back
For my voice, and the other pricked out on his track;
And one eye's black intelligence,—ever that glance
O'er its white edge at me, his own master, askance!
And the thick heavy spume-flakes which aye and anon
His fierce lips shook upwards in galloping on.

By Hasselt, Dirck groaned; and cried Joris " Stay
    spur!
Your Roos galloped bravely, the fault's not in her,
We'll remember at Aix "—for one heard the quick
    wheeze
Of her chest, saw the stretched neck and staggering
    knees,
And sunk tail, and horrible heave of the flank,
As down on her haunches she shuddered and sank.

So, we were left galloping, Joris and I,
Past Looz and past Tongres, no cloud in the sky;
The broad sun above laughed a pitiless laugh,
'Neath our feet broke the brittle bright stubble like
    chaff;
Till over by Dalhem a dome-spire sprang white,
And " Gallop," gasped Joris, " for Aix is in sight!

" How they'll greet us! "—and all in a moment his roan
Rolled neck and croup over, lay dead as a stone;
And there was my Roland to bear the whole weight
Of the news which alone could save Aix from her fate,
With his nostrils like pits full of blood to the brim,
And with circles of red for his eye-sockets' rim.

Then I cast loose my buffcoat, each holster let fall,
Shook off both my jack-boots, let go belt and all,
Stood up in the stirrup, leaned, patted his ear,
Called my Roland his pet-name, my horse without peer;
Clapped my hands, laughed and sang, any noise, bad or
    good,
Till at length into Aix Roland galloped and stood.

And all I remember is,—friends flocking round
As I sat with his head 'twixt my knees on the ground;
And no voice but was praising this Roland of mine,
As I poured down his throat our last measure of wine,
Which (the burgesses voted by common consent)
Was no more than his due who brought good news from
    Ghent.

THE BELL OF ATRI

By Henry Wadsworth Longfellow

At Atri in Abruzzo, a small town
Of ancient Roman date, but scant renown,
One of those little places that have run
Half up the hill, beneath a blazing sun,
And then sat down to rest, as if to say,
" I climb no farther upward, come what may,"—
The Re Giovanni, now unknown to fame,
So many monarchs since have borne the name,
Had a great bell hung in the market-place,
Beneath a roof, projecting some small space,
By way of shelter from the sun and rain.
Then rode he through the streets with all his train,
And, with the blasts of trumpets loud and long,
Made proclamation, that whenever wrong
Was done to any man, he should but ring
The great bell in the square, and he, the King,
Would cause the Syndic to decide thereon.
Such was the proclamation of King John.

How swift the happy days in Atri sped,
What wrongs were righted, need not here be said.
Suffice it that, as all things must decay,
The hempen rope at length was worn away,
Unravelled at the end, and, strand by strand,
Loosened and wasted in the ringer's hand,
Till one, who noted this in passing by,
Mended the rope with braids of briony,
So that the leaves and tendrils of the vine
Hung like a votive garland at a shrine.

By chance it happened that in Atri dwelt
A knight, with spur on heel and sword in belt,
Who loved to hunt the wild-boar in the woods,
Who loved his falcons with their crimson hoods,
Who loved his hounds and horses, and all sports
And prodigalities of camps and courts;—
Loved, or had loved them; for at last, grown old,
His only passion was the love of gold.

He sold his horses, sold his hawks and hounds,
Rented his vineyards and his garden-grounds,
Kept but one steed, his favorite steed of all,
To starve and shiver in a naked stall,
And day by day sat brooding in his chair
Devising plans how best to hoard and spare.

At length he said: " What is the use or need
To keep at my own cost this lazy steed,
Eating his head off in my stables here,
When rents are low and provender is dear?
Let him go feed upon the public ways;
I want him only for the holidays."
So the old steed was turned into the heat
Of the long, lonely, silent, shadeless street;
And wandered in suburban lanes forlorn,
Barked at by dogs, and torn by brier and thorn.

One afternoon, as in that sultry clime
It is the custom in the summer time,
With bolted doors and window-shutters closed,
The inhabitants of Atri slept or dozed;
When suddenly upon their senses fell
The loud alarum of the accusing bell!

The Syndic started from his deep repose,
Turned on his couch, and listened, and then rose
And donned his robes, and with reluctant pace
Went panting forth into the market-place,
Where the great bell upon its cross-beams swung,
Reiterating with persistent tongue,
In half-articulate jargon, the old song:
" Some one hath done a wrong, hath done a
  wrong! "

But ere he reached the belfry's light arcade
He saw, or thought he saw, beneath its shade,
No shape of human form of woman born,
But a poor steed, dejected and forlorn,
Who with uplifted head and eager eye
Was tugging at the vines of briony.
" Domeneddio! " cried the Syndic straight,
" This is the Knight of Atri's steed of state!
He calls for justice, being sore distressed,
And pleads his cause as loudly as the best."

Meanwhile from street and lane a noisy crowd
Had rolled together like a summer cloud,
And told the story of the wretched beast
In five-and-twenty different ways at least,
With much gesticulation and appeal
To heathen gods, in their excessive zeal.
The Knight was called and questioned; in reply
Did not confess the fact, did not deny;
Treated the matter as a pleasant jest,
And set at naught the Syndic and the rest
Maintaining, in an angry undertone,
That he should do what pleased him with his own.

And thereupon the Syndic gravely read
The proclamation of the King; then said:
" Pride goeth forth on horseback grand and gay,
But cometh back on foot, and begs its way;
Fame is the fragrance of heroic deeds,
Of flowers of chivalry and not of weeds!
These are familiar proverbs; but I fear
They never yet have reached your knightly ear.
What fair renown, what honor, what repute
Can come to you from starving this poor brute?
He who serves well and speaks not, merits more
Than they who clamor loudest at the door.
Therefore the law decrees that as this steed
Served you in youth, henceforth you shall take heed
To comfort his old age, and to provide
Shelter in stall, and food and field beside."

The Knight withdrew abashed; the people all
Led home the steed in triumph to his stall.
The King heard and approved, and laughed in glee,
And cried aloud: " Right well it pleaseth me!
Church-bells at best but ring us to the door;
But go not in to mass; my bell doth more:
It cometh into court and pleads the cause
Of creatures dumb and unknown to the laws;
And this shall make, in every Christian clime,
The Bell of Atri famous for all time."

SIR BAT-EARS

By Helen Parry Eden

Sir Bat-Ears was a dog of birth
   And bred in Aberdeen,
But he favoured not his noble kin
   And so his lot is mean,
And Sir Bat-Ears sits by the alms-houses
   On the stones with grass between.

Under the ancient archway
   His pleasure is to wait
Between the two stone pine-apples
   That flank the weathered gate;

And old, old alms-persons go by,
   All rusty, bent and black,
" Good day, good day, Sir Bat-Ears! "
   They say and stroke his back.

And old, old alms-persons go by,
   Shaking and well-nigh dead,
" Good night, good night, Sir Bat-Ears!"
   They say and pat his head.

So courted and considered
   He sits out hour by hour,
Benignant in the sunshine
   And prudent in the shower.

(Nay, stoutly can he stand a storm
  And stiffly breast the rain,
That rising when the cloud is gone
He leaves a circle of dry stone
  Whereon to sit again.)

A dozen little door-steps
  Under the arch are seen,
A dozen agèd alms-persons
  To keep them bright and clean;

Two wrinkled hands to scour each step
  With a square of yellow stone—
But print-marks of Sir Bat-Ears' paws
  Bespeckle every one.

And little eats an alms-person,
  But, though his board be bare,
There never lacks a bone of the best
  To be Sir Bat-Ears' share.

Mendicant muzzle and shrewd nose,
  He quests from door to door;
Their grace they say, his shadow grey
  Is instant on the floor—
Humblest of all the dogs there be,
  A pensioner of the poor.

FIDELITY

By William Wordsworth

A barking sound the shepherd hears,
   A cry as of a dog or fox;
He halts, and searches with his eyes
   Among the scattered rocks;
And now at distance can discern
A stirring in a brake of fern;
And instantly a dog is seen
Glancing from that covert green.

The dog is not of mountain breed;
   Its motions, too, are wild and shy;
With something, as the shepherd thinks,
   Unusual in its cry:
Nor is there any one in sight
All round, in hollow or on height;
Nor shout, nor whistle strikes his ear;
What is the creature doing here?

It was a cove, a huge recess,
   That keeps, till June, December's snow;
A lofty precipice in front,
   A silent tarn below!
Far in the bosom of Helvellyn,
Remote from public road or dwelling,
Pathway or cultivated land,
From trace of human foot or hand.

There sometimes doth a leaping fish
   Send through the tarn a lonely cheer;
The crags repeat the raven's croak
   In symphony austere;

Thither the rainbow comes—the cloud—
And mists that spread the flying shroud;
And sunbeams, and the sounding blast,
That, if it could, would hurry past,
But that enormous barrier binds it fast.

Not free from boding thoughts, a while
    The shepherd stood; then makes his way
Towards the dog, o'er rocks and stones,
    As quickly as he may;
Not far had gone before he found
A human skeleton on the ground;
The appalled discoverer with a sigh
Looks round, to learn the history.

From those abrupt and perilous rocks
    The man had fallen, that place of fear!
At length upon the shepherd's mind
    It breaks, and all is clear:
He instantly recalls the name,
And who he was, and whence he came;
Remembered, too, the very day
On which the traveller passed this way.

But hear a wonder, for whose sake
    This lamentable tale I tell!
A lasting monument of words
    This wonder merits well.
The dog, which still was hovering nigh,
Repeating the same timid cry,—
This dog had been through three months' space
A dweller in that savage place.

Yes, proof was plain that since the day
   On which the traveller thus had died
The dog had watched about the spot,
   Or by his master's side:
How nourished here through such long time
He knows, who gave that love sublime,
And gave that strength of feeling, great
Above all human estimate!

" HOLD "

By Patrick R. Chalmers

I know, where Hampshire fronts the Wight,
   A little church, where " after strife "
Reposes Guy de Blanquely, Knight,
   By Alison his wife:
I know their features' graven lines
   In time-stained marble monotone,
While crouched before their feet reclines
   Their little dog of stone!

I look where Blanquely Castle still
   Frowns o'er the oak wood's summer state,
(The maker of a patent pill
   Has purchased it of late),
And then through Fancy's open door
   I backward turn to days of old,
And see Sir Guy—a bachelor
   Who owns a dog called " Hold " !

I see him take the tourney's chance,
   And urge his coal-black charger on
To an arbitrament by lance
   For lovely Alison;

I mark the onset, see him hurl
  From broidered saddle to the dirt
His rival, that ignoble Earl—
  Black-hearted Massingbert!

Then Alison, with down-dropped eyes,
  Where happy tears bedim the blue,
Bestows a valuable prize
  And adds her hand thereto;
My lord, his surcoat streaked with sand,
  Remounts, low muttering curses hot,
And with a base-born, hireling band
  He plans a dastard plot!

. . . .

'Tis night—Sir Guy has sunk to sleep,
  The castle keep is hushed and still—
See, up the spiral stairway creep,
  To work his wicked will,
Lord Massingbert of odious fame,
  Soft followed by his cut-throat staff;
Ah, " Hold " has justified his name
  And pinned his lordship's calf!

A growl, an oath, then torches flare;
  Out rings a sentry's startled shout;
The guard are racing for the stair,
  Half-dressed, Sir Guy runs out;
On high his glittering blade he waves,
  He gives foul Massingbert the point,
He carves the hired assassin knaves
  Joint from plebeian joint!

. . . .

The Knight is dead—his sword is rust,
  But in his day I'm certain " Hold "
Wore, as his master's badge of trust,
  A collarette of gold:
And still I like to fancy that,
  Somewhere beyond the Styx's bound,
Sir Guy's tall phantom stoops to pat
  His little phantom hound!

BETH GÊLERT

By Robert William Spencer

The spearmen heard the bugle sound,
  And cheerily smil'd the morn;
And many a brach, and many a hound,
  Obey'd Llewelyn's horn.

And still he blew a louder blast,
  And gave a lustier cheer;
" Come, Gêlert, come, wert never last
  Llewelyn's horn to hear."—

Oh where does faithful Gêlert roam,
  The flower of all his race;
So true, so brave, a lamb at home,
  " A lion in the chase " ?

'Twas only at Llewelyn's board
  The faithful Gêlert fed;
He watch'd, he served, he cheer'd his lord,
  And sentinel'd his bed.

In sooth he was a peerless hound,
  The gift of royal John;
But now no Gêlert could be found,
  And all the chase rode on.

And now, as o'er the rocks and dells
  The gallant chidings rise,
All Snowdon's craggy chaos yells
  The many-mingled cries!

That day Llewelyn little lov'd
  The chase of hart and hare;
And scant and small the booty prov'd,
  For Gêlert was not there.

Unpleas'd Llewelyn homeward hied;
  When, near the portal seat,
His truant Gêlert he espied
  Bounding his lord to greet.

But, when he gain'd his castle door,
  Aghast the chieftain stood;
The hound all o'er was smear'd with gore,
  His lips, his fangs, ran blood.

Llewelyn gaz'd with fierce surprise;
  Unus'd such looks to meet,
The favorite check'd his joyful guise,
  And couch'd, and lick'd his feet.

Onward, in haste, Llewelyn pass'd,
  And on went Gêlert too;
And still, where'er his eyes he cast,
  Fresh blood-gouts shocked his view.

O'erturn'd his infant's bed he found,
  With bloodstain'd covert rent;
And all around the walls and ground
  With recent blood besprent.

He call'd his child, no voice replied—
  He search'd with terror wild;
Blood, blood he found on every side,
  But nowhere found his child.

" Hellhound! my child's by thee devour'd,"
  The frantic father cried;
And to the hilt his vengeful sword
  He plung'd in Gêlert's side.

His suppliant looks, as prone he fell,
  No pity could impart;
But still his Gêlert's dying yell
  Pass'd heavy o'er his heart.

Arous'd by Gêlert's dying yell,
  Some slumb'rer waken'd nigh;—
What words the parent's joy could tell
  To hear his infant's cry!

Conceal'd beneath a tumbled heap
  His hurried search had miss'd,
All glowing from his rosy sleep,
  The cherub boy he kissed.

Nor scath had he, nor harm, nor dread;
  But, the same couch beneath,
Lay a gaunt wolf, all torn and dead,
  Tremendous still in death.

Ah, what was then Llewelyn's pain!
  For now the truth was clear;
His gallant hound the wolf had slain,
  To save Llewelyn's heir.

Vain, vain was all Llewelyn's woe;
  " Best of thy kind, adieu!
The frantic blow which laid thee low,
  This heart shall ever rue."

And now a gallant tomb they raise,
  With costly sculpture deck'd;
And marbles storied with his praise
  Poor Gêlert's bones protect.

There never could the spearman pass,
  Or forester, unmov'd;
There, oft the tear-besprinkled grass
  Llewelyn's sorrow prov'd.

And there he hung his horn and spear,
  And there, as evening fell,
In fancy's ear, he oft would hear
  Poor Gêlert's dying yell.

And, till great Snowdon's rocks grow old,
  And cease the storm to brave,
The consecrated spot shall hold
  The name of " Gêlert's grave."

THE BIRDS OF KILLINGWORTH

By Henry Wadsworth Longfellow

It was the season, when through all the land
  The merle and mavis build, and building sing
Those lovely lyrics, written by His hand,
  Whom Saxon Cædmon calls the Blithe-heart King;
When on the boughs the purple buds expand,
  The banners of the vanguard of the Spring,
And rivulets, rejoicing, rush and leap,
And wave their fluttering signals from the steep.

The robin and the bluebird, piping loud,
  Filled all the blossoming orchards with their glee;
The sparrows chirped as if they still were proud
  Their race in Holy Writ should mentioned be;
And hungry crows, assembled in a crowd,
  Clamored their piteous prayer incessantly,
Knowing who hears the ravens cry, and said:
" Give us, O Lord, this day our daily bread! "

Across the Sound the birds of passage sailed,
  Speaking some unknown language strange and sweet
Of tropic isle remote, and passing hailed
  The village with the cheers of all their fleet;
Or quarrelling together, laughed and railed
  Like foreign sailors, landed in the street
Of seaport town, and with outlandish noise
Of oath and gibberish frightening girls and boys.

Thus came the jocund Spring in Killingworth,
  In fabulous days, some hundred years ago;

And thrifty farmers, as they tilled the earth,
  Heard with alarm the cawing of the crow,
That mingled with the universal mirth,
  Cassandra-like, prognosticating woe;
They shook their heads, and doomed with dreadful
    words
To swift destruction the whole race of birds.

And a town-meeting was convened straightway
  To set a price upon the guilty heads
Of these marauders, who, in lieu of pay,
  Levied black-mail upon the garden beds
And cornfields, and beheld without dismay
  The awful scarecrow, with his fluttering shreds;
The skeleton that waited at their feast,
Whereby their sinful pleasure was increased.

Then from his house, a temple painted white,
  With fluted columns, and a roof of red,
The Squire came forth, august and splendid sight!
  Slowly descending, with majestic tread,
Three flights of steps, nor looking left nor right,
  Down the long street he walked, as one who said,
" A town that boasts inhabitants like me
Can have no lack of good society!"

The Parson, too, appeared, a man austere,
  The instinct of whose nature was to kill;
The wrath of God he preached from year to year,
  And read, with fervor, Edwards on the Will;
His favorite pastime was to slay the deer
  In Summer on some Adirondac hill;
E'en now, while walking down the rural lane,
He lopped the wayside lilies with his cane.

From the Academy, whose belfry crowned
　　The hill of Science with its vane of brass,
Came the Preceptor, gazing idly round,
　　Now at the clouds, and now at the green grass,
And all absorbed in reveries profound
　　Of fair Almira in the upper class,
Who was, as in a sonnet he had said,
As pure as water, and as good as bread.

And next the Deacon issued from his door,
　　In his voluminous neck-cloth, white as snow;
A suit of sable bombazine he wore;
　　His form was ponderous, and his step was slow;
There never was so wise a man before;
　　He seemed the incarnate " Well, I told you so!"
And to perpetuate his great renown
There was a street named after him in town.

These came together in the new town-hall,
　　With sundry farmers from the region round.
The Squire presided, dignified and tall,
　　His air impressive and his reasoning sound;
Ill fared it with the birds, both great and small;
　　Hardly a friend in all that crowd they found,
But enemies enough, who every one
Charged them with all the crimes beneath the sun.

When they had ended, from his place apart,
　　Rose the Preceptor, to redress the wrong,
And, trembling like a steed before the start,
　　Looked round bewildered on the expectant throng;
Then thought of fair Almira, and took heart
　　To speak out what was in him, clear and strong,

Alike regardless of their smile or frown,
And quite determined not to be laughed down.

" Plato, anticipating the Reviewers,
    From his Republic banished without pity
The Poets; in this little town of yours,
    You put to death, by means of a Committee,
The ballad-singers and the Troubadours,
    The street-musicians of the heavenly city,
The birds, who make sweet music for us all
In our dark hours, as David did for Saul.

" The thrush that carols at the dawn of day
    From the green steeples of the piny wood;
The oriole in the elm; the noisy jay,
    Jargoning like a foreigner at his food;
The bluebird balanced on some topmost spray,
    Flooding with melody the neighborhood;
Linnet and meadow-lark, and all the throng
That dwell in nests, and have the gift of song.

" You slay them all! and wherefore? for the gain
    Of a scant handful more or less of wheat,
Or rye, or barley, or some other grain,
    Scratched up at random by industrious feet,
Searching for worm or weevil after rain!
    Or a few cherries, that are not so sweet
As are the songs these uninvited guests
Sing at their feast with comfortable breasts.

" Do you ne'er think what wondrous beings these?
    Do you ne'er think who made them, and who taught
The dialect they speak, where melodies
    Alone are the interpreters of thought?

Whose household words are songs in many keys,
　　Sweeter than instrument of man e'er caught!
Whose habitations in the tree-tops even
Are half-way houses on the road to heaven!

" Think, every morning when the sun peeps through
　　The dim, leaf-latticed windows of the grove,
How jubilant the happy birds renew
　　Their old, melodious madrigals of love!
And when you think of this, remember too
　　'Tis always morning somewhere, and above
The awakening continents, from shore to shore,
Somewhere the birds are singing evermore.

" Think of your woods and orchards without birds!
　　Of empty nests that cling to boughs and beams
As in the idiot's brain remembered words
　　Hang empty 'mid the cobwebs of his dreams!
Will bleat of flocks or bellowing of herds
　　Make up for the lost music, when your teams
Drag home the stingy harvest, and no more
The feathered gleaners follow to your door?

" What! would you rather see the incessant stir
　　Of insects in the windrows of the hay,
And hear the locust and the grasshopper
　　Their melancholy hurdy-gurdies play?
Is this more pleasant to you than the whir
　　Of meadow-lark, and her sweet roundelay,
Or twitter of little field-fares, as you take
Your nooning in the shade of bush and brake?

" You call them thieves and pillagers; but know,
　　They are the wingèd wardens of your farms,

Who from the cornfields drive the insidious foe,
  And from your harvests keep a hundred harms;
Even the blackest of them all, the crow,
  Renders good service as your man-at-arms,
Crushing the beetle in his coat of mail,
And crying havoc on the slug and snail.

"How can I teach your children gentleness,
  And mercy to the weak, and reverence
For Life, which, in its weakness or excess,
  Is still a gleam of God's omnipotence,
Or Death, which, seeming darkness, is no less
  The selfsame light, although averted hence,
When by your laws, your actions, and your speech,
You contradict the very things I teach?"

With this he closed; and through the audience went
  A murmur, like the rustle of dead leaves;
The farmers laughed and nodded, and some bent
  Their yellow heads together like their sheaves;
Men have no faith in fine-spun sentiment
  Who put their trust in bullocks and in beeves.
The birds were doomed; and, as the record shows,
A bounty offered for the heads of crows.

There was another audience out of reach,
  Who had no voice nor vote in making laws,
But in the papers read his little speech,
  And crowned his modest temples with applause;
They made him conscious, each one more than each,
  He still was victor, vanquished in their cause.
Sweetest of all the applause he won from thee,
O fair Almira at the Academy!

And so the dreadful massacre began;
  O'er the fields and orchards, and o'er woodland
     crests,
The ceaseless fusillade of terror ran.
  Dead fell the birds, with blood-stains on their
     breasts,
Or wounded crept away from sight of man,
  While the young died of famine in their nests;
A slaughter to be told in groans, not words,
The very St. Bartholomew of Birds!

The Summer came, and all the birds were dead;
  The days were like hot coals; the very ground
Was burned to ashes; in the orchards fed
  Myriads of caterpillars, and around
The cultivated fields and garden beds
  Hosts of devouring insects crawled, and found
No foe to check their march, till they had made
The land a desert without leaf or shade.

Devoured by worms, like Herod, was the town,
  Because like Herod, it had ruthlessly
Slaughtered the Innocents. From the trees spun down
  The canker-worms upon the passers-by,
Upon each woman's bonnet, shawl, and gown,
  Who shook them off with just a little cry;
They were the terror of each favorite walk,
The endless theme of all the village talk.

The farmers grew impatient, but a few
  Confessed their error, and would not complain,
For after all, the best thing one can do
  When it is raining, is to let it rain.

Then they repealed the law, although they knew
  It would not call the dead to life again;
As schoolboys, finding their mistake too late,
Draw a wet sponge across the accusing slate.

That year in Killingworth the Autumn came
  Without the light of his majestic look,
The wonder of the falling tongues of flame,
  The illumined pages of his Doom's-Day book.
A few lost leaves blushed crimson with their shame,
  And drowned themselves despairing in the brook,
While the wild wind went moaning everywhere,
Lamenting the dead children of the air!

But the next Spring a stranger sight was seen,
  A sight that never yet by bard was sung,
As great a wonder as it would have been
  If some dumb animal had found a tongue!
A wagon, overarched with evergreen,
  Upon whose boughs were wicker cages hung,
All full of singing birds, came down the street,
Filling the air with music wild and sweet.

From all the country round these birds were brought,
  By order of the town, with anxious quest,
And, loosened from their wicker prisons, sought
  In woods and fields the places they loved best,
Singing loud canticles, which many thought
  Were satires to the authorities addressed,
While others, listening in green lanes, averred
Such lovely music never had been heard!

But blither still and louder carolled they
  Upon the morrow, for they seemed to know

It was the fair Almira's wedding-day,
  And everywhere, around, above, below,
When the Preceptor bore his bride away,
  Their songs burst forth in joyous overflow,
And a new heaven bent over a new earth
Amid the sunny farms of Killingworth.

PEARL SEVENTY-EIGHT

(From Pearls of the Faith)

By Edwin Arnold

.   .   .   .

High noon it was, and the hot khamseen's breath
Blew from the desert sands and parched the town.
The crows gasped, and the kine went up and down
With lolling tongues; the camels moaned; a crowd
Passed with their pitchers, wrangling high and loud,
About the tank; and one dog by a well,
Nigh dead with thirst, lay where he yelped and fell,
Glaring upon the water out of reach,
And praying succor in a silent speech,
So piteous were its eyes; which when she saw
This woman from her foot her shoe did draw,
Albeit death-sorrowful, and, looping up
The long silk of her girdle, made a cup
Of the heel's hollow, and thus let it sink
Until it touched the cool, black water's brink;
So filled th' embroidered shoe, and gave a draught
To the spent beast, which whined, and fawned and
        quaffed
Her kind gift to the dregs; next licked her hand,
With such glad looks that all might understand

He held his life from her; then, at her feet
He followed close all down the cruel street,
Her one friend in that city.

                           But the king,
Riding within his litter, marked this thing,
And how the woman, on her way to die,
Had such compassion for the misery
Of that parched hound: "Take off her chain, and
    place
The veil once more above the sinner's face,
And lead her to her home in peace!" he said.
"The law is that the people stone thee dead
For that which thou hast wrought; but there is come,
Fawning around thy feet, a witness dumb,
Not heard upon thy trial; this brute beast
Testifies for thee, sister! whose weak breast
Death could not make ungentle. I hold rule
In Allah's stead, who is 'the Merciful,'
And hope for mercy; therefore go thou free —
I dare not show less pity unto thee!"

ONE OF HIS ANIMAL STORIES

By James Whitcomb Riley

Now, Tudens, you sit on *this* knee—and 'scuse
It having no side-saddle on;—and, Jeems,
You sit on *this*—and don't you wobble so
And chug my old shins with your coppertoes;—
And, all the rest of you, range round someway,—
Ride on the rockers and hang to the arms
Of our old-time splint-bottom carryall!—

Do anything but *squabble* for a place,
Or push or shove or scrouge, or breathe *out loud*,
Or chew wet, or knead taffy in my beard!—
Do *any*thing almost—act *any*way,—
Only *keep still*, so I can hear myself
Trying to tell you " just one story more! "

One winter afternoon my father, with
A whistle to our dog, a shout to us—
His two boys—six and eight years old we were,—
Started off to the woods, a half a mile
From home, where he was chopping wood. We raced,
We slipped and slid; reaching, at last the north
Side of Tharp's corn-field.—There we struck what
    seemed
To be a coon-track—so we all agreed:
And father, who was not a hunter, to
Our glad surprise, proposed we follow it.
The snow was quite five inches deep; and we,
Keen on the trail, were soon far in the woods.
Our old dog, " Ring," ran nosing the fresh track
With whimpering delight, far on ahead.
After following the trail more than a mile
To northward, through the thickest winter woods
We boys had ever seen,—all suddenly
He seemed to strike *another* trail; and then
Our joyful attention was drawn to
Old " Ring "—leaping to this side, then to that,
Of a big, hollow, old oak-tree, which had
Been blown down by a storm some years before.
There—all at once—out leapt a lean old fox
From the black hollow of a big bent limb,—
Hey! how he scudded!—but with our old " Ring "

Sharp after him—and father after " Ring "—
We after father, near as we could hold!
And father noticed that the fox kept just
About four feet ahead of " Ring "—just *that*—
No farther, and no nearer! Then he said:—
" There are young foxes in that tree back there,
And the mother-fox is drawing ' Ring ' and us
Away from their nest there! " " Oh, le' 's go back!—
Do le' 's go back! " we little vandals cried,—
" Le' 's go back, quick, and find the little things—
Please, father!—Yes, and take 'em home for pets—
'Cause ' Ring ' he'll kill the old fox anyway! "
So father turned at last, and back we went,
And father chopped a hole in the old tree
And about ten feet below the limb from which
The old fox ran, and—Bless their little lives!—
There, in the hollow of the old tree-trunk—
There, on a bed of warm dry leaves and moss—
There, snug as any bug in any rug—
We found—one—two—three—four, and, yes-sir, *five*
Wee, weenty-teenty baby foxes, with
Their eyes just barely opened—*Cute?*—my-oh!—
The cutest—the most cunning little things
Two boys ever saw, in all their lives!
" Raw weather for the little fellows *now!* "
Said father, as though talking to himself,—
" Raw weather, and no home *now!* "—And off came
His warm old " waumus " ; and in that he wrapped
The helpless little animals, and held
Them soft and warm against him as he could,—
And home we happy children followed him.—
Old " Ring " did not reach home till nearly dusk:
The mother-fox had led him a long chase—

" Yes, and a fool's chase, too!" he seemed to say,
And looked ashamed to hear us *praising* him.
But, *mother*—well, we *could not* understand
Her acting as she did—and we so *pleased!*
I can see yet the look of pained surprise
And deep compassion of her troubled face
When father very gently laid his coat,
With the young foxes in it, on the hearth
Beside her, as she brightened up the fire.
She urged—for the old fox's sake and theirs—
That they be taken back to the old tree;
But father—for *our* wistful sakes, no doubt—
Said we would keep them, and would try our **best**
To raise them. And at once he set about
Building a snug home for the little things
Out of an old big bushel-basket, with
Its fractured handle and its stoven ribs:
So, lining and padding this all cosily,
He snuggled in its little tenants, and
Called in John Wesley Thomas, our hired man,
And gave him in full charge, with much advice
Regarding the just care and sustenance of
Young foxes.—" John," he said, " you feed 'em *milk*—
Warm milk, John Wesley! Yes, and *keep 'em by*
The stove—and keep your stove *a-roarin'*, too,
Both night and day!—And keep 'em *covered* up—
Not *smothered*, John, but snug and comfortable.—
And now, John Wesley Thomas, first and last,—
You feed 'em *milk*—*fresh* milk—and always *warm*—
Say five or six or seven times a day—
Of course we'll grade that by the way they *thrive*."
But, for all sanguine hope, and care, as well,
The little fellows *did not* thrive at all.—

Indeed, with *all* our care and vigilance,
By the third day of their captivity
The last survivor of the fated five
Squeaked, like some battered little rubber toy
Just clean worn out.—And that's just what it was!
And—nights,—the cry of the mother-fox for her
　　young
Was heard, with awe, for long weeks afterward.
And we boys, every night, would go to the door
And, peering out in the darkness, listening,
Could hear the poor fox in the black bleak woods
Still calling for her little ones in vain.
As, all mutely, we returned to the warm fireside,
Mother would say: "How would you like for *me*
To be out there, this dark night, in the cold woods,
Calling for *my* children?"

THE EMPEROR'S BIRD'S-NEST

By Henry Wadsworth Longfellow

Once the Emperor Charles of Spain,
　　With his swarthy, grave commanders,
I forget in what campaign,
Long besieged, in mud and rain,
　　Some old frontier town of Flanders.

Up and down the dreary camp,
　　In great boots of Spanish leather,
Striding with a measured tramp,
These Hidalgos, dull and damp,
　　Cursed the Frenchmen, cursed the weather.

Thus as to and fro they went
  Over upland and through hollow,
Giving their impatience vent,
Perched upon the Emperor's tent,
  In her nest, they spied a swallow.

Yes, it was a swallow's nest,
  Built of clay and hair of horses,
Mane, or tail, or dragoon's crest,
Found on hedgerows east and west,
  After skirmish of the forces.

Then an old Hidalgo said,
  As he twirled his gray mustachio,
" Sure this swallow overhead
Thinks the Emperor's tent a shed,
  And the Emperor but a Macho!"

Hearing his imperial name
  Coupled with those words of malice,
Half in anger, half in shame,
Forth the great campaigner came
  Slowly from his canvas palace.

" Let no hand the bird molest,"
  Said he solemnly, " nor hurt her!"
Adding then, by way of jest,
" Golondrina is my guest,
  'Tis the wife of some deserter!"

Swift as bowstring speeds a shaft,
  Through the camp was spread the rumor,
And the soldiers, as they quaffed
Flemish beer at dinner, laughed
  At the Emperor's pleasant humor.

So unharmed and unafraid
　　Sat the swallow still and brooded,
Till the constant cannonade
Through the walls a breach had made,
　　And the siege was thus concluded.

Then the army, elsewhere bent,
　　Struck its tents as if disbanding,
Only not the Emperor's tent,
For he ordered, ere he went,
　　Very curtly, " Leave it standing! "

So it stood there all alone,
　　Loosely flapping, torn and tattered,
Till the brood was fledged and flown,
Singing o'er those walls of stone
　　Which the cannon-shot had shattered.

THE MILAN BIRD-CAGES

A. D. 1485

By Margaret J. Preston

I

Just four hundred years ago,
　　　　(You may like to know)—
In a city old and quaint,
Lived a painter who could paint
Knight or lady, child or saint,
　　　　With so rich a glow,
And such wondrous skill as none
In the Land of Art had done.

II

Should you ever chance to take
(As you will) a foreign tour,
Milan you will see, I'm sure,
    For the Master's sake,
And be shown, in colors dim,
One grand picture drawn by him—
Christ's *Last Supper*. If your eyes
Fill, while gazing, no surprise
Need be either yours or mine,
    O'er that face divine.

III

Then in Paris, if you go
To the great Louvre Gallery, where
Miles of paintings make you stare
Till your eyes ache, they will show
As they point the finest out,
One the world goes mad about—
Such a portrait, all the while
How it haunts you with its smile,
    Lovely *Mona Lisa!* she
Can't be bought for gold, you see;
Not if kings should come to buy,
    —Let them try!

IV

Oft the Master used to go
(Old Vasari tells us so)
To the market where they sold
Birds, in cages gay with gold,

Brightly tipped on wing and crest,
Trapped just as they left the nest.
Thither went he day by day,
Buying all within his way,
Making the young peasants glad,
Since they sold him all they had;
And no matter what his store,
Counting birds and cages o'er,
He was always buying more.

V

"Wherefore buy so many?" Well,
That's just what I'm going to tell.
Soon as he had bought a bird,
O'er his upturned head was heard
Such a trill, so glad, so high,
Dropped from out the sunny sky
Down into his happy heart;
Filling it as naught else could—
Naught save his belovèd Art—
Full of joy, as there he stood
Holding wide the wicker door,
Watching the bright captives soar
Deep into the blue. You see
Why he bought so many: He
Did it just to set them free.

VI

Love I Leonardo so
For his splendid pictures?—No!
But for his sweet soul, so stirred
By a little prisoned bird.

WALTER VON DER VOGELWEID

By Henry Wadsworth Longfellow

Vogelweid the Minnesinger,
    When he left this world of ours,
Laid his body in the cloister,
    Under Würtzburg's minster towers.

And he gave the monks his treasures,
    Gave them all with this behest:
They should feed the birds at noontide
    Daily on his place of rest;

Saying, " From these wandering minstrels
    I have learned the art of song;
Let me now repay the lessons
    They have taught so well and long."

Thus the bard of love departed;
    And, fulfilling his desire,
On his tomb the birds were feasted
    By the children of the choir.

Day by day, o'er tower and turret,
    In foul weather and in fair,
Day by day, in vaster numbers,
    Flocked the poets of the air.

On the tree whose heavy branches
    Overshadowed all the place,
On the pavement, on the tombstone,
    On the poet's sculptured face,

On the cross-bars of each window,
  On the lintel of each door,
They renewed the War of Wartburg,
  Which the bard had fought before.

There they sang their merry carols,
  Sang their lauds on every side;
And the name their voices uttered
  Was the name of Vogelweid.

Till at length the portly abbot
  Murmured, " Why this waste of food?
Be it changed to loaves henceforward
  For our fasting brotherhood."

Then in vain o'er tower and turret,
  From the walls and woodland nests,
When the minster bells rang noontide,
  Gathered the unwelcome guests.

Then in vain, with cries discordant,
  Clamorous round the Gothic spire,
Screamed the feathered Minnesingers
  For the children of the choir.

Time has long effaced the inscriptions
  On the cloister's funeral stones,
And tradition only tells us
  Where repose the poet's bones.

But around the vast cathedral,
  By sweet echoes multiplied,
Still the birds repeat the legend,
  And the name of Vogelweid.

FOR VANITY

Yet there in distant forests, where
The little fur-clad creatures fare,
Shrill cries of torture rend the air!

To a Lady in Her Furs.   JAMES BEEBE CARRINGTON.

FOR VANITY

FOUR LITTLE FOXES

By Lew Sarett

Speak gently, Spring, and make no sudden sound;
For in my windy valley yesterday I found
Newborn foxes squirming on the ground—
      Speak gently.

Walk softly, March, forbear the bitter blow;
Her feet within a trap, her blood upon the snow,
The four little foxes saw their mother go—
      Walk softly.

Go lightly, Spring, oh, give them no alarm;
When I covered them with boughs to shelter them
      from harm,
The thin blue foxes suckled at my arm—
      Go lightly.

Step softly, March, with your rampant hurricane;
Nuzzling one another, and whimpering with pain,
The new little foxes are shivering in the rain—
      Step softly.

THE KIND LADY'S FURS

By Strickland Gillilan

The white wolves belled on the ermine's trail
    'Way up in the heart of the heartless north.

The ermine must haste ere his strength should fail;
In spite of the danger, he hurried forth.
He saw some food in a tempting cache;
He hastened to gulp it and hurry on—
Two jaws of a demon of steel went "Smash!"
And the animal's hope of life was gone!
A white man came ere the wolves might come,
And he carried that ermine's peltry home.
Milady she wears it with joy and pride,
Not caring a whit how the ermine died!
(He had tugged at the trap for hours—ha, ha!
Had struggled with all of his powers—la, la!
So laugh as you wear your furs, ma chère,
Laugh as you flaunt your furs!)

The small boy placed by the meadow creek
A steel trap held by a long strong chain.
For there the muskrats, he knew, would seek
Their nightly food—might they seek in vain!
A muskrat came, and the jaws went "Crunch!"
And the night—ah, the cruel night was young!
He gnawed at his leg—'twas a hideous lunch!—
But the terrible trap-jaws clung and clung.
The little lad at the dawning came,
(He was kind when he wasn't in search of
"game");
He ripped from his victim the velvet hide,
For milady's wardrobe must be supplied!
(He had writhed in the grisly grip—ha, ha!
Nearly gnawed off his leg at the hip—la, la!
So merrily wear your furs, ma chère,
Merrily wear your furs!)

TO A LADY IN HER FURS

By J. B. Carrington

The furs you wear are rich and rare,
Your face is smiling, sweet and fair,
Dear TENDERNESS seems biding there.

And as you step adown the way,
Of fashion's pageant and display,
You've not a care in all the day.

Yet there in distant forests, where
The little fur-clad creatures fare,
Shrill cries of torture rend the air!

MY LADY'S FUR

By F. Ursula Payne

'Tis midnight in the forest cold and bleak,
  The north wind drives the snow, the icy reeds
Bend o'er a cruel trap where faint and weak
  A timid furry creature slowly bleeds.

Faintly above the wind she seems to hear
  Her little babies crying for her care;
She writhes in agony, and moans in fear.
  For two long nights she has been dying there.

'Tis midnight in the city. Cold and keen
  The north wind blows the sparkling snow about.
Before the opera house a limousine
  Stops to receive a lady coming out.

Her rich, warm cloak she draws about her, so ;
　　The soft fur rests against her glowing cheek.
This is the fur that just a year ago
　　Clad that poor forest creature, stiff and weak.

Could she but see that forest far away,
　　Could she but hear the suff'ring creature's cry,
The lady's laughter would not be so gay,
　　Her lips would breathe a sympathetic sigh.

She, who can move the very hearts of men,
　　Would storm great Congress at its mighty door,
Till legislation she would gain, and then
　　The cruel, cruel trap would be no more.

FOR VANITY

By Hannah J. Dawtrey

I would the scene might flash before your eye
Of bonnie mother birds that bleed and die,
　　When you with plumage rare
　　　　Bedeck your hair,
　　　　For Vanity.

I would the piteous cry might haunt your ear,
Of helpless orphan broods that pine in fear,
　　When you white feathers wear,
　　　　Ye ruthless fair,
　　　　For Vanity.

I would these sights and sounds of useless pain
Might burn themselves upon your heart and brain,
When you, unblushingly, dare
Such spoils to share
For Vanity.

Who loves the birdlings, gave them the plumage gay
For their own joy,—the God to whom ye pray;
Remember when at prayer—
He does not care
For Vanity.

DEAD BIRDS AND EASTER

By May Riley Smith

God thought it worth His while to make a bird—
A joyous creature that could soar and float
With sweetest melody man ever heard,
Caught in the feathered meshes of its throat.
And this rare thing with God's own touch upon it
Is rended wing from wing to trim a bonnet!

It is an Easter morning, holy, calm,—
And life, not death, is the glad theme to-day.
The air is full of Spring's delicious balm,
The maple buds are dropping on the way.
And one I saw, with flush of crimson on it,
Fall on the dead birds of a woman's bonnet!

What say the bells at these good Easter times?
They tell of vanquished death, and risen life!
Hush then, O bells, your inconsistent chimes.

You and the dull old world are hard at strife;
For surely when the crimson leaf fell on it,
I saw dead birds upon a woman's bonnet!

What does it cost, this garniture of death?
It costs the life that God alone can give,
It costs dull silence where was music's breath,
It costs dead joy that foolish pride may live;
Ah, Life and Love and Joy, depend upon it,
Are costly trimmings for a woman's bonnet!

Who would arrest the sweet pulse of a lark
That flutters in such ecstasy of bliss,
Or lay a robin's bright breast cold and stark
For such a petty recompense as this?
O, you who love your babies, think upon it.
Mothers are slaughtered just to trim your bonnet!

Will Herod never cease to rule the land
That we should slay sweet innocency so?
Is joy so cheap, or happiness sure planned?
Tell me, you who are intimate with woe—
Does your sad heart proclaim no ban upon it?
Would you slay happiness just for a bonnet?

And must God's choirs that through His forests rove
Whose matinees are free to high and low,—
Must His own orchestra of fields and grove,
Himself their leader, be disbanded so?
Nay, nay, O God, proclaim thy ban upon it.
Protect thy birds from sport, and greed, and bonnet!

Dead birds, and dead for gentle woman's sake
To feed awhile her vanity's poor breath!
And yet the foolish bells sweet clamor make
And tell of One whose power has vanquished death.
Ah, Easter time has a reproach upon it
While birds are slain to trim a woman's bonnet!

OUR BROTHERS OF THE FIELDS AND TREES

By Charles Keeler

I dreamed that I was Francis of Assisi
In shadowy daisy field of misty dawn,
The children of the air, my ministrants,
Flocking about with matins of sweet song.

" My tiny choristers of field and tree,
Blithe winged disciples," so my sermon ran,
" I bring the word of God to comfort you,
Good tidings of our Savior Christ, the risen."

And thereupon wings flapped about my face
And cries derisive rang from feathered throats.
" You of the Titan race," they shrilly called,
" Who preach of love and seek us but to slay,
Apostates revelling in lust of blood!"

A mother robin 'plained: " What bliss was mine,
What hope, what promise in those eggs of blue,
Snug in my plastered cradle hid away
Until the prying bandit eyes had pierced
My leafy screen and my dear home despoiled!"

" Alas," outpiped the quail, " the huntsman came
And slew my chosen mate, and called it sport,
While I am left in lonely copse to mourn."

Then with a wail of anguish winged anigh
A snowy egret like an angel white
Out of the mist of heaven to challenge me:
" A host of wings erstwhile amid the trees,
A throng of mothers' hearts about the nests!
Ah, little did they dream of ravage drear,
That mothers of the lordlier race of men
So craved our nuptial dower of airy plumes
That they should have us slain in wantonness
While all our little ones with piteous cries
Awaited the slow stealing on of death."

Thereat the frantic birds came clamoring round
To mob me from the grove with mocking scorn,
When loud a gun pealed forth its breath of doom,
Some passing sportsman's challenge to the throng,
And lifeless fluttered down a feathery form.
Startled I roused me from my sombre dream
But shook not off the woodland reverie.

What is this life we take so wantonly?
A spark of God's great love so stamped upon
Because we have the craft and lust to kill!
What Golden Rule is made for man alone?
The beast looks in your eyes and cries you shame.
Let us renounce blood sacraments and dare
To live untainted by corrupting flesh,
And in the might of tenderness rejoice.
Methinks that Buddha's way leads unto peace

Through kinship with the least and lowliest lives.
All are God's children, even as thou and I,
United in the spirit of brotherhood,
And in th' eternal reckoning shall be
Accounted in the great Creator's plan.

"BRAVES of the HUNT"

Sport! to slay with no cause to slay—not even the pride
of hate!
Courage? then stand to an even chance, facing a
foeman's gun
Out in the open, eye to eye, for Honor of Kin or State,
Oh, ye who slink in the woven blind seeking to kill—
for fun!

Braves of the Hunt.　　　　　Henry Herbert Knibbs.

"BRAVES OF THE HUNT"

IN COOL, GREEN HAUNTS

By Mahlon Leonard Fisher

A sweet, deep sense of mystery filled the wood.
  A star, like that which woke o'er Bethlehem,
  Shone on the still pool's brow for diadem—
  The first to fall of summer's multitude!
In cool, green haunts, where, haply, Robin Hood
  Ranged royally, of old, with all his train,
  A hushed expectance, such as augurs rain,
  Enthralled me and possessed me where I stood.

Then came the wind, with low word as he went;
  The quick wren, swift repeating what he said;
  A chattering chipmunk lured me on and led
Where scented brakes 'neath some wee burden bent:—
  One look—'twas this those wild things yearned to say:
  "A little brown-eyed fawn was born to-day!"

THE CATCH

By John Kendrick Bangs

I've enjoyed the chase to-day
  Through the woodland wild.
Fortune in a lavish way
  Hath my heart beguiled.

I have filled my game-bag well—
  Better than I thought.
Fat and teeming it doth swell
  With the things I sought.

Songs of birds, and songs of trees.
Gentle whisperings of the breeze.
Splendid mess of mountain air.
Odors of wild-flowers rare.
Happy thoughts that grew apace
As I watched the rillets race.
Wondrous pictures in the skies.
Vistas soft for tired eyes.
Hints of peace, and hints of rest.
Gorgeous colors in the west.
Stores of gold flung far and wide
O'er the gleaming country-side,
As the sun smiled on the scene,
Lighting up the forest green.

O the joy, the glad delight,
   O the taste of bliss,
Making homeward through the night
   With a catch like this.

THE QUAILS

By Francis Brett Young

(In the South of Italy the peasants put out the eyes of a captured quail so that its cries may attract the flocks of spring migrants into their nets.)

All through the night
I have heard the stuttering call of a blind quail,
A caged decoy, under a cairn of stones,
Crying for light as the quails cry for love.

Other wanderers,
Northward from Africa winging on numb pinions, dazed

With beating winds and the sobbing of the sea,
Hear, in a breath of sweet land-herbage, the call
Of the blind one, their sister. . . .
Hearing, their fluttered hearts
Take courage, and they wheel in their dark flight,
Knowing that their toil is over, dreaming to see
The white stubbles of Abruzzi smitten with dawn,
And split grain lying in the furrows, the squandered gold
That is the delight of quails in their spring mating.

Land-scents grow keener,
Penetrating the dank and bitter odour of brine
That whitens their feathers;
Far below, the voice of their sister calls them
To plenty, and sweet water, and fulfillment:
Over the pallid margin of dim seas breaking,
Over the thickening in the darkness that is land,
They fly. Their flight is ended. Wings beat no more.
Downward they drift, one by one, like dark petals,
Slowly, listlessly falling,
Into the mouth of horror:
The nets . . .

Where men come trampling and crying with bright
    lanterns
Plucking their weak, entangled claws from the meshes of
    net,
Clutching the soft brown bodies mottled with olive,
Crushing the warm, fluttering flesh, in hands stained
    with blood,
Till their quivering hearts are stilled, and the bright
    eyes,
That are like a polished agate, glazed in death.

But the blind one, in her wicker cage, without ceasing
Haunts this night of spring with her stuttering call,
Knowing nothing of the terror that walks in darkness,
Knowing only that some cruelty has stolen the light
That is life, and that she must cry until she dies.

I, in the darkness,
Heard, and my heart grew sick. But I know that to-
  morrow
A smiling peasant will come with a basket of quails
Wrapped in vine-leaves, prodding them with blood-
  stained fingers
Saying, " Signore, you must cook them thus, and thus,
With a sprig of basil inside them." And I shall thank
  him,
Carrying the piteous carcases into the kitchen
Without a pang, without shame.

" Why should I be ashamed? Why should I rail
Against the cruelty of men? Why should I pity,
Seeing that there is no cruelty which men can imagine
To match the subtle dooms that are wrought against
  them
By blind spores of pestilence: seeing that each of us,
Lured by dim hopes, flutters in the toils of death
On a cold star that is spinning blindly through space
Into the nets of time? "

So cried I, bitterly thrusting pity aside,
Closing my lids to sleep. But sleep came not,
And pity, with sad eyes,
Crept to my side, and told me
That the life of all creatures is brave and pitiful

Whether they be men, with dark thoughts to vex them,
Or birds, wheeling in the swift joys of flight,
Or brittle ephemerids, spinning to death in the haze
Of gold that quivers on dim evening waters;
Nor would she be denied.
The harshness died
Within me, and my heart
Was caught and fluttered like the palpitant heart
Of a brown quail, flying
To the call of her blind sister,
And death, in the spring night.

THE BLOODLESS SPORTSMAN

By Sam Walter Foss

" Hast thou named all the birds without a gun?
Loved the wood-rose and left it on its stalk? "
EMERSON.

I go a-gunning, but take no gun;
 I fish without a pole;
And I bag good game and catch such fish
 As suit a sportsman's soul;
For the choicest game that the forest holds,
 And the best fish of the brook,
Are never brought down by a rifle shot
 And never are caught with a hook.

I bob for fish by the forest brook,
 I hunt for game in the trees,
For bigger birds than wing the air
 Or fish that swim the seas.

A rodless Walton of the brooks
  A bloodless sportsman, I—
I hunt for the thoughts that throng the woods,
  The dreams that haunt the sky.

The woods were made for the hunters of dreams,
  The brooks for the fishers of song;
To the hunters who hunt for the gunless game
  The streams and the woods belong.
There are thoughts that moan from the soul of the
    pine,
  And thoughts in a flower bell curled;
And the thoughts that are blown with the scent of
    the fern
  Are as new and as old as the world.

So, away! for the hunt in the fern-scented wood
  Till the going down of the sun;
There is plenty of game still left in the woods
  For the hunter who has no gun.
So, away! for the fish in the moss-bordered brook
  That flows through the velvety sod;
There are plenty of fish still left in the streams
  For the angler who has no rod.

POEM FOR PRUE

By Norman Gale

Bound, Hare, bound!
  Here's a bully with a hound.
If you'd *really* rather not
Smell delicious in a pot,

Over briar and streamlet vault,
Far from pepper, far from salt,
Till at last your toothy foe
Cannot see which way you go.
    Bound, Hare, bound!
        Here's a bully—
Yes, a bully with a yard or two of hound.

Look, Salmon, look!
    Here's a bully with a hook.
If it's *really* not your wish
Soon to decorate a dish,
        Don't, by playing tug-of-war,
        Help this man to carry more
Silvered beauty home, and bite
Far too much of it at night.
        Look, Salmon, look!
            Here's a bully—
Yes, a bully with a minnow on his hook.

Back, Fox, back!
    Here are bullies in a pack.
If you *really* want to be
Safe at home in time for tea,
        Bid your pads and brain and breath
        Hold you half a mile from Death
Hunting you since middle-day
All along your twisty way.
        Back, Fox, back!
            Here are bullies—
Here are bullies with a horsey-doggy pack.

Run, Rabbit, run!
  Here's a bully with a gun.
If you *really* dread to lie
Close to onions in a pie,
  Quit that turnip, and begin
  Legging homeward with the skin
Just as dear, of course, to you,
Powderpuff, as hers to Prue.
  Run, Rabbit, run!
    Here's a bully—
Yes, a bully with a cartridge in his gun.

HOW TO CATCH A BIRD

By Leland B. Jacobs

Don't hunt him with a sling or gun
For that would surely spoil the fun;
For when all life has left his breast
You then can pick up all the rest—
A crumpled body, red and small,
A bit of plumage, that is all.
You haven't got his song or call!

  Don't kill him!

I'll tell a secret that I heard—
The perfect way to catch a bird.
Just get a bird book, called a guide,
And with field-glasses at your side
Go out into the woods and see
The bird perched up in some tall tree;
Stop, too, and hear his melody—

  You've got him!

WOUNDED

By Florence Wilkinson

Let her creep to earth again, my children,
She will never heed our signal calls.
Do not whine along her track,
She will not come footing back.
She is wounded to the heart of her, my children,
And the red blood follows where she falls.

Let her be, forget her steps, my children,
Forgotten be the anguish and the length:
Let her find a covert place,
There to hide her glazing face
And to stretch her grievous paws in silence, chil-
dren,
Dripping drop by drop her scarlet strength.

She will dread the common trail, my children,
Crouching where the deepest shade is cast.
Creatures of the earth and sky—
None can comfort when we die
Only dark and unremembering, my children,
For we feel the Hour is come at last.

She will creep wet-foot and slow, my children;
She will never heed the signal call.
She will voiceless be and blind
To her kin and to her kind,
Waiting in the shadow, O my children,
Wounded—For that is the End of all.

THE PUZZLED GAME-BIRDS

By Thomas Hardy

They are not those who used to feed us
When we were young—they cannot be—
These shapes that now bereave and bleed us?
They are not those who used to feed us,
For did we then cry, they would heed us.
—If hearts can house such treachery
They are not those who used to feed us
When we were young—they cannot be!

TO A WILD GOOSE OVER DECOYS

By Lew Sarett

" O lonely trumpeter, coasting down the sky,
Like a winter leaf blown from the bur-oak tree
By whipping winds, and flapping silverly
Against the sun,—I know your lonely cry.

I know the worn wild heart that bends your flight
And circles you above this beckoning lake,
Eager of neck, to find the honking drake
Who speaks of reedy refuge for the night.

I know the sudden rapture that you fling
In answer to our friendly gander's call—
Halloo! Beware decoys!—or you will fall
With a silver bullet whistling in your wing!

Beat on your weary flight across the blue!
Beware, O traveller, of our gabbling geese!
Beware this weedy counterfeit of peace!—
Oh, I was once a passing bird like you."

From "WINDSOR FOREST"

By Alexander Pope

With slaughtering guns the unwearied fowler roves,
When frosts have whiten'd all the naked groves;
Where doves in flocks the leafless trees o'ershade,
And lonely woodcocks haunt the watery glade,
He lifts the tube, and levels with his eye;
Straight a short thunder breaks the frozen sky.
Oft, as in airy rings they skim the heath,
The clamorous lapwings feel the leaden death:
Oft, as the mounting larks their notes prepare,
They fall, and leave their little lives in air.

WOUNDS

By Arthur C. Benson

The wounded bird sped on with shattered wing,
    And gained the holt, and ran a little space,
    Where briar and bracken twined a hiding-place;
There lay and wondered at the grievous thing.

With patient filmy eye he peeped, and heard
    Big blood-drops oozing on the fallen leaf;
    There hour by hour in uncomplaining grief
He watched with pain, but neither cried nor stirred.

The merry sportsmen tramped contented home,
  He heard their happy laughter die away;—
    Across the stubble by the covert-side
    His merry comrades called at eventide;
  They breathed the fragrant air, alert and gay,
And he was sad because his hour was come.

NO SANCTUARY

(An event that happened in November, 1924)

By Edwin Markham

  Over the hills with terror-cry,
  An eagle burst into the sky.
  Thousands of crows pursued him, filling
  The heavens with sounds of curse and killing.
  They rusht in raucous murder crowds,
  Stung by some madness of the clouds.
  Over my head there came to me
  The thunder of an upper sea.

  The noble bird in desperate hope,
  Fled to a camp upon the slope,
  Crasht down upon the men, that they
  Might keep his enemies at bay.
  It was good reasoning to suppose
  That men have higher souls than crows.

  What happened as a crowning proof
  Of how divine a thing is man?
  The men saw tragedy and ran
  To shield the bird beneath their roof.
  They scared away the murder bands,

Taking him in with happy hands.
They brought him food and water, glad
To soothe a fugitive, terror-mad.
They felt the thrill of his great eyes
That still burned with the upper skies.
They loost him then to the airy spaces,
To gladden upward-looking faces. . . .

No, no, you're wrong, my pen! Instead,
They got their guns and shot him dead!
And now, in bitter shame, I know
How little a man transcends a crow!

THE WIDOWED EAGLE

By Edith M. Thomas

Out from the aerie beloved we flew,
Now through the white, and now through the blue;
Glided beneath us hilltop, and glen,
River, and meadow, and dwellings of men!

We flew, we flew through the regions of light
And the wind's wild pæan followed our flight!
Free of the world, we flew, we flew—
Bound to each other alone,—we two!

To the shivering migrant we called, " Adieu!"
Mid the frost-sweet weather, we flew, we flew!
Till, hark from below! the hiss of lead,
And one of us dropped, as a plume is shed!

Around and around I flew, I flew,
Wheeling my flight, ever closer I drew!
There, on the earth, my belovèd lay,
With a crimson stain on her breast-plumes gray!

And creatures of earth we had scorned before,
Now measured the wings that would lift no more:
And I stooped, as an arrow is shot from the height,
And sought to bear her away in my flight—

Away to our aerie far to seek!
Well did I fight with talons and beak;
But the craven foe, in their numbers and might,
Bore her in triumph out of my sight!

THE WOUNDED HARE

By Robert Burns

Inhuman man! curse on thy barbarous art,
  And blasted be thy murder-aiming eye;
  May never pity soothe thee with a sigh,
Nor ever pleasure glad thy cruel heart!

—Go, live, poor wanderer of the wood and field,
  The bitter little that of life remains;
  No more the thickening brakes and verdant plains
To thee shall home, or food, or pastime yield.

Seek, mangled wretch, some place of wonted rest,
  No more of rest, but now thy dying bed!
  The sheltering rushes whistling o'er thy head,
The cold earth with thy bloody bosom prest.

Oft as by winding Nith, I, musing, wait
  The sober eve, or hail the cheerful dawn,
  I'll miss thee sporting o'er the dewy lawn,
And curse the ruffian's aim, and mourn thy hapless fate.

THE BEAVER

By Mary Howitt

Up in the north if thou sail with me,
A wonderful creature I'll show to thee;
As gentle and mild as a lamb at play,—
Skipping about in the month of May;
Yet wise as any old learned sage
Who sits turning over a musty page!

Come down to the lonely river's bank,
See driven-in stake and riven plank;
'Tis a mighty work before thee stands
That would do no shame to human hands.
A well-built dam to stem the tide
Of this northern river so strong and wide;
Look! the woven bough of many a tree,
And a wall of fairest masonry.
The waters cannot o'erpass this bound,
For a hundred keen eyes watch it round;
And the skill that raised can keep it good
Against the peril of storm and flood.

And yonder the peaceable creatures dwell,
Secure in their watery citadel!
They know no sorrow, have done no sin;
Happy they live 'mong kith and kin,—

As happy as living things can be,
Each in the midst of his family!
Ay, there they live, and the hunter wild
Seeing how they were kind and good,
Hath felt his stubborn soul subdued;
And the very sight of their young at play
Hath put his hunter's heart away;
And a mood of pity hath o'er him crept,
As he thought of his own dear babes and wept.

THE SNARE

By James Stephens

I hear a sudden cry of pain!
    There is a rabbit in a snare:
Now I hear the cry again,
    But I cannot tell from where.

But I cannot tell from where
    He is crying out for aid;
Crying on the frightened air,
    Making everything afraid.

Making everything afraid,
    Wrinkling up his little face,
As he cries again for aid;
    And I cannot find the place.

And I cannot find the place
    Where his paw is in the snare:
Little one! Oh, little one!
    I am searching everywhere.

THE DEER-TRAPPER

By Francis Sterne Palmer

At sight of him the birds berate;
The blackbird points him to her mate,
The bluejay screams a scathing word,
Even the thrush is anger-stirred;—
Stealthy his step by wood-path dim,
Yet they know and jeer at him.

His coming makes the fields less gay;
The men who work there look away,
No welcome, only a half-hid sneer,
For Paul who loafs—and traps the deer!

When night-mist softens clearings rough,
And men who work have worked enough,
Around the shanty doors you hear
Laughing girls make music clear;
Jest answers jest, heart's cheer to heart,—
But Paul Fineffe still keeps apart!

Sleepin' he dreams, and seems to hide
Close by a spruce-tree's shadowy side;
A slender doe through the mosses stepped,
Under her foot a deer-trap leapt
And fastened on her, biting deep,
Biting deeper at each wild leap!
She is no stolid, brutish bear
To crouch and wait the trapper there;

Frantic she plunges, crazed with fright,
Bruised and broken, a piteous sight!—
Paul sees and shudders and would away,
But something holds him—he too must stay!

Such day-time joy, such night-time cheer,
For Paul Fineffe who traps the deer!

BRAVES OF THE HUNT

By Henry Herbert Knibbs

Braves! that go out with your guides and gold and the
    polished tube of steel,
  Playing safe with the hunting-pack, the trap and the
    prism-glass;
Slaying the Moose or the Silver-tip, e'en as you pause
    and kneel
  Loosing the power that ye wield for shame. . . .
    So do our monarchs pass.

Not for the hunger of babes ye hunt; for mother or
    aged sire;
  Not to the Red Gods offering the blood of your lust
    to kill;
Not with the strength of your brawn and thew match-
    ing the fury-fire
  Of the beast that fights for the life it loves; nay! but
    with sneaking skill

Ye speed the sting of the spreading slug, giving your
    lust a name;
  Sport! to shatter the buoyant life, to sever the liver
    thread!

Then ye stand with a gun in hand, grinning your pic-
tured shame;
"See at my feet the mighty thing that I, yea, that *I*
struck dead!"

When ye have toiled on the foot-worn trail till the
hunger-pinch is keen;
When ye have stood as a man with men earning your
wage through strife
Of the outland ways, ye have fair excuse to kill—an
the kill be clean;
Then, perchance, will the vaunt be lost in fostering
life with life.

Sport! to slay with no cause to slay—not even the
pride of hate!
Courage? then stand to an even chance, facing a foeman's gun
Out in the open, eye to eye, for Honor of Kin or State,
Oh, ye who slink in the woven blind seeking to kill—
for fun!

Would that ye lay by the wounded thing that crawls
to the brush to die;
Would that ye knew the biting pain and that linger-
ing thirst of hell,
Writhing down to the darksome pit as ye vainly im-
plored the sky,
Asking It if there once was God that made ye and
loved ye well!

Perhaps, when the Hand that fashioned all shall strike,
and the earth be dumb

Out of the dim and the voiceless vast—back to their
    own again—
Herd and band and the mated beasts, fearless and free,
    shall come,
    Knowing naught of the ancient fear of a tribe that
    were named as men.

THE HUNT

By Gertrude Huntington McGiffert

Crash and off and away together
Over the moors and the purple heather,
Over the moors in the golden weather!
Huntsmen, gentlemen, hunters, all
Loosed at last by the harbourer's call!
Off and away! Like a swinging lash
Two score pitiless staghounds crash
Out through the broom with hot fixed eyes,
And surer and clearer and deadlier rise
Over the hills where the fresh track lies.

Hound to hound and horse to horse,
Mile on mile through the yellow gorse,
The scarlet coats, the bits agleam,
The reeking flanks, the froth, the steam,
The reddening spurs and the daring leap
Down treacherous foothold of mountain sheep,
Up perilous steep, from ledge to ledge,
Around the covert and over the hedge,
Through wooded coomb and baffling glen,
Through glen and coomb—pack, hunters, and
    men!

Beyond, the lordly wild red Deer,
Gaining the cliff where the rocks fall sheer,
Clears crag and chasm with breathless spring,
Wheels down the wind like a bird on wing—
Noble mile on mile with eyes on fire,
Noble mile on mile through ooze and mire,
Till his hide is black and his staunch limbs tire!
At bay at last in brave defeat
On a rocky ledge where the waters meet
He turns on his foes with striking feet.

He rips a hound from flank to flank,
The stream runs red from bank to bank.
Hound after hound he grapples and turns,
With tossing crest he fends and spurns,
A death-trapped knight he fends and spurns.
Death-trapped! The white blade at his throat!
His proud head lowers, the hot hounds gloat,
His royal antlers are borne away,
A stately prize—brow, bay, and tray!

. . . .

Had God walked over His hills to-day!

IN CAPTIVITY

Exiles, they tread their narrow bounds
    Behind the iron bars.
Where'er they turn the hand of man
    Their straining vision mars,
Save only when at night they gaze
    Upon the friendly stars.

In the Zoo.   GEORGE T. MARSH.

IN CAPTIVITY

AT THE ZOO

By Israel Zangwill

The sky is gray with rain that will not fall,
The clayey paths are oozing ghostly mist.
Reeking with sadness immemorial,
The gray earth saps the courage to exist.

Poor tropic creatures, penned in northern land,
I, too, desire the sun and am a slave.
My heart is with you, and I understand
The lion turning in his living grave.

IN THE ZOO

By George T. Marsh

Exiles, they tread their narrow bounds
    Behind the iron bars.
Where'er they turn the hand of man
    Their straining vision mars,
Save only when at night they gaze
    Upon the friendly stars.

See! there a golden eagle broods
    With glazed, unseeing eyes
That never more will sweep the snows
    Where blue Sierras rise;
And there, sick for his native hills,
    A sullen panther lies.

What dreams of silent polar nights
   Disturb the white bear's sleep?
Roams he once more unfettered where
   Eternal ice-floes sweep?
What memories of the jungle's ways
   Does that gaunt tiger keep?

Exiles, they tread their narrow bounds
   Behind the iron bars,
For thus the ruthless hand of man
   Each God-made creature mars.
But oh, what hungry eyes they raise
   Up to the friendly stars!

TO A CAGED LION

By Oliver Wendell Holmes

Poor conquered monarch! though that haughty glance
   Still speaks thy courage unsubdued by time,
And in the grandeur of thy sullen tread
   Lives the proud spirit of thy burning clime;—
Fettered by things that shudder at thy roar,
Torn from thy pathless wilds to pace this narrow floor!

Thou wast the victor, and all nature shrunk
   Before the thunders of thine awful wrath;
The steel-armed hunter viewed thee from afar,
   Fearless and trackless in thy lonely path!
The famished tiger closed his flaming eye,
And crouched and panted as thy step went by!

Thou art the vanquished, and insulting man
  Bars thy broad bosom as a sparrow's wing;
His nerveless arms thine iron sinews bind,
  And lead in chains the desert's fallen king.
Are these the beings that have dared to twine
Their feeble threads around those limbs of thine?

So must it be; the weaker, wiser race,
  That wields the tempest and that rides the sea,
Even in the stillness of thy solitude
  Must teach the lesson of its power to thee;
And thou, the terror of the trembling wild,
Must bow thy savage strength, the mockery of a child!

THE DROMEDARY

By A. Y. Campbell

In dreams I see the Dromedary still,
  As once in a gay park I saw him stand:
  A thousand eyes in vulgar wonder scanned
His humps and hairy neck, and gazed their fill
At his lank shanks and mocked with laughter shrill.
  He never moved: and if his Eastern land
  Flashed on his eye with stretches of hot sand,
It wrung no mute appeal from his proud will.
He blinked upon the rabble lazily;
  And still some trace of majesty forlorn
And a coarse grace remained: his head was high,
    Though his gaunt flanks with a great mange were
      worn:
There was not any yearning in his eye,
  But on his lips and nostril infinite scorn.

THE CAPTIVE POLAR BEAR

By Stephen Gwynn

His dam lay, powerless now to help,
   White fur on snow with one red stain;
A sailor caught the snarling whelp,
   Who never swam the seas again.

Huge now, he lies behind the bars,
   Stretches, and gapes, and idly rolls:
Too soft to face the winds and stars
   That freeze above the icy poles.

Mangy and yellow-toothed and old
   He lies, and lolls an inky tongue;
Yet in his brain's most inward fold
   Still lives the world where he was young.

For still he keeps the sharp fish-head,
   The sloping shoulder, the round limbs,
To cleave the water, for the dread
   Of all that by the icefield swims.

Still upon keen, clear frosty days
   There comes a stirring in his blood,
Inklings of his forefathers' ways,
   Of prey and battle in the flood.

He scents the blood of what they slew,
   He dreams, what he can never feel,
How the snatched salmon quivers through,
   And how they tore the oily seal.

Forward and backward, like the tide,
  With ceaseless motion shambling slow,
He sways himself from side to side,
  As if he rode the rocking floe.

Or in his tank—how cramped and small
  After wide waters of the pole!
Contemptuously from wall to wall
  He surges with great wallowing roll.

He loves no keeper's hand; cold rage
  Haunts him for ever in his cell;
Thus far he keeps his heritage,
  Tameless and unapproachable.

A JAPANESE SONG

THE HEART OF A BIRD

By Dorothea MacKellar

What does the bird-seller know of the heart of a bird?

There was a bird in a cage of gold, a small red bird
  in a cage of gold;
The sun shone through the bars of the cage, out of
  the wide heaven;
The depths of the sky were soft and blue, greatly to be
  longed for.
The bird sang for desire of the sky, and her feathers
  shone redder for sorrow;
And many passed in the street below, and they said one
  to another:
" Ah, that we had hearts as light as a bird's! "

But what does the passer-by know of the heart of a bird?

What does the bird-seller know of the heart of a bird?

" I have given grain for you to eat and water that you
may bathe."

Shall not this bird be content? is there need to clip
her wings?

No, for her cage is very strong, the golden bars are
set close;

Yet the real bird has flown away, very far away over
the rice-fields;

There is only the shadow-body in the cage.

What does the bird-seller care for the heart of the bird?

THE CAPTURED EAGLE

By Janet Gargan

He broods upon the highest perch
   Within the wire-encircled run—
And motionless, his fierce eyes search
   The dazzling glory of the sun;
He deigns no glance at curious crowds—
   Their speech comes like the muffled roar
Below the sea cliffs wreathed in clouds,
   Far on a bleak and icy shore.

There was his nest, and from its height
   He watched, majestic as a king—
The sun could blind not with its light,
   Nor feared he any living thing;
A life in glorious freedom spent,
   To feed the eaglets all his care—
But here he sickens, prison-pent,
   Untamed, though, in his fierce despair.

TO A CAPTIVE CRANE

By Hamlin Garland

Ho, brother! Art thou prisoned too?
  Is thy heart hot with restless pain?
I heard the call thy bugle blew
  Here by the bleak and chilling main
(Whilst round me shaven parks are spread
  And cindered drives wind on and on);
And at thy cry, thy lifted head,
  My gladdened heart was westward drawn.

O splendid bird! your trumpet brings
To my lone heart the prairie springs.

From " THE MANCIPLE'S TALE "

By Geoffrey Chaucer

Take any brid, and put it in a cage,
And do all thin entente, and thy corage,
To foster it tendrely with mete and drinke
Of alle deintees that thou canst bethinke,
And kepe it al so clenely as thou may;
Although the cage of gold be never so gay,
Yet had this brid, by twenty thousand fold,
Lever in a forest, that is wilde and cold,
Gon eten wormes, and swiche wretchednesse.
For ever this brid will don his besinesse
To escape out of his cage whan that he may:
His liberty the brid desireth ay.

THE CAGE

By James Stephens

It tried to get from out the cage;
   Here and there it ran, and tried
   At the edges and the side,
In a busy, timid rage.

Trying yet to find the key
   Into freedom, trying yet,
   In a timid rage, to get
To its old tranquillity.

It did not know, it did not see,
   It did not turn an eye, or care
   That a man was watching there
While it raged so timidly.

It ran without a sound, it tried,
   In a busy, timid rage,
   To escape from out the cage
By the edges and the side.

CAGED

By Grace Denio Litchfield

It was born behind bars, but it knew it had wings,
And it felt God had meant it for happier things;
And it sang of the joys that it never had known—
Of fetterless flights over fields flower-strown:
Of the green of the forest and gold of the wheat:

Of the thrill of the tree-top, just touched by its feet:
Of the feel of a lily-leaf, brushed by its breast,
And the splash of a raindrop, caught on its crest.
It sang of the beauty, the rapture of flying,
The palpitant air to its heart-beats replying,
Naught over, naught under, save limitless blue
And the music of wing-strokes, rhythmic and true.
It sang, and men said that its song was good;
       But not one understood.

They then brought in a wild bird, entrapped in a snare,
And a day and a night held it prisoner there.
And a night and a day, unbelieving, distraught,
With impassible fate for its freedom it fought,
Though it bled at the breast blindly beating the bars
As if strength of desire should force way to the stars.
And men pitied, and said: It was free its life long;
Who could bid it endure but a day of such wrong?
And they flung wide the door, and the bird, flashing
    through,
Swept away, like a leaf in a gale, from their view.

Then the other, behind the closed bars of its fate,
Once again sang its heart out—its need, co-create,
Of the Broad and the Boundless. In passionate song
It besought men to right for one day its life's wrong—
To bestow for a day, or for one only hour,
The leave to make proof of its God-given power;
For one hour only to float on free wings
In the world where its soul lived—the world of best
    things,
Of commensurate effort and gain, of desire,
Unlinked from despair, mounting higher and higher

Till lost in attainment—the world of clear visions,
True measures, high aims, and untrammelled decisions—
The world God had made it for. So its song rose,
Ecstatic, tumultuous, thrilled with wild woes
And delicious complainings, until the last note
Broke off in an exquisite cry in its throat.—
And men listened, and said that the song was good.
      But not one understood.

TO A LINNET IN A CAGE

By Francis Ledwidge

When Spring is in the fields that stained your wing,
   And the blue distance is alive with song,
And finny quiets of the gabbling spring
   Rock lilies red and long,
At dewy daybreak, I will set you free
   In ferny turnings of the woodbine lane,
Where faint-voiced echoes leave and cross in glee
   The hilly swollen plain.

In draughty houses you forget your tune,
   The modulator of the changing hours,
You want the wide air of the moody noon,
   And the slanting evening showers.
So I will loose you, and your song shall fall
   When morn is white upon the dewy pane,
Across my eyelids, and my soul recall
   From worlds of sleeping pain.

THE SKY-LARK CAGED

By Alfred Noyes

I

Beat, little breast, against the wires,
  Strive, little wings and misted eyes
Which one wild gleam of memory fires
  Beseeching still the unfettered skies,
Whither at dewy dawn you sprang
Quivering with joy from this dark earth and
    sang.

II

And still you sing—your narrow cage
  Shall set at least your music free!
Its rapturous wings in glorious rage
  Mount and are lost in liberty,
While those who caged you creep on earth
Blind prisoners from the hour that gave them
    birth.

III

Sing! The great City surges round.
  Blinded with light, thou canst not know.
Dream! 'Tis the fir-woods' windy sound
  Rolling a psalm of praise below.
Sing, o'er the bitter dust and shame,
And touch us with thine own transcendent flame.

IV

Sing, o'er the City dust and slime;
  Sing, o'er the squalor and the gold,
The greed that darkens earth with crime,
  The spirits that are bought and sold.
O, shower the healing notes like rain,
And lift us to the height of grief again.

V

Sing! The same music swells your breast,
  And the wild notes are still as sweet
As when above the fragrant nest
  And the wide billowing fields of wheat
You soared and sang the livelong day,
And in the light of heaven dissolved away.

VI

The light of heaven! Is it not here?
  One rapture, one ecstatic joy,
One passion, one sublime despair,
  One grief which nothing can destroy,
You—though your dying eyes are wet
Remember, 'tis our blunted hearts forget.

VII

Beat, little breast, still beat, still beat,
  Strive, misted eyes and tremulous wings;
Swell, little throat, your *Sweet! Sweet! Sweet!*
  Thro' which such deathless memory rings:
Better to break your heart and die,
Than, like your gaolers, to forget your sky.

MOTHER CAREY'S CHICKEN

By Theodore Watts-Dunton

I cannot brook thy gaze, belovèd bird;
  That sorrow is more than human in thine eye;
Too deeply, brother, is my spirit stirr'd
  To see thee here, beneath the landsmen's sky,
Coop'd in a cage with food thou canst not eat,
Thy " snow-flake " soil'd, and soil'd those conquering
    feet
That walk'd the billows, while thy " *sweet-sweet-sweet* "
    Proclaim'd the tempest nigh.

Bird whom I welcomed while the sailors cursed,
  Friend whom I bless'd wherever keels may roam,
Prince of my childish dreams, whom mermaids nursed
  In purple of billows—silver of ocean-foam,
Abash'd I stand before the mighty grief
That quells all other: Sorrow's King and Chief,
Who rides the wind and holds the sea in fief,
    Then finds a cage for home!

From out thy jail thou seest yon heath and woods,
  But canst thou hear the birds or smell the flowers?
Ah, no! those rain-drops twinkling on the buds
  Bring only visions of the salt sea-showers.
" The sea! " the linnets pipe from hedge and heath;
" The sea! " the honeysuckles whisper and breathe,
And tumbling waves, where those wild-roses wreathe,
    Murmur from inland bowers.

These winds so soft to others—how they burn!
  The mavis sings with gurgle and ripple and plash,
To thee yon swallow seems a wheeling tern;
  And when the rain recalls the briny lash,
Old Ocean's kiss we love—oh, when thy sight
Is mocked with Ocean's horses—manes of white,
The long and shadowy flanks, the shoulders bright—
      Bright as the lightning's flash—

When all these scents of heather and brier and whin,
  All kindly breaths of land-shrub, flower, and vine,
Recall the sea-scents, till thy feather'd skin
  Tingles in answer to a dream of brine—
When thou, remembering there thy royal birth,
Dost see between the bars a world of dearth,
Is there a grief—a grief on all the earth—
      So heavy and dark as thine?

But I can buy thy freedom—I (Thank God!),
  Who loved thee more than albatross or gull—
Loved thee, and loved the waves thy footsteps trod—
  Dream'd of thee when, becalm'd, we lay a-hull—
'Tis I, thy friend, who once, a child of six,
To find where Mother Carey fed her chicks,
Climb'd up the boat and then with bramble sticks
      Tried all in vain to scull—

Thy friend who shared thy Paradise of Storm—
  The little dreamer of the cliffs and coves,
Who knew thy mother, saw her shadowy form
  Behind the cloudy bastions where she moves,
And heard her call: " Come! for the welkin thickens,

And tempests mutter and the lightning quickens!"
Then, starting from his dream, would find the chickens
Were daws or blue rock-doves—

Thy friend who owned another Paradise,
    Of calmer air, a floating isle of fruit,
Where sang the Nereids on a breeze of spice,
    While Triton, from afar, would sound salute:
There wast thou winging, though the skies were calm;
For marvellous strains, as of the morning's shalm,
Were struck by ripples round that isle of palm
        Whose shores were Ocean's lute.

And now to see thee here, my king, my king,
    Far-glittering memories mirror'd in those eyes,
As if there shone within each iris-ring
    An orbèd world—ocean and hills and skies!—
Those black wings ruffled whose triumphant sweep
Conquer'd in sport!—yea, up the glimmering steep
Of highest billow, down the deepest deep,
        Sported with victories!—

To see thee here!—a coil of wilted weeds
    Beneath those feet that danced on diamond spray,
Rider of sportive Ocean's reinless steeds—
    Winner in Mother Carey's Sabbath-fray
When, stung by magic of the Witch's chant,
    They rise, each foamy-crested combatant—
They rise and fall and leap and foam and gallop and
        pant
    Till albatross, sea-swallow, and cormorant
        Must flee like doves away!

And shalt thou ride no more where thou hast ridden,
　And feast no more in hyaline halls and caves,
Master of Mother Carey's secrets hidden,
　Master and monarch of the wind and waves,
Who never, save in stress of angriest blast,
Ask'd ship for shelter—never till at last
The foam-flakes hurled against the sloping mast
　　　　Slash'd thee like whirling glaives?

Right home to fields no seamew ever kenn'd,
　Where scarce the great sea-wanderer fares with thee,
I come to take thee—nay, 'tis I, thy friend!
　Ah, tremble not—I come to set thee free;
I come to tear this cage from off this wall,
And take thee hence to that fierce festival
Where billows march and winds are musical,
　　　　Hymning the Victor-Sea!

　　·　·　·　·　·　·　·　·　·　·　·

Yea, lift thine eyes to mine.　Dost know me now?
　Thou'rt free! thou'rt free!　Ah, surely a bird can
　　smile!
Dost know me, Petrel?　Dost remember how
　I fed thee in the wake for many a mile,
Whilst thou wouldst pat the waves, then, rising, take
The morsel up and wheel about the wake?
Thou'rt free, thou'rt free, but for thine own dear sake
　　　　I keep thee caged awhile.

Away to sea! no matter where the coast:
　The road that turns for home turns never wrong;
Where waves run high my bird will not be lost:
　His home I know: 'tis where the winds are strong—
Where, on a throne of billows, rolling hoary

And green and blue and splash'd with sunny glory,
Far, far from shore—from farthest promontory—
Prophetic Nature bares the secret of the story
    That holds the spheres in song!

THE CAGED SQUIRREL

By Janet Gargan

As 'round and 'round he spins the wheel
    Within his cage of woven wires,
What haunting memories may steal
    Across his heart—of forest spires,
Of mossy banks, of bubbling springs
    That trickle from the fern-grown glades;
Of happy furred and feathered things
    Within the silent, cloistered shades.

And thus when cold eyes ofttimes stare
    To watch his flashing, agile dart,
His treadmill 'round, then like a flare
    Of beating drums, his timid heart
Will urge him on and on; perhaps,
    This cage is but a dream that holds,
And he will wake to tree-trunk gaps
    And stores of nuts in mossy folds.

An evil dream that clutches tight
    And prisons in a tiny space,
Where falls no golden, dusky light
    That softly sifts through leafy lace—
Where are no great branched trees to run,
    No ripened nuts to fill his bin,
Nor singing birds to greet the sun—
    Only a wheel that he must spin.

PERFORMING ANIMALS

Their cause I plead,—plead it in heart and mind;
A fellow-feeling makes one wondrous kind.

DAVID GARRICK.

Prologue on Quitting the Stage in 1776.

PERFORMING ANIMALS

BABOON

By Charles Hanson Towne

At eight o'clock in the evening,
　And at two in the afternoon
The monster curtains open,
　The fiddles creak and croon;
And then I bow to the people—
　A lumbering baboon.

I wonder why I do it?
　Why do the humans stare
From even rows of shadow
　Behind the footlights' glare?
Why do I go through my weary tricks
　On a table and a chair?

They laugh and clap and giggle,
　They never seem to tire,
For I am quite amusing
　As I dance upon a wire,
Or leap, at my master's signal,
　Through golden hoops of fire.

I cannot smile, like the people,
　I cannot speak at all;
I pirouette insanely
　In the foolish carnival;
Yet could I laugh, oh, I would laugh
　When the velvet curtains fall!

For I wonder why those people
    Sit in such even rows,
And smile at my useless knowledge,
    Laugh at my mincing toes,
And dream that they have wisdom!—
    How little a human knows!

And why do they always gather
    In houses bright and hot,
When they might be out in the open
    In a place I've never forgot?
Why do they live in a shell like this,
    And bid me share their lot?

And why is my life a schedule,
    Run by rote and rule?
I was not meant for theaters,
    I was not made for school;
I was not meant to caper here,
    A thing of ridicule!

I was not meant to be the slave
    Of a man in a shiny suit,
Or bring the golden dollars in,
    To stand up and salute;
The good God put me in the world
    To be a happy brute!

But at eight o'clock each evening,
    And at two in the afternoon
The monster curtains open,
    The fiddles creak and croon;
And I bow to the senseless people—
    A sensible baboon!

LITTLE DOG OF AMUSEMENT ZOO

By Alice Jean Cleator

Little dog of amusement zoo,
Who looks with quivering lips at you?
Instead they laugh at your tricks and say:
" Well, how do they learn 'em anyway? "
" How do they learn 'em? " O let me tell,
Hot irons, wire whips, and a life of hell!
We say they are " learned." They are clubbed and
    gripped
And dragged and tortured and choked and whipped.
Behind the scenes they are ruled by Fear.
A " rehearsal hour " would you care to hear?
" How do they learn 'em? " By pain, I say,
Whose cries would haunt you for many a day.
Who is to blame that these things are so?
Managers, trainers, *and you who go!*
Decree, O statutes, with righteous scorn
A stop to " pleasures " of torture born.
Then no more tricks for all such as you,
Little dog of amusement zoo!

TIGERS

By Louise Morgan Sill

I saw eight royal tigers in a ring
    Barred round with iron like a monstrous cage,
And in the midst a man, a puny thing,
    With whip, pole, pistol shot defied their rage.

Their golden bodies, like the cage black-barred,
  Were lithe as houris in a paradise,
With sneering nose and snarling lips to guard
  The deathless fire of hatred in their eyes.

And for their righteous hate I loved them. Power
  Had violated, mangled—to its shame—
Unconquerable beings for an hour.
  My spirit joined with theirs as flame to flame.

God-made they were. Let man respect their right!
  God-taught were they to love their freedom so.
And, tragic puppets, prisoners of might,
  They were unchanged as water in its flow.

Whatever force may be in love or hate,
  The soul is scarless, and resists forever,
Man's soul is like the tiger soul, its mate,
  That may be trapped and bent, but broken never.

FOR the CHILDREN

The wolf also shall dwell with the lamb, and the leopard shall lie down with the kid; and the calf and the young lion and the fatling together; and a little child shall lead them.

Isaiah 11: 6.

FOR THE CHILDREN

LITTLE FRIENDS IN FAIRYLAND

By Edith M. Thomas

When I was a child I used to roam
In wonderful regions, though near at home;
For I feigned that the Queen of Fairyland
Made me a Knight, by the stroke of her wand—
A Knight whose mission it was to seek
And rescue the captive and the weak,
Wherever I found them in her domain,
Bind up their wounds and relieve their pain!

Now the cat, that under the trumpet-vine lay
Was a tiger that crouched for a royal prey;
For the humming-bird, with his ruby gem,
Was heir to a fairy diadem!
So I drove Grimalkin far away,
And the bird flew back to his mother fay.

If a fly was caught in a net of gauze,
The spider a wicked enchanter was;
So I broke the net, and the fly went free;
But if ever the spider I chanced to see
Adrift on the stream—a luckless rover—
With a leaf for a raft, I helped him over!

If a honey-bee fell by the way, overladen,
I saw in her a patient maiden,
One of the toilers that gather nectar
For my Queen and her Court, so I must protect
    her!
So I made a staff of a stem of grass,
And helped to her feet the fairy lass!

If I met a tortoise, clumsy and slow,
I took him along where he wished to go.
If a merry hopper by chance was lamed,
If a grig by some careless foot was maimed,
A litter of leaves I quickly made,
And carried the sufferer into the shade.

So I travelled abroad, the long summer days,
In the wonderful realm of the Queen of Fays.
Though I never came yet to the Court of the
    Queen,
I have heard her voice, her smile I have seen!
Her voice, in the whispering leaves, I have heard,
In the hum of insect and twitter of bird;
And her smile with the sunny landscape blends,
And all of her subjects are my true friends.

NURSERY RHYMES

I had a little pony,
    His name was Dapple-grey
I lent him to a lady,
    To ride a mile away.

She whipped him, she slashed him,
    She rode him through the mire;
I would not lend my pony now
    For all the lady's hire.

————

A man went a-hunting at Reigate,
    And wished to leap over a high gate;
Says the owner, " Go round,
With your gun and your hound,
For you never shall leap over my gate."

————

Shoe the horse, and shoe the mare;
But let the little colt go bare.

————

Come hither, sweet Robin,
    And be not afraid,
I would not hurt even a feather;
Come hither, sweet Robin,
    And pick up some bread,
    To feed you this very cold weather.

I don't mean to frighten you,
    Poor little thing,
    And pussy-cat is not behind me;
So hop about pretty,
    And drop down your wing,
    And pick up some crumbs, and don't mind
        me.

There came to my window,
　One morning in spring,
A sweet little robin;
　It came there to sing.
And the tune that it sang
　Was prettier far
Than ever I heard
　On flute or guitar.

————

Mary had a little lamb,
　Its fleece was white as snow;
And everywhere that Mary went,
　The lamb was sure to go.

He followed her to school one day,
　Which was against the rule;
It made the children laugh and play
　To see a lamb at school.

And so the teacher turned him out,
　But still he lingered near,
And waited patiently about
　Till Mary did appear.

Then he ran to her, and laid
　His head upon her arm,
As if he said, " I'm not afraid—
　You'll keep me from all harm."

" What makes the lamb love Mary so? "
　The eager children cried.
" Oh, Mary loves the lamb, you know,"
　The teacher quick replied.

And you each gentle animal
  In confidence may bind,
And make them follow at your will,
  If you are only kind.

I had a little Doggy that used to sit and beg;
But Doggy tumbled down the stairs and broke his
    little leg.
Oh! Doggy, I will nurse you, and try to make you well,
And you shall have a collar with a little silver bell.

Ah! Doggy, don't you think that you should very
    faithful be,
For having such a loving friend to comfort you as me?
And when your leg is better, and you can run and play,
We'll have a scamper in the fields and see them making
    hay.

But, Doggy, you must promise (And mind your word
    you keep)
Not once to tease the little lambs, or run among the
    sheep;
And then the little yellow chicks that play upon the
    grass,
You must not even wag your tail to scare them as you
    pass.

A QUESTION

By Fairmont Snyder

When you go to get a drink,
Do you ever stop to think,
That dogs and cats, and squirrels, too,
Get just as thirsty, dear, as you?

They cannot turn a faucet,—so—
All parched and thirsty they must go.
Oh, did you ever stop to think,
They cannot ASK you for a drink?

THE WISTFUL WAIF

By Fairmont Snyder

Edward found a homeless dog
Out on Lonesome street,
Edward took it home with him
And gave it food to eat.
Quite unhappy seemed the dog—
It whined and sadly fretted;
All that ailed that poor dog was—
It wanted to be petted!

THE PETS' CHRISTMAS CAROL

By Winifred Sackville Stoner
(Countess de Bruche)

" Tweet-tweet-tweet! " sang the canary,
Which meant that he was very merry
Because his little mistress Nell
On Christmas eve had fed him well.

" Bow-wow-wow! " sang the gay young pup,
" My master's gone away to sup,
But though he won't be here for tea,
Just see the meal he left for me! "

" Mew-mew-mew ! " sang the mama cat,
" Such milk as this will make me fat,
And I am feeling very gay
This cold and frosty Christmas Day."

THREE THINGS TO REMEMBER

By William Blake

A Robin Redbreast in a cage
Puts all Heaven in a rage.

A skylark wounded on the wing
Doth make a cherub cease to sing.

He who shall hurt the little wren
Shall never be beloved by men.

KINDNESS TO ANIMALS

Anonymous

Little children, never give
Pain to things that feel and live:
Let the gentle robin come
For the crumbs you save at home,—
As his meat you throw along
He'll repay you with a song;
Never hurt the timid hare
Peeping from her green grass lair,
Let her come and sport and play
On the lawn at close of day;

The little lark goes soaring high
To the bright windows of the sky,
Singing as if 'twere always spring,
And fluttering on an untired wing,—
Oh! let him sing his happy song,
Nor do these gentle creatures wrong.

HIAWATHA'S CHICKENS

By Henry Wadsworth Longfellow

Then the little Hiawatha
Learned of every bird its language,
Learned their names and all their secrets,
How they built their nests in Summer,
Where they hid themselves in Winter,
Talked with them whene'er he met them,
Called them " Hiawatha's Chickens."

HIAWATHA'S BROTHERS

By Henry Wadsworth Longfellow

Of all beasts he learned the language,
Learned their names and all their secrets,
How the beavers built their lodges,
Where the squirrels hid their acorns,
How the reindeer ran so swiftly,
Why the rabbit was so timid,
Talked with them whene'er he met them,
Called them " Hiawatha's Brothers."

LITTLE GUSTAVA

By Celia Thaxter

Little Gustava sits in the sun,
Safe in the porch, and the little drops run
From the icicles under the eaves so fast,
For the bright spring sun shines warm at last,
　　And glad is little Gustava.

She wears a quaint little scarlet cap,
And a little green bowl she holds in her lap,
Filled with bread and milk to the brim,
And a wreath of marigold round the rim:
　　" Ha! ha! " laughs little Gustava.

Up comes her little gray coaxing cat
With her little pink nose, and she mews, " What's
　　that? "
Gustava feeds her,—she begs for more;
And a little brown hen walks in at the door:
　　" Good day! " cries little Gustava.

She scatters crumbs for the little brown hen.
There comes a rush and a flutter, and then
Down fly her little white doves so sweet,
With their snowy wings and crimson feet:
　　" Welcome! " cries little Gustava.

So dainty and eager they pick up the crumbs.
But who is this through the doorway comes?
Little Scotch terrier, little dog Rags,
Looks in her face, and his funny tail wags:
　　" Ha! ha! " laughs little Gustava.

" You want some breakfast, too? " and down
She sets her bowl on the brick floor brown;
And little dog Rags drinks up her milk,
While she strokes his shaggy locks, like silk;
    " Dear Rags! " says little Gustava.

Waiting without stood sparrow and crow,
Cooling their feet in the melting snow;
" Won't you come in, good folk? " she cried.
But they were too bashful, and stood outside,
    Though " Pray come in! " cried little Gustava.

So the last she threw them, and knelt on the mat
With doves and biddy and dog and cat.
And her mother came to the open house-door:
" Dear little daughter, I bring you some more.
    My merry little Gustava! "

Kitty and terrier, biddy and doves,
All things harmless Gustava loves.
The shy, kind creatures 'tis joy to feed,
And oh, her breakfast is sweet indeed
    To happy little Gustava!

NATURE'S FRIEND

By William H. Davies

Say what you like,
    All things love me!
I pick no flowers—
    That wins the Bee.

The Summer's Moths
    Think my hand one—
To touch their wings—
    With Wind and Sun.

The garden Mouse
    Comes near to play;
Indeed, he turns
    His eyes away.

The Wren knows well
    I rob no nest;
When I look in,
    She still will rest.

The hedge stops Cows.
    Or they would come
After my voice
    Right to my home.

The Horse can tell,
    Straight from my lip,
My hand could not
    Hold any whip.

Say what you like,
    All things love me!
Horse, Cow, and Mouse,
    Bird, Moth, and Bee.

DINAH

By Norman Gale

Our Dinah is a Persian cat
    Too beautiful for words!
She wears about her neck a bell
    To warn the garden-birds.

Her eyes are blue as thrushes' eggs,
    Her coat is brown as cloves,
And when she's wakeful, in my lap
    She kneads her little loaves.

If you could see how diligent
    Her paws are when they knead,
You'd think she had at least a score
    Of kittycats to feed.

And often, lying in my lap,
    So velvety and still,
With steadiness she grinds and grinds
    A little coffee-mill.

To hear the lovely miller grind,
    To watch her knead, is sweet;
It makes me want to pick her up
    To kiss her face and feet.

I love her sleeping in the sun,
    A hot and silky bale;
I love her when she tries to pounce
    Upon her shadow's tail.

I'd rather have her for my pet
  Than guinea-pigs or birds;
For Dinah is a Persian cat
  Too beautiful for words!

I LIKE LITTLE PUSSY

By Jane Taylor

I like little Pussy,
  Her coat is so warm;
And if I don't hurt her
  She'll do me no harm.
So I'll not pull her tail,
  Nor drive her away,
But Pussy and I
  Very gently will play;
She shall sit by my side,
  And I'll give her some food;
And she'll love me because
  I am gentle and good.

I'll pat little Pussy,
  And then she will purr,
And thus show her thanks
  For my kindness to her;
I'll not pinch her ears,
  Nor tread on her paw,
Lest I should provoke her
  To use her sharp claw;
I never will vex her,
  Nor make her displeased,
For Pussy can't bear
  To be worried or teased.

THE GRAY KITTEN

By Jane Campbell

A homeless little kitten
Came to the door one day,
" I'm cold and starved, oh, let me in ! "
Its sad cries seemed to say.

I took it up and shut the door
Upon the bitter storm,
And put the little shiv'ring thing
Before the fire to warm.

I gave it milk to drink, and smoothed
Its pretty, soft gray fur,
" Poor pussy, stay with me," I said.
It answered with a purr.

And ever since that winter day
I have so happy been;
I gained a merry playmate when
I let my pussy in.

'F I WAS ER HORSE!

By Burges Johnson

'F I was er horse I'd hate t' wear
A collar what didn't fit,
An' blinder-things, an' I wouldn't care
To chew on a iron bit.
It ain't a way 'at I'd wanter live,
To just go everywhere I was driv.

'F I was er horse, I guess you'd see
I'd run away pretty quick!
I'd tear my harness an' wriggle free
An' go where th' grass was thick.
I'd kick my heels, an' I'd neigh fer joy,
But I ain't er horse, I'm er little boy!

THE COW

By Robert Louis Stevenson

The friendly cow all red and white,
    I love with all my heart;
She gives me cream with all her might,
    To eat with apple-tart.

She wanders lowing here and there,
    And yet she cannot stray,
All in the pleasant open air,
    The pleasant light of day;

And blown by all the winds that pass
    And wet with all the showers,
She walks among the meadow grass
    And eats the meadow flowers.

THE LAMB

By William Blake

Little Lamb, who made thee?
Dost thou know who made thee?
Gave thee life and bade thee feed
By the stream and o'er the mead;

Gave thee clothing of delight,
Softest clothing, woolly, bright;
Gave thee such a tender voice,
Making all the vales rejoice:
　Little Lamb, who made thee?
　Dost thou know who made thee?

Little Lamb, I'll tell thee!
Little Lamb, I'll tell thee.
He is callèd by thy name,
For He calls Himself a Lamb:—
He is meek, and He is mild;
He became a little child:
I, a child, and thou, a lamb,
We are callèd by His name.
　Little Lamb, God bless thee;
　Little Lamb, God bless thee.

THE BEST FRIEND

By Norman Gale

My Daddy is the truest friend
　The birds have anywhere;
If swimming on the beamy lake
　Or flying in the air.

He knows their beaks and wings and tails,
　Their topknots and their legs,
And how they make with clever bills
　The cups to hold the eggs.

And sometimes when he sees a nook
    Of safety in the quick
He says that he should build a home
    Just there, if he were Dick!

He gently peeps, and sure enough
    He very often spies
A mother looking straight at him
    With rather worried eyes.

Thus every summer Daddy knows
    A thousand nests, or more,
Among the lanes, upon the hills,
    And all along the shore.

He tells me where the chaffinch hides
    Away from all his foes
The lovely cottage that he built
    So quickly with his nose!

He never shoots; he never steals
    The babies or the eggs,
And never uses sticky stuff
    To worry little legs.

He even throws a kiss to birds
    Assembled overhead
To gossip for a little while
    Before they go to bed;

And when they start for Africa,
    And other foreign lands,
My Daddy watches from a hill
    The flitter-flutter bands.

He hates to lose them, but he knows
  The Spring will come again
And toss a thousand thousand dears
  To field and wood and lane.

My Daddy is the closest friend
  The birds have anywhere;
If swimming on the beamy lake
  Or twittering in the air.

TIT FOR TAT

By Walter de la Mare

Have you been catching of fish, Tom Noddy?
  Have you snared a weeping hare?
Have you whistled, " No Nunny," and gunned a poor
    bunny,
  Or a blinded bird of the air?

Have you trod like a murderer through the green
    woods,
  Through the dewy deep dingles and glooms,
While every small creature screamed shrill to Dame
    Nature,
  " He comes—and he comes! " ?

Wonder I very much do, Tom Noddy,
  If ever, when you are a-roam,
An Ogre from space will stoop a lean face,
  And lug you home;

Lug you home over his fence, Tom Noddy,
  Of thorn-stocks nine yards high,
With your bent knees strung around his old iron gun
  And your head dan-dangling by:

And hang you up stiff on a hook, Tom Noddy,
  From a stone-cold pantry shelf,
Whence your eyes will glare in an empty stare,
  Till you are cooked yourself!

THE BLUE-TIT

By Norman Gale

He is nothing but a blue-tit,
  Just a bright and fluffy blue-tit,
And he comes to peck my suet half a hundred
    times a day.
  If he makes me mope or grumble
  'Tis because he will not tumble
In my pinafore, and stop with me to whistle or
    to play.

He is hanging noddle downward,
  With his velvet noddle downward,
And is staring at a sparrow that has found a
    crumb of bread.
  I can guess what he is jotting
  In the tiny brain that's plotting
How to drive away the sparrow and to eat the
    crumb instead!

As I watch him in the ivy,
Soft as leaf upon the ivy,
I am sorry that his mother cannot give him
sweets and toys.
If he wore a little pocket
I suppose he wouldn't stock it
Full of sugar-plums and lollipops, like happy
girls and boys.

He is nothing but a blue-tit,
Just a shy and silky blue-tit,
And I love to watch his antics half a hundred
times a day.
If he makes me sigh or grumble
'Tis because he will not tumble
In my pinafore, and stop with me to whistle or
to play!

IF EVER I SEE

By Lydia Maria Child

If ever I see,
On bush or tree,
Young birds in their pretty nest,
I must not in play,
Steal the birds away,
To grieve their mother's breast.

My mother, I know,
Would sorrow so,
Should I be stolen away;
So I'll speak to the birds
In my softest words,
Nor hurt them in my play.

And when they can fly
In the bright blue sky,
They'll warble a song to me;
And then if I'm sad
It will make me glad
To think they are happy and free.

THE BROWN THRUSH

By Lucy Larcom

There's a merry brown thrush sitting up in the tree.
He's singing to me! He's singing to me!
And what does he say, little girl, little boy?
"Oh, the world's running over with joy!
Don't you hear? Don't you see?
Hush! Look! In my tree,
I'm as happy as happy can be!"

And the brown thrush keeps singing, "A nest do
you see
And five eggs, hid by me in the juniper-tree?
Don't meddle! Don't touch! little girl, little boy,
Or the world will lose some of its joy!
Now I'm glad! now I'm free!
And I always shall be,
If you never bring sorrow to me."

So the merry brown thrush sings away in the tree,
To you and to me, to you and to me;
And he sings all the day, little girl, little boy,
"Oh, the world's running over with joy!
But long it won't be,
Don't you know? Don't you see?
Unless we're as good as can be."

THE SNOW-BIRD

By Frank Dempster Sherman

When all the ground with snow is white,
    The merry snow-bird comes,
And hops about with great delight
    To find the scattered crumbs.

How glad he seems to get to eat
    A piece of cake or bread!
He wears no shoes upon his feet,
    Nor hat upon his head.

But happiest is he, I know,
    Because no cage with bars
Keeps him from walking on the snow
    And printing it with stars.

NEST EGGS

By Robert Louis Stevenson

Birds all the sunny day
    Flutter and quarrel
Here in the arbour-like
    Tent of the laurel.

Here in the fork
    The brown nest is seated;
Four little blue eggs
    The mother keeps heated.

While we stand watching her,
    Staring like gabies,
Safe in each egg are the
    Bird's little babies.

Soon the frail eggs they shall
    Chip, and upspringing,
Make all the April woods
    Merry with singing.

Younger than we are,
    O children, and frailer,
Soon in blue air they'll be
    Singer and sailor.

We, so much older,
    Taller and stronger,
We shall look down on the
    Birdies no longer.

They shall go flying
    With musical speeches
High overhead in the
    Tops of the beeches.

In spite of our wisdom
    And sensible talking,
We on our feet must go
    Plodding and walking.

LITTLE BIRD

By Madison Cawein

I

A little bird sits in our cottonwood tree,
And perks his head and sings;
And this is the song he pipes to me
While he flirts his tail and wings:—

" Hello! hello!
You jolly little fellow!
Hello! hello! I say!
Do you hear me every morning
How I try to give you warning?
With my little song adorning
Every day, every day;
With my little song adorning every day.
I want to tell you this, sir:
You are sweeter than a kiss, sir,
You are fairer than a posy,
With your face so fresh and rosy;
Oh, I love to see you merry at your play,
        Every day;
I love to see you laughing at your play.
        Hello! hello!
You merry little fellow! "

II

And I run to the tree where he sings and sits,
High up on the topmost limb;
And he cocks his eye and flirts and flits
While I reply to him:—

"Hello! hello!
You cunning little fellow!
Hello! hello! I say!
You are complimenting early;
And your song is clear and pearly
As the dewdrop dripping nearly
From the spray, from the spray;
As the dewdrop dripping nearly from the
 spray.
Your singing is far sweeter
Than any rhyme or metre:
Oh, I love to hear you whistle,
Swinging lighter than a thistle,
And I hope you'll come and see me every day,
 Every day;
I hope you'll come and see me every day.
 Hello! hello!
You darling little fellow!"

MEADOW TALK

By Nora Archibald Smith

"Don't pick all the flowers!" cried Daisy one day
To a rosy-cheeked boy who was passing her way.
"If you take every one, you will very soon see
That when next summer comes, not a bud will there
 be!"

 "Quite true!" said the Clover,
 "And over and over
 I've sung that same song
 To whoe'er came along."

Quoth the Buttercup, " I
Have not been at all shy
In impressing that rule
On each child of the school."

" I've touched the same subject,"
  Said Timothy Grass.
" ' Leave just a few flowers! '
  I beg, as they pass."

Sighed a shy little Fern,
  From her home in the shade,
" About pulling up roots,
  What a protest I've made! "

" The children are heedless! "
  The Gentian declared.
" When my blossom-time comes,
  Not a bud will be spared."

" Take courage, sweet neighbor! "
  The Violet said;
And raised in entreaty
  Her delicate head.

" The children are thoughtless,
  I own, in my turn;
But if we *all* teach them,
  They cannot but learn."

" The lesson," said the Alders,
  " Is a simple one, indeed,
Where no root is, blooms no flower,
  Where no flower is, no seed."

" 'Tis very well said!'" chirped the Robin,
  From the elm-tree fluttering down;
" If you'll write on your leaves such a lesson,
  I'll distribute them over the town."

" Oh, write it, dear Alders!" the Innocents cried,
  Their pretty eyes tearfully blue;
" You are older than we are; you're strong and
      you're wise—
  There's none but would listen to you!"

But, ah! the alders could not write;
  And though the Robin knew
The art as well as any bird—
  Or so he said—he flew
Straight up the hill and far away,
  Remarking as he went,
He had a business errand
  And was not on pleasure bent.

Did the children learn the lesson,
  Though 'twas never written down?
We shall know when, gay and blithesome,
  Lady Summer comes to town.

THE MISCHIEVOUS MORNING-GLORY

(*Adapted from the Japanese*)

By Mary Fenollosa

It was the rosy flush of dawn
  In beautiful Japan,
When, from the house with swinging pail,

Came little Noshi-San,
Her strapped and lacquered wooden clogs
A-clicking as she ran.

She hurried to the mossy well,
Then paused, for—what a sight!—
Her bucket-pole was held secure
By tendrils curling tight,
And one great, dewy, purple bloom
Had opened to the light.

The dainty thief, with smile and nod,
Looked up as if to say,
" I got here first; and don't you think
That really I should stay? "
And Noshi gravely answered, " Yes,
I'll find another way."

She sought a kindly neighbor's well
And, laughing, told her plight.
" Gift-water I must beg of you! "
The neighbor's smile was bright;
But, being Japanese, she thought
The child exactly right.

THE SEED

By Mary Fenollosa

(Good-Night)

Here's a sleepy little seed
Wants to go to bed.
Tightly shut the little eye
In his sleepy head.

Dig a couch in earth for him,
   Soft and warm and deep;
Tuck the cover gently in—
   Now he's fast asleep.

(Good-Morning)

What a yawn of little leaves!
   What a stretch of root!
Baby seed is up at last;
   Now he wants to shoot!

Bring him bath of rosy dew,
   Give him yards of twine,
Hear him laugh his tendrils out!
   Soon he'll be a vine.

(Growth)

Leaves are crowding thick and fast.
   Stems are brittle things!
Grave responsibility
   High position brings.

Earth-worm dragons must be slain,
   Humming-birds defied.
" Would I were a seed again!"
   Morning-glory cried.

(Blossoms)

Ah, a bud! all blue and white,
   Twisted like a shell.
Something strange must happen soon,
   Any one can tell!

Something stirs against the dawn!—
　　Is it bird or bee?
Or a purple-hearted song
　　Blown for you and me?

IN MEMORIAM

                    And when the stream
Which overflowed the soul was passed away,
A consciousness remained that it had left,
Deposited upon the silent shore
Of memory, images and precious thoughts,
That shall not die, and cannot be destroyed.

Excursion.   WILLIAM WORDSWORTH.

IN MEMORIAM

LADDIE

By Katharine Lee Bates

Lowly the soul that waits
At the white, celestial gates,
A threshold soul to greet
Belovèd feet.

Down the streets that are beams of sun
Cherubim children run;
They welcome it from the wall;
Their voices call.

But the Warder saith: " Nay, this
Is the City of Holy Bliss.
What claim canst thou make good
To angelhood? "

" Joy," answereth it from eyes
That are amber ecstasies,
Listening, alert, elate,
Before the gate.

> *Oh, how the frolic feet*
> *On lonely memory beat!*
> *What rapture in a run*
> *'Twixt snow and sun!*

" Nay, brother of the sod,
What part hast thou in God?
What spirit art thou of? "
It answers: " Love,"

Lifting its head, no less
Cajoling a caress,
Our winsome collie wraith,
Than in glad faith

The door will open wide,
Or kind voice bid: " Abide,
A threshold soul to greet
The longed-for feet."

Ah, Keeper of the Portal,
If Love be not immortal,
If Joy be not divine,
What prayer is mine?

TO SIGURD

By Katharine Lee Bates

Not one blithe leap of welcome?
          Can you lie
Under this woodland mould,
More still
Than broken daffodil,
When I,
Home from too long a roving,
Come up the silent hill?
Dear, wistful eyes,
White ruff and windy gold

Of collie coat so oft caressed,
Not one quick thrill
In snowy breast,
One spring of jubilant surprise,
One ecstasy of loving?

Are all our frolics ended?   Never more
Those royal romps of old,
When one,
Playfellow of the sun,
Would pour
Adventures and romances
Into a morning run;
Off and away,
A flying glint of gold,
Startling to wing a husky choir
Of crows whose dun
Shadows would tire
Even that wild speed?   Unscared to-day
They hold their weird seances.

Ever you dreamed, legs twitching, you would
    catch
A crow, O leaper bold,
Next time,
Or chase to branch sublime
That batch
Of squirrels daring capture
In saucy pantomime;
Till one spring dawn,
Resting amid the gold
Of crocuses, Death stole on you

From that far clime
Where dreams come true,
And left upon the starry lawn
Your form without your rapture.

And was Death's whistle then so wondrous
    sweet
Across the glimmering wold
That you
Would trustfully pursue
Strange feet?
When I was gone, each morrow
You sought our old haunts through,
Slower to play,
Drooping in faded gold;
Now it is mine to grieve and miss
My comrade true
Who used to kiss
With eager tongue such tears away,
Coaxing a smile from sorrow.

I know not what life is, nor what is death,
Nor how vast Heaven may hold
All this
Earth-beauty and earth-bliss.
Christ saith
That not a sparrow falleth
—O songs of sparrow faith!—
But God is there.
May not a leap of gold
Yet greet me on some gladder hill,

A shining wraith,
Rejoicing still,
As in those hours we found so fair,
To follow where love calleth?

HIS NAME WAS BOB

By M. V. Caruthers

A little mongrel dog—he couldn't boast
  The smallest trace of blooded pedigree—
All legs and feet, a no'count tail, that thumped
  Its joyous greeting at the sight of me—

But loving! There's no dictionary prints
  The word which, to my thinking, can express
That look that shone in his brown eyes of trust,
  Solicitude and wistful tenderness!

O' nights his tawny head against my knee,
  We'd sit together—yesterday he died—
And every one who loves a dog will know
  Just why, a lonely-hearted man—I cried!

A FAITHFUL DOG

By Richard Burton

My merry-hearted comrade on a day
Gave over all his mirth, and went away
Upon the darksome journey I must face
Sometime as well. Each hour I miss his grace,

His meek obedience and his constancy.
Never again will he look up to me
With loyal eyes, nor leap for my caress
As one who wished not to be masterless;
And never shall I hear his pleading bark
Outside the door, when all the ways grow dark,
Bidding the house-folk gather close inside.
It seems a cruel thing, since he has died,
To make his memory small, or deem it sin
To reckon such a mate as less than kin.

O faithful follower, O gentle friend,
If thou art missing at the journey's end,
Whate'er of joy or solace there I find
Unshared by thee I left so far behind,
The gladness will be mixed with tears, I trow,
My little crony of the long ago!
For how could heaven be home-like, with the door
Fast-locked against a loved one, evermore?

IN MEMORY OF A DUMB FRIEND

By Amelia Josephine Burr

Strange that so small mortality should leave
So large an emptiness! for as we grieve
Your little life of seven happy years
Ended for us, one who could understand
Each subtle word, and answer hand with hand
Had hardly taken greater toll of tears.

Yet why should we not mourn as for a friend?
That name was yours; if every man would spend

His life as well, earth were not hard to save.
Grant that God made your heart and brain but
  small.
What more has an archangel than his all?
And all God gave to you, to us you gave.

TO THE DOGS OF THE GREAT ST. BERNARD

By Abbie Farwell Brown

*(From the French of Chanoine Jules Gross of St.
Bernard)*

Brave dogs of St. Bernard, companions dear
On the pale mountains through the livelong year,
To you, the hardy squires of our King,
Who scorn the storm and hail, to you I sing!

Here in the misty cloudlands where we dwell,
What matters avalanche and tempest fell?
Our realm of pure white snow and ice is best;
Our task to save the wanderer, cheer the guest.

Many have sung of Barry, good and great,
His was a hero's life, a martyr's fate.[1]
  And so, dear dogs, you all will live and die!
Ah, you are dowered with beauty, strength and skill;
Obedience, devotion and good will.
  What wonder all men love you, as do I?

---

[1] The noble dog Barry saved the lives of forty persons and
was killed by the forty-first.

A DOG'S GRAVE

By W. M. Letts

He sleeps where he would wish, in easy call,
Here in a primrose nook beside the wall,
And near the gate, that he may guard us all
Even in death, our faithful seneschal.

I do not think the courteous Cherubim
Will chide him if he waits, nor Seraphim
Summon him hence till we may follow him
Who knew no heav'n without—faithful Tim.

A HORSE'S EPITAPH

By Lord Sherbrooke

Soft lies the turf on those who find their rest
Beneath our common mother's ample breast,
Unstained by meanness, avarice, or pride;
They never cheated, and they never lied.
They ne'er intrigued a rival to dispose;
They ran, but never betted on the race;
Content with harmless sport and simple food,
Boundless in faith and love and gratitude;
Happy the man, if there be any such,—
Of whom his epitaph can say as much.

INSCRIPTION ON THE MONUMENT OF A NEWFOUNDLAND DOG

By Lord Byron

NEAR THIS SPOT
ARE DEPOSITED THE REMAINS OF ONE
WHO POSSESSED BEAUTY WITHOUT VANITY,
STRENGTH WITHOUT INSOLENCE,
COURAGE WITHOUT FEROCITY,
AND ALL THE VIRTUES OF MAN WITHOUT HIS VICES.
THIS PRAISE, WHICH WOULD BE UNMEANING FLATTERY
IF INSCRIBED OVER HUMAN ASHES,
IS BUT A JUST TRIBUTE TO THE MEMORY OF
BOATSWAIN, A DOG,
WHO WAS BORN AT NEWFOUNDLAND, MAY, 1803,
AND DIED AT NEWSTEAD ABBEY, NOV. 18, 1808.

POEM TO THE SAME

When some proud son of man returns to earth,
Unknown to glory, but upheld by birth,
The sculptor's art exhausts the pomp of woe,
And storied urns record who rests below;
When all is done, upon the tomb is seen,
Not what he was, but what he should have been:
But the poor dog, in life the firmest friend,
The first to welcome, foremost to defend,
Whose honest heart is still his master's own,
Who labors, fights, lives, breathes for him alone,
Unhonored falls, unnoticed all his worth,
Denied in heaven the soul he held on earth:

. . . .

Ye! who perchance behold this simple urn,
Pass on—it honors none you wish to mourn;
To mark a friend's remains these stones arise;
I never knew but one—and here he lies.

THE C. W. DANIEL COMPANY—"The Little Red Bullock" from *The Wide Garden and Other Poems* by Herbert Tremaine.

J. M. DENT AND SONS, LTD.—"My Dog and I" from *Spun Yarn and Spindrift* by Norah M. Holland, published by J. M. Dent and Sons, Ltd., London and Toronto. "Thrushes" from *Theophanies* by Evelyn Underhill.

DODD, MEAD AND COMPANY, INC.—Poems from *Poems* by Arthur Christopher Benson, *Complete Works* of William Blake, *Poems of Rupert Brooke, Complete Poems* of Paul Laurence Dunbar, *Coal and Candle Light* by Helen Parry Eden, *The Queen's Chronicler* by Stephen Gwynn, *Hail! Men* by Angela Morgan, *The Child World* by Gabriel Setoun, and *Poems* by Rosamund M. Watson. Copyright by Dodd, Mead and Company, Inc.

GEORGE H. DORAN COMPANY—"In Memory of a Dumb Friend" from *In Deep Places* by Amelia Josephine Burr, copyright, 1914; "The Loon" from *Roadside Fire* by Amelia Josephine Burr, copyright, 1912; "Trees" from *Trees and Other Poems* by Joyce Kilmer, copyright, 1914; "At the Dog Show" and "In Honor of Taffy Topaz" from *Songs for a Little House* by Christopher Morley, copyright, 1917; "The Birds" from *The Birds and Other Poems* by J. C. Squire, copyright, 1920.

DOUBLEDAY, PAGE AND COMPANY—Poems from *Shoes of Happiness* by Edwin Markham, and *The Far Country* by Florence Wilkinson.

DOUBLEDAY, PAGE AND COMPANY (America) and A. P. WATT AND SON (England)—"Toomai of the Elephants" and "Lukannon" from *The Jungle Book,* copyright, 1893, 1894, by Rudyard Kipling, published by Doubleday, Page & Company. "Beast and Man in India" by John Lockwood Kipling, from *Chapter Headings* from *Rudyard Kipling's Verse, Inclusive Edition, 1885–1918.* These poems are used by permission, authorized by Mr. Rudyard Kipling.

DUFFIELD AND COMPANY—"The Deer Trapper" by Francis Sterne Palmer from *Camp Fire Verse* by William Haynes.

E. P. DUTTON COMPANY—"The First Bluebirds," "The Horses" and "Only Mules" by permission from *The Retinue* by Katharine Lee Bates. Copyright by E. P. Dutton and Company. "To Sigurd" and "Laddie" by permission from *Sigurd: Our Golden Collie* by Katharine Lee Bates. Copyright by E. P. Dutton and Company. "The Donkey" by permission from *The Wild Knight and Other Poems* by G. K. Chesterton. Published by E. P. Dutton and Company.

"'F I Was Er Horse" by permission from *Youngsters* by Burges Johnson. Copyright by E. P. Dutton and Company. "Pensioners" and "A Dog's Grave" by permission from *The Spires of Oxford* by Winifred M. Letts. Published by E. P. Dutton and Company. "The Heart of a Bird" by permission from *The Witch Maid* by Dorothea MacKellar. Published by E. P. Dutton and Company. "A B C's in Green" by permission from *A Canopic Jar* by Leonora Speyer. Copyright by E. P. Dutton and Company.

THE FORUM—"Polo Ponies" by Eleanor Baldwin. Copyrighted by *The Forum* magazine.

THE FOUR SEAS COMPANY—"To Some Philadelphia Sparrows" from *Willow Pollen* by Jeanette Marks, published by The Four Seas Company, Boston.

ROBERT FROTHINGHAM—"A Horse's Epitaph" from *Songs of Horses* by Robert Frothingham.

FUNK AND WAGNALLS COMPANY—"At the Zoo" from *Blind Children* by Israel Zangwill. Copyright, 1903, by Funk and Wagnalls Company, New York and London.

NORMAN GALE—Poems from *A Flight of Fancies, A Merry-Go-Round of Song,* and *Collected Poems.*

M. H. GILL AND SON, LTD.—"A Health to the Birds" from *Ballads of a Country Boy* by Seumas MacManus.

HARCOURT, BRACE AND COMPANY—"Da Pup Een Da Snow" from *McAronie Ballads* by T. A. Daly. Reprinted by permission of Harcourt, Brace and Company, Inc., holders of the copyright.

HARPER AND BROTHERS—"The Road to Vagabondia" from *Poems* by Dana Burnet, "The Dialogue of the Horses" from *Farm Festivals* by Will Carleton, "Tigers" from *Poems* by Louise Morgan Sill, and "To a Cat" from *Selected Lyrical Poems* by Algernon Swinburne. Harper and Brothers, publishers. "A Boy and a Pup" and "Little Lost Pup" by Arthur Guiterman, from *The Laughing Muse,* copyright, 1915, by Harper and Brothers, and "A Mascot" by Arthur Guiterman, from *The Mirthful Lyre,* copyright, 1918, by Harper and Brothers.

HENRY HOLT AND COMPANY—"The Nightingales of Flanders" from *Wilderness Songs* by Grace Hazard Conkling, "The Marsh" and "Cattle before the Storm" from *The Enchanted Mesa* by Glenn Ward Dresbach, "A Brook in the City" from *Poems* by Robert Frost, and "Four Little Foxes" and "To a Wild Goose Over Decoys" from *Slow Smoke* by Lew Sarett.

THE JOHN HOPKINS PRESS—"The Burthen of the Ass" from *Father Tabb: A Study of His Life and Works, with Ten Hundred Unpublished Poems* by Francis A. Litz.

HOUGHTON MIFFLIN COMPANY—The extracts from *Heart of New England* by Abbie Farwell Brown, *Songs of Sixpence* by Abbie Farwell Brown, *Out Where the West Begins* by Arthur Chapman, *Poems* by Ralph Waldo Emerson, *Complete Poems* by Oliver Wendell Holmes, *Riders of the Stars* by Henry Herbert Knibbs, *Poems* by Lucy Larcom, *Complete Works* of Henry Wadsworth Longfellow, *Sword Blades and Poppy Seed* by Amy Lowell, *The Lifted Cup* by Jessie B. Rittenhouse, *Little-Folk Lyrics* by Frank Dempster Sherman, *The Christmas Child and Other Poems for Children* by Nora Archibald Smith, *Poems* by Celia Thaxter, and *Poems* by Bayard Taylor are used by permission of, and special arrangements with Houghton Mifflin Company, the authorized publishers.

KELLY AND WALSH, Shanghai, China, and CHARLES SCRIBNER'S SONS, New York—"Wild Geese" from *Chinese Lyrics* by Frederick Peterson.

MITCHELL, KENNERLEY—Poems from *Songs of the Army of the Night* by Francis Adams, *Man-Song* by John G. Neihardt, and *Sixteen Dead Men and Other Poems of Easter Week* by Dora Sigerson Shorter.

THE LADIES' HOME JOURNAL,—"The Fate of the Fur-Folk" by Edwin Markham.

LIFE—"The Kind Lady's Furs" by Strickland Gillilan.

J. B. LIPPINCOTT COMPANY—"Sheridan's Ride" by Thomas Buchanan Read, courtesy of J. B. Lippincott Company, publishers, Philadelphia.

THE LONDON MERCURY—"The Quails" by Francis Brett Young.

LONGMANS, GREEN AND COMPANY—"The Mother Bird" from *Songs of Childhood* by Walter de la Mare, and "Tapestry Trees" from *By the Way* by William Morris.

THE MACMILLAN COMPANY—"My Dog," "The Catch," and "The Seeing Eye" from *The Foothills of Parnassus* by John Kendrick Bangs; "The Sea Mew" from *Poems* by Elizabeth Barrett Browning; "How They Brought the Good News from Ghent" from *Poems* by Robert Browning; "Indifference" from *Garden Grace* by Louise Driscoll, copyright, 1924, The Macmillan Company; "A Yoke of Steers" from *Skylines and Horizons* by DuBose Heyward, copyright, 1924, The Macmillan Company; "The Bells of Heaven" and "Stupidity Street" from *Poems* by Ralph Hodgson, copyright, 1917, The Macmillan Company; "The Broncho That Would Not Be Broken" from *Collected Poems* by Vachel Lindsay; "Tewkesbury Road" from *Poems* by John Masefield, copyright, 1925, The Macmillan Company; "Birds" and "A Bee Sets Sail" from *A Gate of Cedar* by Katharine Morse, copyright, 1922, The Macmillan Company; "The Last Antelope" from *Barbed Wire and Wayfarers* by Edwin Ford Piper, copyright, 1924, The Macmillan Company; "Fur and Feather," "Hurt No Living Thing," "The City Mouse" and "These All Wait Upon Thee" from *Complete Works* of Christina Rossetti; "The Snare" and "The Cage" from *Songs from the Clay* by James Stephens, copyright, 1915, The Macmillan Company; "The Army Horse" from *The Little Flag on Main Street* by McLandburgh Wilson.

ROBERT M. McBRIDE AND COMPANY—"The Turkish Trench Dog" from *Poems* by Geoffrey Dearmer.

DAVID McKAY COMPANY—"The Kerry Cow" from *Songs from Leinster* by Winifred M. Letts.

THE MOSHER PRESS—"April in the City" from *Candle and Cross* by Elizabeth Scollard.

THE MUSSON BOOK COMPANY, LTD.—"On the Companionship of Nature" from *Lyrics of Earth* by Archibald Lampman, published by arrangement with The Musson Book Company, Ltd., Toronto.

THE NORMAN, REMINGTON COMPANY—"The Gardener's Cat" and "Hold" from *Green Days and Blue Days* by Patrick R. Chalmers.

G. P. PUTNAM'S SONS—Poems from *The Marble House* by Ellen M. Huntington Gates, *Songs in Cities and Gardens* by Helen Granville-Barker, *In Woods and Fields* by Augusta Larned, *Collected Poems* by Grace Denio Litchfield, and *Florentine Cyle* by Gertrude Huntington McGiffert.

REILLY AND LEE COMPANY—"Bob White" and "A Boy and His Dog" from *When Day Is Done* by Edgar A. Guest, copyrighted, Reilly and Lee Company; "The Pup" from *Just Folks* by Edgar A. Guest, copyrighted, Reilly and Lee Company; "The Yellow Dog" from *The Passing Throng* by Edgar A. Guest, copyrighted, Reilly and Lee Company.

THE ROYAL SOCIETY FOR THE PREVENTION OF CRUELTY TO ANIMALS—"Compassion" by Thomas Hardy from *A Century of Work for Animals* by Edward G. Fairholme and Wellesley Pain.

CHARLES SCRIBNER'S SONS—Poems from *Collected Poems* by Edmund Gosse, *A Child's Garden of Verses* by Robert Louis Stevenson, *The Builders* and *Songs Out of Doors* by Henry van Dyke, and "In the Zoo" by George T. Marsh from *Scribner's Magazine.*

THOMAS SELTZER—"Snake" from *Birds, Beasts and Flowers* by D. H. Lawrence.

SMALL, MAYNARD AND COMPANY—"To a Buffalo Skull" and "To a Rattlesnake" from *Cowboy Lyrics* by Robert V. Carr; "Little Bird" from *The Giant and the Star* by Madison Cawein; "Feedin' the Stock" from *Pine Tree Ballads* by Holman F. Day and "I've Got Them Calves to Veal" and "The Stock in the Tie-Up" from *Up in Maine* by Holman F. Day; "Thou Little God Within the Brook" from *The Poems of Philip Henry Savage;* "Is Thy Servant a Dog?" from *Poems* by John B. Tabb.

THE SONNET—"Oxen" and "The Old Plough-Horse" by Mahlon Leonard Fisher, and "In Cool, Green Haunts" from *Sonnets: A First Series* by Mahlon Leonard Fisher.

FREDERICK A. STOKES COMPANY—"Chickadee" reprinted by permission from *Poems by a Little Girl* by Hilda Conkling. Copyright, 1920, by Frederick A. Stokes Company. "The Seed" and "The Mischievous Morning-Glory" reprinted by permission from *Blossoms from a Japanese Garden* by Mary Fenollosa. Copyright, 1913, by Frederick A. Stokes Company. "To a Tree-Frog" reprinted by permission from *As the Wind Blew* by Amélie Rives. "The Bee in Church" reprinted by permission from *The Elfin Artist and Other Poems* by Alfred Noyes. Copyright, 1920, by Frederick A. Stokes Company. "The Skylark Caged" reprinted by permission from *Collected Poems,* Volume II, by Alfred Noyes. Copyright, 1910, by Frederick A. Stokes Company.

THE P. F. VOLLAND COMPANY—Verses from *Rhymes for Kindly Children* by Fairmont Snyder.

FREDERICK WARNE AND COMPANY, LTD.—A poem from *The Poetical Works of Charles Mackay.*

YALE UNIVERSITY PRESS—Poems from *Blue Smoke* by Karle Wilson Baker.

The list of acknowledgments should include tribute to the friendly interest of Honorable Percival H. Baxter, Miss Esther M. Davis, Mrs. Minnie Maddern Fiske, Mr. Albert F. Gilmore, Mr. William K. Horton, Miss

Emma L. Johnston, Dr. Francis H. Rowley, and the late Mrs. Ellin Prince Speyer; to the gracious coöperation of members of the staff of Pratt Institute Free Library, especially Mr. Edward F. Stevens, librarian, and Miss Annie Mackenzie and Miss Elin J. Lindgren; and to the clerical devotion of Miss Ruth Sasuly.

INDEX OF AUTHORS

INDEX OF TITLES

412

INDEX OF FIRST LINES

A

B